Fallers

D1287073

The Catholic
Theological Union
LIBRARY
Chicago, Ill.

BUGANDA IN MODERN HISTORY

BUGANDA
IN MODERN HISTORY

D. A. LOW

WITHDRAWN

The Catholic
Theological Union
LIBRARY
Chicago, Ill.

UNIVERSITY OF CALIFORNIA PRESS
Berkeley and Los Angeles 1971

University of California Press
Berkeley and Los Angeles, California
© 1971 by D. A. Low

*All rights reserved. No part of this
publication may be reproduced, stored in
a retrieval system, or transmitted, in
any form or by any means, electronic,
mechanical, photocopying, recording or
otherwise, without the prior permission
of the copyright owner.*

Copyright to Chapter 1, which originally
appeared in *Christianity in Tropical Africa*,
rests with the International African Institute,
London.

ISBN 0 520 01640 8
Library of Congress Catalog Card Number 73 10019
Printed in Great Britain

Contents

	Preface	xi
	Introduction	1
1	Conversion, Revolution and the New Regime in Buganda 1860–1900	13
2	British Public Opinion and 'The Uganda Question': October–December 1892	55
3	The British and the Baganda	84
4	The Namirembe Conferences 1954	101
5	The Advent of Populism in Buganda	139
6	Political Parties in Uganda 1949–1962	167
7	Buganda and Uganda: the Parameters of a Relationship	227
	Bibliographical note	256
	Index	259

Illustrations

Between pages 148 and 149

1 Kabaka Daudi Chwa and company at Namirembe Cathedral on the day of the British King Edward VII's Coronation, 1902
2 Martin Luther Nsibirwa, Katikiro of Buganda (1928–41, 1945), and Serwano Kulubya, Omuwanika of Buganda (1928–45)

Between pages 180 and 181

3 The Namirembe Conference 1954
4 'Populism' in Buganda. Waiting outside the Lukiko hall, Mengo, 1954

To D.P.L. and W.P.L.
in gratitude

Preface

The chapters in this book comprise several of the attempts I have made over the last decade or so to try to understand a number of episodes and themes relating to the modern history of Buganda. They are for the most part 'essays'. There are some overlaps; their concern over detail varies; and they leave many gaps. But I hope that in their present form they provide something of a sequence, and that their appearance together may be of both some interest and some convenience.

The first and the last appear here for the first time. The final chapter on 'Buganda and Uganda' is completely new, though I am very much indebted to seminars in Oxford, Northwestern, Toronto and Aberdeen for their assistance in helping me to put it into shape. Part of the first chapter has appeared as 'Converts and Martyrs in Buganda' in C. G. Bäta, *Christianity in Tropical Africa*, London 1968, and I am most grateful to both Professor Bäta and Professor Daryll Forde of the International African Institute for permission to reincorporate it here; the whole essay was, however, originally cast in its present, longer, form, and its overall purport is in several respects substantially different. I am very grateful to seminars in Canberra, Sussex, Cambridge, Manchester and Wisconsin for their helpful comments upon it. (Perhaps I should say that it only deals very partially with the issues I tried to discuss in 'Religion and Society in Buganda 1875–1900', *East African Studies No. 8*, which I have not sought to reproduce here). Chapter 4 on 'The Namirembe Conferences 1954' was originally published in Australia as 'The Buganda Mission 1954' in a special number of *Historical Studies* which was prepared in honour of Sir Keith Hancock. I am very grateful to the editor for permission to reprint it here. Chapter 3 began as a tract for the times in *International Affairs*, XXXII, 3, (July 1956). I have somewhat recast it for inclusion here, and I am very grateful to the editor for permission to do so. I am also very grateful to the editors of the *Uganda Journal* and *Comparative Studies in Society and History* who originally published Chapters 2 and 5 for their kindness in allowing me to republish them. Thanks – in more ways than one – to Professor Kenneth Robinson, Chapter 6, 'Political Parties in Uganda 1949–62', originally appeared as Commonwealth Paper No. 8, published by the Athlone Press. Friends of mine have rightly objected that it deals more with Buganda than Uganda. I hope, therefore, that its appearance here may not be thought inappropriate. It has been out of print for some time, and as there appears to be some continuing demand for it, I am very much indebted to Professor Robinson's successor, Professor W. H. Morris-Jones, to the Athlone Press, and to the University of London for permission to reproduce it. Because of the passage of time I have in places altered a tense here, or added a phrase there – as I have indeed in Chapter 2 as well. The substance of each, however, remains as originally presented.

I wish I could effectively thank all those who have helped me to come thus far in my understanding of Buganda. I can only affirm that I know of no brotherhood equal in generosity to that which has concerned itself with its study, and it continues to be an undiminishing delight to participate in it. I must, however, thank as well all those very many Baganda who during the 1950s gave me so unstintingly of their time and their confidence, often indeed when it was far from their interest to do so. I should also like to thank those in the four Universities of which I have been a member – at Exeter and Nuffield Colleges, Oxford; Makerere; the Australian National University; and Sussex – who have so often been so generous with their assistance. Belle, my wife, has been my most cheerful and – in all conscience – long-suffering helper. At the end, Yvonne Wood has once again alone made the final version possible. My thanks are very heartfelt.

Sussex
November 1969   D. A. LOW

Introduction

Of all the kingdoms of east, central and south Africa that persisted through the colonial period and into the immediate aftermath of independence, none was of greater significance than the kingdom of Buganda. By the nineteenth century, after perhaps four centuries of continuous history[1], its ruler, the Kabaka, had developed a substantial royal supremacy over his kingdom. Within a very short time, however, of the first contact with alien visitors from beyond the immediate horizon, some remarkable conversions to Islam and to Christianity were taking place at his court; and in the last years of the nineteenth century a revolution of seminal importance occurred there. This became coupled with the extension of British imperial authority over the kingdom which was marked both by a close alliance between its victorious Christian elite and the British in the country, and by a greater degree of autonomy for Buganda than was possessed by any other African kingdom during the colonial period. Throughout the first half of the twentieth century this made it the cynosure of a great many other African peoples, not only in the immediate vicinity, but in many other parts of Africa as well.

Throughout the colonial period – which stretched in this area from 1890 to 1962 – Buganda was by far the most important part of the British Protectorate of Uganda. It saw the greatest European impact. It possessed the largest population. It enjoyed the most privileged constitution. It was the breeding ground for many of the most notable features of Uganda's modern development. Administratively it constituted one of Uganda's four Provinces, whereas the other dozen component parts of the Protectorate were not more than Districts, even the three western kingdoms of Bunyoro, Toro and Ankole, which

I

shared with Buganda the distinction of having treaty relations with the British that were not enjoyed elsewhere. In a great many senses it stood at the heart of the Uganda Protectorate, and was the prime element in ensuring that in the half century before independence it retained a greater 'African' character than any other part of eastern, central or southern Africa. With the coming of independence, however, Buganda found itself overwhelmed by the greatest crisis in its history. This eventually culminated in May 1966 in the fateful assault by the independent Government of Uganda upon the palace of its Kabaka. Thereafter the kingdom lay in ruins.

In a series of essays this book discusses the major themes and episodes in this eventful story. It does so with an eye to the social and political organisation of Buganda; to the conventional explanations of religious conversion; to the debates about 'imperialism'; to the theorising about the rise of nationalist parties; to the sequence in the world-wide advent of independence; to the conditions affecting African states upon its attainment; and to the exigencies of writing societal history. It traverses the critical period from just after the middle of the nineteenth century to just after the middle of the twentieth – from, that is, the last decades of the pre-colonial period, through the colonial, and into the first decade of the post-colonial era.

By way of introduction three sets of considerations may be offered.

First, it is worth emphasising that at most the events with which this book is concerned took place within something less than three generations. Grandsons of Apolo Kagwa (who for so many of the earlier decades was *Katikiro*, that is Chief Minister, of Buganda) were still relatively young professional men when they faced the events of the 1950s and 1960s. Kagwa himself had held important positions in Buganda before the colonial advent; his most prominent son Kawalya Kagwa (who in the late 1940s held his father's old office of Katikiro) only died in 1968 after the seminal post-independence events had already occurred. Viewed in these terms the manifold occurrences to which this book refers take on some of the breathless quality which they possessed; and the resilience with which they were met – and the vividness with which they are recalled – may be the more readily appreciated. When Apolo Kagwa was a boy his countrymen were still making their first few contacts with the first alien visitors from Egypt and the Sudan, and from Europe and North America; and it was not so long since they had welcomed the first visitors to their country from the East African coast. Just a century later one of his grandsons – a professional lawyer and a university graduate, attributes of a very particular kind, unknown in Buganda hitherto – was his country's permanent representative on the Security Council of the United Nations in New York. The radical changes in the framework within which the thoughts of such a family revolved and within which their actions operated – 'the enlargement of scale' as it has been termed – are not hard to envisage. The intervening century had in so many ways been tumultuous.

This was the common experience of most east and central African peoples.

It is tempting to believe that their most profound political experience centred upon the advent, persistence, and departure of their colonial rulers. Superficially this was patently the case, and a good deal of recent writing has been devoted to some of the features of this story which have hitherto been inadequately explored.[2] It is becoming clear, however – and this is the second set of considerations to be offered here – that there was a much more fundamental theme to the political history of Africa during the century considered here – a theme which runs forward into the post-colonial, as it runs back into the colonial, and in certain quarters to the pre-colonial period as well. What I have in mind is the profound process of multiple 'aggregation', comprising, in particular, the erection, often for the first time, of an ambitious series of successively inclusive polities. Indeed the significance of the colonial period looks increasingly to lie precisely in its relationship to this process.

Since the colonial period did not see Africa subjected to one colonial power, but to many, the overall unification of Africa was not much advanced during it; and for all the enthusiasm devoted to Pan-Africanism since independence, Pan-African unity has not proved to be a flourishing enterprise. There were some 'regional' aggregations – if we may term them that – which were mounted by the colonialists: but their endeavours at this level were not unequivocal, as the post-independence experience of Nigeria or the Sudan, East Africa, francophone

3

West Africa and francophone Equatorial Africa all indicate. A great deal of colonialist activity did, however, go into creating a comprehensive series of 'territorial' aggregations in Africa. It was within these that the nation-states of Africa took shape. They owe indeed not only their curious dimensions, and many of their key institutions, but much of their political leadership (some of it, of course, largely by reaction) to the colonialist intrusion – as well as a good deal of their political fragility. On this last point it should be remembered that colonial rule did not seek to secure its 'territorial' aggregations in any social reality. Only very tardily were there efforts to man its key institutions at this level with local people from the aggregated parts; throughout the colonial period indeed they were very largely monopolised by transient alien bureaucrats.

There was some attention given by the colonial powers to what we may call – on the next level down the pyramid – 'provincial' aggregations; but for the most part these were accorded considerably less attention than 'territorial' or 'district' aggregations: and with very few exceptions – like the 'regional' aggregations – turned into nothing. The most striking aggregations occurred below this at what we may call the 'district' level.

These did not by any means always proceed smoothly. There were in fact frequently 'sub-district' aggregations that militated against successful 'district' aggregations. Sometimes indeed precisely as 'district' aggregations proceeded some minority peoples within them felt increasingly uncomfortable and strove very vehemently to break away from them. (In Uganda – to take just two examples – the Sebei succeeded in breaking away from Bugisu in 1962, while the Bakonjo came out in open revolt against being incorporated in Toro around the same time).[3] Even so there were a great many effective 'district' aggregations, and it has so often been these which have constituted the major occurrences of political history, at all events in East Africa, during the course of the past century. In Kenya for example the Kamba peoples of Machakos District became increasingly the Kamba people; Luo peoples the Luo people; Luyia peoples the Luyia people; Gusii peoples the Gusii people. Sometimes the beginnings of aggregation preceded the colonial advent – amongst for example (thanks to their *orkoiyots*) the Nandi and the Kipsigis. Sometimes it took an abortive path, as when

4

Wanga chiefs were sent to lord it over other Luyia peoples, till they had to be withdrawn. In all this the influence of the imposition of the colonialists' district-focused administration seems to have been substantial, as also the cohesive proclivities of successive generations of the local elites. The strength of the 'district' model can be seen very clearly, and most paradoxically, in the Kikuyu instance. Given the size and extent of the Kikuyu people 'provincial' aggregation could here have had a very real basis in social reality. Kikuyu country was divided, however, by the colonial régime into the three districts of Kiambu, Fort Hall and Nyeri – with consequences which persisted; and over several decades there were a series of drives towards Kikuyu solidarity by the Kikuyu themselves which look to have owed more to their reaction to this division than has been generally allowed.

Where there was no intractable minority problem the development of a 'district' aggregation was often substantial. It was usually aided by the fact that the administrative and political institutions which the colonialists erected were almost always manned – as they were not at the 'territorial' level – by people with all sorts of local connections. It was aided too because it was often based in a latent or actual social reality. And it looks as if it was assisted as well both by an awareness amongst the peoples concerned that aggregation at this level was accepted as legitimate by the colonialists – who assumed that all Africans were members of cohesive tribes – and could thus hope to make headway with their support (as cults, or independent churches, or inter-tribal nationalism only could with difficulty), as well as by the sense that in an era when one's horizons were enlarging very extensively 'district' aggregation – given the other concerns with which it coincided – could provide the now greatly needed new measure of psychological security. At all events this became an increasingly major preoccupation, amongst the Chagga and Haya of Tanganyika, amongst the Bagisu and Lango of Uganda, to name but four other East African instances from amongst a great many.[4]

Seen in this context Buganda's really very special position becomes very plain. In the first place it was that very rare phenomenon – a 'provincial' aggregation. This put it out of line with most of its contemporaries, sometimes to its advantage, sometimes (especially at the end) to its disadvantage. For a long time, moreover, Buganda played a much more substantial part than any other 'tribal' aggregation at the 'territorial' level. Part of its activity here went back to the pre-colonial period when it exercised a measure of political pre-eminence over many of its neighbours. It was sustained, however, and even enlarged, during the colonial period. Contemporaneously with the onset of colonial rule one of its most famous sons, Semei Kakunguru, established his own Buganda-like dominion over several of the peoples away to the northwest.[5] Thereafter he and many of his contemporaries were used by the British administration as agents of imperial dominion there and elsewhere. With them went many of the values, including the new values of Buganda – and many of the institutions, including the new institutions of Buganda as well. Under the British the Baganda indeed had an immense influence in the very much wider territory which perhaps appropriately enough found itself named Uganda. And it was very largely because of these things that Buganda found itself so vulnerable when, with independence, the other peoples being aggregated within Uganda secured access to the key institutions at its centre. For by that stage, Buganda not only seemed to stand for the old régime: in very many respects it was the very quintessence of the old régime.

Buganda's most notable difference from most of the other large tribal aggregations lay, however, in the fact that while for most of them their aggregation has been an occurrence of the last century or so, Buganda's prime aggregation had occurred several centuries before. Further south in Africa there were other pre-colonial kingdoms which persisted into the twentieth century; but virtually all of them, even when they were built on previous foundations, were creations of the nineteenth century, and not of any earlier period.[6] Buganda's continuous history stretched back far behind that. This meant that it had a much more substantial political solidarity, a much more elaborated political style, and a much weightier political tradition. It meant too that – apart from peripheral aggregations to it during the colonial period of, for example, the Koki people and the islanders of Buvuma – it was not pre-occupied during the colonial period with the major strains of aggregation. Its major concern was to uphold the particular aggregation which had already occurred. Several of its immediately neighbouring kingdoms were in a somewhat similar position,[7] but few of them on quite the same scale as Buganda. Bunyoro was licking its wounds. Toro was, at most, a nineteenth century creation, and was still involved in aggregating with some of its neighbours – as indeed was Ankole.[8] All in all in fact, whilst Buganda was enmeshed in a good deal of the aggregating process, its relation to it was really very particular and unusual.

Yet if it happened that in these respects Buganda's experience was out of line with that of the other peoples of eastern, central and southern Africa, it seems clear (now that more is coming to be known about these other peoples) that in other ways – and this brings us to the third set of considerations – its experience was strikingly similar to theirs, only – if we may put it like this – more so. Few African peoples displayed, for example, a more active and articulate initiative *vis-à-vis* the colonial intrusion than Buganda, not merely at the beginning of the colonial period, but all the way through to its end. In an earlier study I have recounted a particularly vivid example of the leaders of Buganda actively fashioning their own destiny in their negotiations with the British administration prior to the so-called Uganda Agreement of 1900.[9] There are other examples of such initiatives to be found later in these pages. Indeed, seen from the vantage point of Buganda there has never been much doubt about the reality of African initiative during the colonial period – though neither, let it be added, of the truth of Professor Ajayi's *caveat* that 'it is probably an exaggeration to suggest that the Europeans were not generally masters of the colonial situation'.[10] The modern history of Buganda reveals very clearly indeed the tensions which ran between these coexistent poles, and is perhaps an object lesson for those making investigations of similar developments elsewhere.

Equally, the modern history of Buganda displays, not just the pre-eminence of its leaders as 'collaborators' with their colonial rulers, or the presence amongst them of 'resisters', but the coexistence of these roles in one and the same person – in Kabaka Mwanga for example – to an extent which is now increasingly coming to be recognised. If Buganda's leaders

7

appear from one angle to have been arch collaborators with their colonial rulers, it is very apparent that they were also amongst the most adroit and successful resisters as well. More than that: their story shows very clearly that collaboration and resistance were not issues which, simply, divided men into two camps: on the Buganda evidence (confirming indeed what one would think *a priori*) these were issues over which many of the same individual and collective minds agonised continuously.[11]

In the nineteenth and twentieth century Buganda saw a substantial 'Christian' revolution – on a much larger scale indeed than almost anywhere else in the region. It saw as well 'improvement' – to take Dr Iliffe's term – again to a greater extent than in most other places. Furthermore its modern history exemplifies – in a fashion which has very few equals – the politics of what Dr Lonsdale has called 'local focus', more particularly in opposition to what he calls 'central focus' (in this instance as symbolised by the Legislative Council of the Uganda Protectorate Government to which it was persistently opposed). It exemplifies too the operation of what he has called 'social communicators', including their decline and fall by the 1940s.

There is some special difficulty, it seems, concerning the term populism. In an otherwise often helpful essay, Dr John Saul has suggested that the characterisation of 'the people', which I have given in an article republished here, is misleading. In Buganda 'the people' were, he – correctly – insists, extensively differentiated. It is obfuscating, he says, to grant a representative character to the politically articulate groups amongst them; while by using the term 'populism' we may well be displaying 'the relative superficiality of our analysis'.[13] I confess to finding all this unwarranted. It is like saying that even in a brief outline analysis of British political history from the late nineteenth century through to the middle of the twentieth – dominated as so much of it was by the Conservatives – we should not make statements like 'Labour came to power in 1945', lest we forget the degree of differentiation within the Labour movement itself, fail to ask apposite questions about the representative character of Labour Members of Parliament, and imagine that we have said all that needs to be said about

Britain in the 1940s. These are important issues – for a full-scale study and in due proportion.

Peter Worsley's paraphrase of Edward Shils' characterisation of populism (which is based on North American examples), seems to serve quite adequately for Buganda.

Populism, for him [so this runs], involves subscription to two cardinal principles: (a) the supremacy of the will of the people 'over every other standard, over the standards of traditional institutions and over the will of other strata. Populism identifies the will of the people with justice and morality'; (b) the desirability of a 'direct' relationship between people and leadership, unmediated by institutions. Such styles of popular participation, it is commonly observed, are generally accompanied by a quasi-religious belief in the virtues of the uncorrupted, simple, common folk, and a converse distrust of the 'smart', effete, supercilious, aristocratic, idle, wealthy, functionally unnecessary and basically degenerate or corrupt; 'an ideology of resentment against the order imposed on society by a long-established ruling class, which is believed to have a monopoly of power, property, breeding and culture.'[14]

Once again Buganda would seem to have seen a much wider East African phenomenon in a rather sharp form, largely one would think, *pace* Dr Saul, because of the unusual authority of its appointed chiefs.

The first of the chapters which follows reviews how this authority was established in the aftermath of the seminal conversions to the new religions which first occurred in Buganda during the last third of the nineteenth century, and of the revolution which ensued both upon them and upon a series of other developments within the body politic of Buganda. The second is largely a content analysis of the original British interest in Buganda (and the areas surrounding it) of a kind which is not often feasible. The third reviews the course of British–Buganda relations over the greater part of the colonial period; while in the fourth detailed attention is given to the moment in the transfer of power in Uganda and East Africa when elected representatives from Buganda appear to have had a preeminently important influence upon the whole process. In the fifth chapter a review is made of the advent of a striking political phenomenon within Buganda itself. In the sixth the chequered history of the political parties of Uganda – all of them originally

9

based in Buganda – is traced through the fifteen years prior to independence. While the final chapter picks up a whole complex of earlier themes with a view to emphasising that the bitter clash between the Kabaka of Buganda and President Obote of Uganda in 1966 was not, simply, just one episode in post-independence politics, but the culmination of a long-gestating encounter in Uganda over social and political values. The publication of President Obote's *Common Man's Charter*[15] as this book goes to press is a logical extension of the analysis which is offered there.

The essays vary in their approach. At least two involve a close concentration on detailed events and detailed analysis. The first is a resumé of my own detailed work on a subject on which several of us are still engaged.[16] The fifth and sixth stem *inter alia* from my having been a newspaper correspondent in Buganda over several years; while the third and the last represent a first and a final attempt to mull over the experiences of Buganda in the past century rather more generally. Taken together they illustrate one series of ways in which it seems possible to attempt to illuminate the modern history of an African kingdom.

NOTES

1. In his work on Apolo Kagwa's *Basekabaka be Buganda* Dr M. S. Kiwanuka is throwing new light on this.
2. For a striking study see John Iliffe, *Tanganyika under German Rule 1905–1912*, Cambridge, 1969.
3. Uganda Government, *Exchange of Despatches between His Excellency the Governor and the Secretary of State for the Colonies concerning the creation of Sebei District*, Entebbe, 1962; Uganda Government, *Report of the Commission of Inquiry into the Recent Disturbances amongst the Baamba and Bakonjo of Toro*, Entebbe 1962.
4. These points are inherent in a good deal of current and as yet still largely unpublished research. For a preliminary review see the introductory chapter in the Oxford *History of East Africa*, Volume III (forthcoming).
5. The researches of Dr Michael Twaddle will illumine this story further than hitherto.
6. See Jan M. Vansina, *Kingdoms of the Savanna*, Madison 1966, and J. D. Omer-Cooper, *The Zulu Aftermath, a Nineteenth Century Revolution in Bantu Africa*, London 1966, for summaries.

7. The closest parallels are probably to be found in Rwanda and Burundi. Since the influence of the two of them seems to have been confined during the colonial period to the limits of their own territory, they probably cannot be compared to Buganda in the other respects mentioned here.

8. D. A. Low, 'Uganda: the Establishment of the Protectorate', in V. T. Harlow and E. M. Chilver, *History of East Africa*, Volume II, 1966.

9. D. A. Low and R. C. Pratt, *Buganda and British Overrule: 1900–1955*, London 1960.

10. See the chapters by John D. Hargreaves (Ch. 6), T. O. Ranger (Ch. 9) and J. F. A. Ajayi (Ch. 15) in L. H. Gann and Peter Duignan, *Colonialism in Africa 1870–1960*, Volume I, Cambridge 1969.

11. R. Rotberg and A. A. Mazrui, *Resistance in Africa* (forthcoming).

12. T. O. Ranger, 'Connexions between "Primary Resistance" Movements and Modern Mass Nationalism in East and Central Africa', *Journal of African History*, XI, 3 and 4 (1968); Iliffe, op. cit.; J. M. Lonsdale, 'Some Origins of Nationalism in East Africa', *Journal of African History*, IX, 1 (1968), pp. 119–146.

13. John Saul, 'Africa', in Ghita Ionescu and Ernest Gellner, *Populism: Its Meanings and National Characteristics*, London 1969, pp. 124–7.

14. Peter Worsley, 'The Concept of Populism', ibid., p. 244, quoting Edward Shils, *The Torment of Secrecy: the Background and Consequences of American Security Policies*, London 1956, pp. 98–104.

15. A. Milton Obote, *The Common Man's Charter*, Kampala 1969.

16. I have particularly in mind the meticulous researches of Dr John A. Rowe of Northwestern University.

Conversion, Revolution and the New Regime in Buganda 1860–1900

I

Buganda lies on the equator, around the northwest shore of Lake Victoria, some eight hundred miles inland from the East African coast. During the nineteenth century it was only one of perhaps forty or fifty neighbouring kingdoms of greater or lesser size. Three or four centuries earlier it seems to have been amongst the smallest of these. But, following the advent of iron smelting techniques, the forest which covered its homeland was steadily cut back to reveal an extraordinarily fertile countryside. This made it possible for the production of food to be left almost entirely to the women, while the men were set free for war, for disputation, for labour service for the kingdom, and for political creativity.

They used their time to good effect. Buganda grew in size and cohesion. After about the sixteenth century it does not seem to have lost territory which it had once secured, and whereas its larger neighbour, Bunyoro-Kitara, seems to have steadily declined in power and dominion, Buganda regularly made headway. By the nineteenth century it had reached indeed the position of *primus inter pares* amongst its neighbours, and had become imbued with a confidence in its pre-eminence, and a desire to scale still greater heights, which had no parallel in the region.

For all that, in the later decades of the nineteenth century, the apex of Baganda society underwent a tumultuous upheaval. Many of the details of this period have been recounted before. But there are themes and features to it which have only partially been analysed, and there still seems to be room for an attempt to adumbrate the ongoing linkages and patterns within it, even while eschewing many of the details.

Here was a society whose controlling centre was so articulated with it as to give those that sat at its centre very considerable authority. It nevertheless possessed within it a number of distinguishable tensions and conflicts. The way in which these were added to by the external forces which impinged upon it in the second half of the nineteenth century conditioned most markedly the tempestuous upheaval which then ensued. Because of the particularities of the situation there were some quite unusual occurrences. Amongst the members of the ruler's court, for instance, there were a number of notable conversions to Islam and Christianity. By 1888, moreover, all these things had conspired to bring about an eruption at court of – in many respects – revolutionary proportions. Many of the protagonists in this upheaval were possessed of some quite fervent notions about the necessity for the reordering of society. A stable restructuring, however, proved to be as difficult to secure as in so many other post-revolutionary situations elsewhere. A fierce struggle for control of the commanding heights of the kingdom ensued, which more than once threatened to bring it down altogether. And it was only after a series of traumatic vicissitudes that a firm resettlement was finally attained. Perhaps its most striking feature was that, whilst embodying most of the quintessential components of the previous order, it effectively linked these with a number of new developments that embodied some of the new principles to which the revolutionary tumult had given expression. Once the dust had settled this gave the new régime, which now found itself installed at the apex of Baganda society, an authority and a security which, *pace* the precedents, had not obtained before. It is the sequences in these events which this essay seeks to point up.[1]

II

In the beginning, if one may put it like that, Baganda society appears to have consisted of a congeries of localised lineages and clans. These came to have their 'heads', chosen in the case of the latter from an innermost lineage which held the right to provide the clan head or *Mutaka*. When, as tradition tells us, Buganda got its ruler the *Kabaka* (seemingly in the first instance as an arbitrator from outside) one of his primary titles came to be *Sabataka*, that is head of the *Bataka*, or in other words head of the heads of clans. For several centuries, moreover, he appears to have maintained what Max Weber would have called a 'patriarchal' régime by exercising local control over different parts of the kingdom primarily through chiefs chosen from within clans who had hereditary ties with particular territorial jurisdictions within the country.[2]

But as during the sixteenth, seventeenth and eighteenth century Buganda grew in size and importance, the localised clans (if that is what they originally were) became dispersed, partly, one may suppose, as a result of the greater internal security which political success brought to the kingdom, and partly too because of the inevitable tendencies of localised clans to fissiparate. Dispersal at all events prevailed, and it would seem to have circumscribed the ability of the Bataka, the clan heads, to control and mobilise their own following, while making it easier, in due course, for successive Kabakas to set about increasing theirs. Although there have patently been many, very important, bonds binding Kabaka and Bataka together, it is difficult to resist the impression that there was always a basic conflict between them. For while the Bataka were concerned to control their own parts, the Kabaka's interest was to control the whole. It was not, however, until about the eighteenth century that, beginning more especially with Kabaka Mawanda, substantial political consequences resulted. Nevertheless by the opening of the nineteenth century, the increase in the authority of the Kabaka over the clans, and the reduction in the hereditary hold of certain clans over the territorial jurisdictions into which the kingdom was divided, was already well advanced. Of particular importance here was the increasing appointment at the Kabaka's own personal instance of territorial chiefs who had no clan or hereditary connections with their jurisdictions. The greatest of these chiefs were called *Bakungu*, and their spread through the territorial jurisdictions of the kingdom symbolised the switch in the Buganda polity from it being one which was pre-eminently 'patriarchal' to one which Weber would have labelled 'patrimonial'.

It does not seem to have been long, however, before this first basic tension within the polity, between the Kabaka on the one

hand and the Bataka and their ilk on the other, was comple-
mented by another tension – between the Kabaka on the one
hand and his own direct appointees on the other, between, to
over-simplify, the Kabaka and his Bakungu. For in so far as
each *Mukungu* chief enjoyed extensive jurisdiction over a
substantial portion of the kingdom, he possessed the opportunity
no less than a 'patriarchal' chief, to turn himself into an
overmighty subject; and from the Kabaka's point of view there
was plainly no point in supplanting men with strong lineal
followings by men who would be free to establish strong localised
followings. Accordingly, or so it would seem, some blurring of
jurisdictional boundaries was allowed to remain. Further
non-hereditary appointed chiefs – generically distinguishable
as *Batongole* chiefs, or stewards of royal estates – were given
territorial jurisdictions scattered across those of the larger
chiefs. All subordinate appointments were made directly by
the Kabaka himself; and royal appointees, small and great
alike, were denied any security of tenure. Although granted
considerable local status they could be raised, and toppled,
and switched around at very little notice; like the *daimyo* in
Japan they were required, moreover, to spend a great deal of
their time at court. As a result it became none too easy to turn
oneself into an overmighty subject outside the Kabaka's
reach; and although there could be much disputation at court,
and although much attention had to be given there to balancing
different forces against each other, nevertheless sitting at the
centre of an elaborately articulated political network, the
Kabaka of Buganda came to possess a remarkable royal
supremacy over his kingdom. Its very elaboration, however,
bred a great deal of tension between the Kabaka and his appointed chiefs, which if it were not to be handled adroitly
could very easily lead to an eruption.[3]

However imperfectly, the network of relationships needs to
be viewed in its totality. The clans were now dispersed. They
continued even so to play a substantial part in the operation of
society. They still gave a man a large part of his identity, and
they were vital to issues concerning his marriage and succession.
Because, moreover, clans were generally exogamous – and there
were only in any event about forty of them – they were very
extensively matted together. But if every *Muganda* was in these

circumstances a member by birth of a dispersed exogamous clan, in most cases he now came to be the subject by choice of residence as well of a non-hereditary appointed chief. Buganda society was thus, as it were, double-knit. This indeed was one of its major characteristics. And the two patterns within it, which we may call the Bataka pattern and the Bakungu pattern, the one based upon the principles of unilineal descent, the other on dyadic relationships between each individual and his appointed chief, were those to which the Baganda seem hereafter to have instinctively returned. Their coexistence within their society seems indeed to have been one of the major explanations for the astonishing cohesion it has displayed during the many vicissitudes of the last hundred years.

It probably provides a major explanation as well for the tremendous emphasis the Baganda so often gave to their Kabaka. For along both axes the ordinary peasantry, the *Bakopi*, owed allegiance to – were in fact bound to – their Kabaka. Moreover, although there were marked tensions in the structure of Baganda society – between Kabaka and Bataka, between Kabaka and Bakungu, between Bataka and Bukungu, and between Bataka and Bakungu and Bakopi – there was no point of tension between Kabaka and Bakopi. Not only was there a double nexus between them; they were the only two components in the total structure which belonged structurally to both of its different patterns. Translated into social, political, and ideological realities, these considerations were of prime importance.

For our present purposes it is not only, however, the cohesion that existed within Baganda society which has to be stressed. It is the points of tension within it as well – and more especially those two to which attention has already been drawn, namely the tension between the Kabaka and the leading figures in the unilineal descent groups (the clans), the Bataka, on the one hand, and that between the Kabaka and his own appointed chiefs on the other.

III

It looks as if the first of these set the scene for the remarkable conversions first to Islam and then to Christianity which took

17

place at the Kabaka's court in the second half of the nineteenth century. Their story has often been told before.[4] But there has not been much attempt to ask the question which will be posited here: 'how was it that these conversions took place at all?' This would seem to be a specially important and necessary question. For although there were conversions in other parts of East Africa at this time, almost everywhere else they were from amongst the 'detribalised', from amongst refugees from tribal wars, freed slaves, and so on. Not so in Buganda: here they took place from within the ranks of the most favoured members of a powerful and burgeoning court. The tendency in most quarters – and especially in missionary histories – has been to proceed on the assumption that having related how some proselytisers went here and some went there, it is unnecessary to explain why the first won converts and the second did not. But will this do? Is it really the case that the creed itself, or the quality of its propagators, or the 'blindness' of the peoples to whom the message was preached, were the only important variables? Can it really be argued that Christian missionaries to the Middle East, for example, who never secured more than a handful of converts, were 'less faithful' than those that went to Buganda who won a great many? But if not, what was so particular about the story in Buganda?

The traditional focus of religious attention in Buganda was a pantheon of instrumental gods – of war, of health, of thunder and so on. According to Baganda tradition these had been mainly taken over from the people of the neighbouring Sesse islands in Lake Victoria at some early period in their history when they had needed supernatural support against Bunyoro-Kitara, their much more powerful neighbour to the west-wards. The gods apparently did their duty. They seem indeed to have played a very prominent part in giving Buganda its earlier cohesion in the first two or three centuries of its history. In a way, moreover, which looks to have been typical of that earlier phase, each of these gods became the particular res-ponsibility of one of the originally localised clans. One clan became responsible for providing the priests and mediums of one particular god. And in this way the gods became intimately linked with particular clans, even while performing their tribal-wide functions as well.[5]

With, however, the development of the Kabaka's own pre-eminent authority, the need to turn to the gods to give the kingdom cohesion became reduced, and this seems to have given later Kabakas the opportunity to challenge the old gods directly. By the nineteenth century they had, in any event, become particularly concerned to do this, for the gods by this time remained the one substantial obstacle to the establishment of the full supremacy of the Kabaka and his henchmen over everybody and everything in the kingdom. Through the mouths of their priests and mediums they could still curse a Kabaka; even, some thought, hound him to death. What was worse, such powers were now being used to support the resistance towards the Kabaka's growing authority which was being conducted by the Bataka (with whom, through their association with the clans, the gods were intimately linked). The inherent conflict, that is, between the Kabaka and the Bataka was being aggravated by and conjoined with a conflict between the Kabaka and the traditional gods – which touched, of course, an issue of great moment in a rural polity like Buganda, the conflict between centre and periphery, that could only be resolved in favour of the centre after some very considerable effort.

On such issues the Kabaka could be assured of the support of the men who clustered about his court, and herein, it would seem, lies the meaning of various reports such as this of a scene at the court in July 1874:

There was an unusual assemblage at the palace, and some great question evidently engaged M'tesa's attention. I leaned feebly against the post behind me, and suddenly there were cries and confusion without, and the fatal cords of the executioners were encircling the necks of seven men, who had just been by turns addressing M'tesa. These were the spirit-guardians of the lake, a terror to all Uganda supposed to exercise control over the lake and the river. The terror they have inspired, the murders they have committed, are a matter of tradition. M'tesa had broken the chain of this superstition in order that his men might take me far out upon the lake. M'tesa said to me: 'It pains my bowels (*batn*) to do this, but they have done me and my people great injury, and I do this for you as well.' This execution was followed by a rush into the palace of a large number of officers of the Army, headed by the Kongowee (General in chief) with clubs in their hands. With wild gesticulations and loud vociferations they rushed towards M'tesa, shouting: 'You are the great M'tesa, we are your faithfuls.' Said and Abdul stood by the door and witnessed with their own eyes these executions.[6]

It is important to try and see what was happening here. Into this society secular values had not yet intruded. The supernatural could not, therefore, be ignored. If a powerful ruler was in conflict with the traditional gods, their priests and mediums and allies, the need, from his point of view, was evidently for a new cult over which he himself would have complete control instead of one which was closely associated with his opponents. In Buganda, however, such a change could not be easily effected. There was not very much the Kabaka could do to reform the traditional gods. There were as it happened no further pantheons of gods belonging to any neighbouring peoples which he could satisfactorily borrow. All Baganda traditions were against the Kabaka turning himself into a god; and there was very little to be said for turning the royal ancestors into gods – their priests and mediums could be as troublesome as the priests and mediums of the existing gods.

IV

This being the position which was reached by the middle of the nineteenth century one can begin to understand how extraordinarily timely it was for the Kabaka of Buganda that Arab traders should have arrived about this time at his court, and that they should, among other things, have spoken about Islam. For here was a ready made religion with immense potentialities which the Kabaka could not only adopt as his own, but which he might hope to control and exploit as well.

There were, moreover, by this time other considerations as well. First – and most important – the Arab penetration heralded the arrival within the relatively closed circle of Baganda existence of a vast new world. To meet such a fearsome threat, many African peoples have sought to conjure up some greatly increased supernatural support: and one of the obvious things for them to do has been to develop quite markedly their own existing religion. In response to the Egyptian advent the Nuer of the southern Sudan for example, as Professor Evans-

Pritchard has told us, developed a wholly new series of pro-
phets.[7] Yet to develop his own religion was precisely what the
Kabaka of Buganda could not do. There has, however, always
been an alternative. It has always been possible to adopt the
formula of the invaders instead; and this is what, it would seem,
the Kabaka of Buganda did in his day with Islam. As it happened such a step fitted in very well with the adventurous
proclivities of the Baganda which from time to time they have
displayed in a quite dramatic way. Here and on other occasions
it becomes of enormous importance to recognise that for the
Baganda the golden age always lay in the future. For some of
their neighbours, who over the centuries had been losing territory and importance (not least to the Baganda), the golden
age lay in the past. Not so for the Baganda. For a good deal of
their history they had had their eyes fixed upon the future.
Something therefore like Islam which was at once purposive,
creative and enlarging of the mind had a very good chance of
producing in them a very favourable response. Once indeed its
initial impact had been carefully considered, its adoption came
to be seriously entertained by the Kabaka and his court.

To adopt Islam looked like solving the internal religious
problem which had arisen. It looked like meeting the external
problem by giving access to the spiritual supports which the
Arabs possessed. It accorded very well with the forward
looking approach which held a very prominent place in
Baganda thinking. And it had the additional advantage of
smoothing the way for the enlarging of the long distance
external trade – for cloth and guns and luxury goods of various
kinds – which the Arabs were now introducing.

As a consequence, it would seem, by the mid 1860s the
Kabaka was encouraging some of his courtiers to embrace
Islam fully. Many were becoming circumcised. The Kabaka
himself adopted the Islamic calendar, started to wear Arabic
dress, and for ten years after 1868 annually observed Ramadan.
He supervised, moreover, the building of mosques not only at
his court but out in the countryside (which suggests that he had
a keen interest in invading the rural strongholds of the Bataka
and their associated gods). At the same time he periodically
took it upon himself to expound the Koran to his court, and
thus displayed not just his intellectual interest in its precepts,

but his determination to be closely associated with their promulgation. Nothing comparable occurred in any of the neighbouring kingdoms in East Africa; but then, it may be argued,
none of them saw quite the same complex of developments as
occurred in Buganda.

By the mid 1870s, however, some of Kabaka Mutesa's
initial enthusiasm for Islam was beginning to die down. Muslim converts, for example, were now beginning to refuse to
obey his orders to eat the meat which he sent to them on the
grounds that it had been killed by his royal butcher who had
not been circumcised. The decretals of Islam were apparently
beginning to take precedence over the orders of the Kabaka,
and if such insubordination were to become rife amongst his
own closest associates, all the efforts which he and his predecessors had made to establish a largely untrammelled supremacy
over their kingdom might very quickly be brought to nought.
The trouble, however, was that his Muslim courtiers were
becoming so deeply attached to their newfound faith that they
were not to be easily persuaded to compromise. In about 1876
Kabaka Mutesa had a hundred or more of them put to death
so as to teach the others to mend their ways. But they met their
death boldly, and, at most, those who survived were only
temporarily cowed.[8]

There was now a further matter as well. For by the mid
1870s it was also becoming clear that the giants of the new
world which was now increasingly impinging upon Buganda
were not the Arabs who brought the new wonders to the
country, but the Europeans who manufactured them. And the
Europeans were not Muslims at all. If therefore one was to
make a successful rapprochement with this second and mightier
alien invasion, Islam was unlikely to be of very much assistance.
It is scarcely surprising therefore that when a number of
Europeans came to Buganda in the mid 1870s the Kabaka
should have insisted upon having urgent discussions with them
about Christianity; and hardly to be wondered at either that
he should have ended one of these (with the explorer Stanley
in 1875) by announcing to his court: 'I say that the white
men are greatly superior to the Arabs, and I think, therefore,
that their book must be a better book than Mohammed's.'[9]

V

The Kabaka did not there and then become a Christian, any more than in the end he had become a circumcised Muslim; no wise Kabaka would jump quite so rapidly to such conclusions. But he did give the missionaries who arrived in his country during the next few years a very warm welcome, even though he was careful to oversee personally the formal worship which they conducted at his court – which suggests once again that he was anxious to secure control over the new religion coming to his country and ensure that he himself became closely linked with its promulgation.[10]

Yet, for the rest, the previous story of the conversions to Islam was not repeated. For when in 1879 Roman Catholic missionaries arrived hard on the heels of Anglican missionaries, it soon appeared that there was not just one kind of Christianity in which the Europeans believed, but two; and their respective adherents were soon denouncing each other at court with often uncontrolled vehemence. This presented the Kabaka and his courtiers with a most baffling problem. For if it was important, as in the general interests of their country many of them now thought it was, to secure access to the same spiritual supports which the Europeans enjoyed, how were they to know which version of Christianity they would be best advised to adopt? The answer could not be given quickly. And the whole situation was very complicated; in the first place because there was at the same time some strong resistance to the Kabaka's readiness to entertain Christianity from the Arab traders in the country, and from those about his court who still adhered strongly to Islam; and in the second, because, late in 1879, the adherents of the old gods seized an opportunity when the Kabaka was ill to launch the most serious counterattack they ever succeeded in mounting against all this flirting with alien gods by bringing the medium of the most important of them, Mukasa, the god of the lake and the god of health, to the Kabaka's court amid the cheering of crowds and the beating of drums.

Amid this mounting confusion the more cautious minds about the Kabaka's court now began to ponder very deeply indeed

whether all this upheaval might not have very serious consequences for their kingdom – might not, indeed, undermine both
the integrity of its social order, and its ability to meet any
external danger; the latter being throughout this period an
especially serious consideration in view of the Egyptian attempt
in the mid 1870s to annex the kingdom to their Sudanese
empire. Unlike the Arabs the missionaries were not traders.
They might offer a few presents, or mend a few guns, but their
contribution to the kingdom's economy was virtually nil.
Why then should they be tolerated? It was not long indeed
before these further questions began to figure very largely in
the interminable debates which, from 1879 onwards, frequently took place at open meetings of the Kabaka's court,
usually in his own presence.

As the confusion increased, the Kabaka himself did nothing
to resolve it. Indeed he made it very much worse by swinging
in every possible direction in turn in swift and bewildering
succession. This was not just because he was beset by genuine
intellectual difficulties. It was also, or so it would seem, because
he was very much afraid that if he took a decisive step in any
one direction he might break his court apart into deeply
divided and perhaps even bitterly warring factions. He seems
in short to have anticipated very clearly indeed the rifts which
eventually overtook his court a few years after his death when a
less circumspect man presided over its fortunes. But his non-
committal attitude had some very serious consequences; for
in effect it meant that upon these now momentous issues he was
abdicating his leadership – something which no Kabaka in
living memory had ever done before; and that was to leave his
courtiers floundering.

One of the consequences was that the missionaries found
themselves free to proselytise on their own, so long as they did
not proceed to openly: the Kabaka evidently felt that if he
took any decisive action against them he might well lose the
support of the more forward-looking elements at his court
whose vision of an expanding future for the Buganda kingdom –
which they saw as being brought within reach by grasping
what the missionaries had to present – he personally shared to
the full.

The missionaries made excellent use of their opportunities.

24

They were often devoted men. Whether Roman Catholic White Fathers, trained, as these were, under the fervent eye of the great Cardinal Lavigerie of Algiers, or evangelical Anglicans of the Church Missionary Society from Britain, they radiated a profound conviction in the truth of their creed. At the same time, though never like the Arabs great traders, they not only taught reading and writing; they displayed many of the elemental skills of western civilisation. The leading Anglican missionary, for example, was at once an engineer, and an expert carpenter, printer and house builder. The technological tasks which he in particular could perform not only provoked a desire at the court to be able to do likewise but a wonder and amazement at how all these things could be. As it chanced the gospel which he and his colleagues preached was typical of its time in stressing the intimate connection between Christianity and 'civilisation'. 'This book', one missionary told the Kabaka in presenting him with the Bible, 'is the source of England's greatness.' It so chanced as well that no 'godless' European traders ever came to Buganda at this time to throw any doubts on such claims. And in all the circumstances of the time, it is not therefore altogether surprising that they should soon have been imbibed in a somewhat uncritical manner by some of the young men about the court, who, in the intervals between military expeditions and running errands for their lords, had time on their hands to cluster about the missionaries, to listen to their teaching, and debate it among themselves. They were plainly by this time very anxious for enlightenment. They had fallen into the morass of a very profound intellectual confusion. For close followers of the Kabaka there could be no going back to the old gods. The supernatural, however, could not be ignored. Some of them might still find satisfaction in Islam. But for a number of others this no longer seemed to be the royal road to the great future for themselves and their kingdom for which as earnest, forward-looking, young Baganda so many of them aspired. To such men the adoption of Christianity seemed in the end the only possible course to take. They appear to have been struck by some quite particular features of Christian doctrine. In Africa the supreme God was usually a very distant creature. To a greater extent than Islam, Christianity brought Him within reach. These young men, moreover, were very greatly impressed by the missionaries personally; by their teaching by their individual kindness, by their considerable self-assurance, and by their mechanical skills. It could very well be tha they held the open sesame to the great new order for the kingdom (and for those who aspired to be its future leaders) a they averred.

In due course the only question which had still to be answered was, to which version of Christianity should one adhere ? Some eventually solved the dilemma here by visiting each mission station in turn, and then opting for the one which, for some quite personal reason, they found to be most congenial Most, however, took the rather different course of talking the whole problem out with their closest friends – given the dangers of life at the court of Buganda that was an elementary precaution – before deciding to attach themselves to one mis sion station or the other as a group. As a result of both proces ses by the early 1880s the first baptisms were taking place a the two mission stations, and by 1884 the Roman Catholic and the Anglicans had each baptised about 200 members o the Kabaka's court, many of whom were already formed into closely linked little clusters. These baptisms were sincerely meant. Personal names have immense symbolic importance here. One prominent convert, whose name was Mukasa and had taken the good Old Testament name of Ham – and who had originally been attracted by the technological achieve ments of which the missionaries had showed themselve capable – was soon telling his missionary sponsor, 'Do not call me Mukasa: my name is Ham.'

There were, of course, grave issues at stake here. The first converts were leading where the Kabaka had not gone before The first conversions to Christianity took place, therefore, in very different circumstances from the first conversions to Islam which had been mainly at the bidding of the Kabaka. They arose out of a great many personal and collective decisions to resolve the enormous intellectual, spiritual and psychic con fusion which had overtaken the Kabaka's court by the early 1880s. At the same time it is no coincidence that many of the first converts were young men who were either still bachelors or at most possessed one wife; for they found it easier to resolve their difficulties by becoming Christians than most of the older men who were faced by the enormous difficulties entailed in the missionaries' insistence on monogamy. Had either mission station been willing to relax its position on this issue it is not impossible that the Kabaka himself would have become baptised. But they refused to make special allowances, and he would not give up his wives, because as he pointed out, to do so would be to undermine much of the existing political, social and economic order in his kingdom. His readiness, however, to consider as he did the possibility of following where his young courtiers had gone before – a most remarkable course for any nineteenth century Kabaka to contemplate – gives some idea of the momentum which Christianity was beginning to enjoy at the Kabaka's court by about 1884.

VI

In that year the old Kabaka died, still unbaptised, and was succeeded by his young son, Mwanga. Mwanga, like any new occupant of a traditional throne, was in an unenviable position. He was a man of the same generation as the majority of the Christian converts. He shared their hostility towards the traditional gods and their traditionally minded supporters. He sympathised with their ambitions for a great new future for his kingdom. And in the nature of things, he was soon looking to them to rid him of the incubus of his father's old chiefs. But in a very short time, in large part because the European scramble for Africa was now getting under way, he began to share the concern of the more cautious minds at his court about their loyalties. He was worried lest, in view of the overall circumstances of the mid 1880s, and in particular because of their close association with the European missionaries, they might become traitors to the long-sought, and hard won, autonomy of the Buganda kingdom. This soon became indeed a further major issue of controversy at the Kabaka's court. And in due course, in June 1886, there was a substantial breach. The particular occasion was an interference by some of the young converts with his practice of sodomy – a practise he had learned from the Arabs – a slight upon him to which he reacted very strongly indeed. His sudden anger was fanned by his father's old chiefs, and together they set on foot a severe persecution of the Christian converts, during which (among other things) thirty-two converts were burnt alive on a single pyre on a single day. Many of the converts went into hiding. Some of them, however, very deliberately courted arrest, and went to their funeral pyres singing hymns as they died.[11]

It is important to try and see why. Life, of course, was still relatively cheap in Buganda. Execution was an occupational hazard at the Kabaka's court. Its members had no illusions about the possibility that a sudden change in the Kabaka's humour could quickly bring them to mutilation or death. 'Religious' holocausts, moreover, were part of its culture. But the victims could, of course, have rebelled, as both the Christians and the Muslims in Buganda were to do two years later. At this stage, however, they seem to have had little of the organisation and few of the guns which they were to employ in 1888; and in any event, amid all the vituperous accusations for insolence and treachery which were being levied against them at this time, they were deeply concerned to display their loyalty. But if so, why did they not apostatise? Part of the answer would seem to lie in the fact that in their ranks there were now a number of people who had resolved the immense spiritual and intellectual confusions into which the Kabaka's court had been thrown in the later years of the previous reign by becoming baptised Christians; who had found great comfort and strength from the assurance which that had given them; and for some of whom at least retreat presented greater difficulties than advance. There is certainly every reason for thinking that their Christian convictions had now become very profound and very far-reaching; and there can be no doubt at all that their devotion and fervour had now reached a very high peak.

The same, however, had been true of the Muslims who had been martyred a decade previously; and in all the circumstances of the time, it is difficult to reach a satisfactory understanding of what was afoot here without taking a further consideration into account as well. This cannot be easily specified but may perhaps be put like this. These men – like the Muslim martyrs before them and like later groups of Baganda in various other situations after them – appear to have seen that the point had come when it was quite vital for the future of the society of which they felt themselves to be no less loyal and responsible members than the Kabaka himself, that some of them should make a stand against the existing régime in the country in the interests of forwarding that greater régime towards which for so many centuries of continuing effort Buganda had been striving. In the terms available to them in the 1860s and 1870s that new régime looked like finding its consummation in Islam and through Islam in the culture which the Arab traders were bringing; by the 1880s it found its hope in Christianity and through Christianity in that new civilisation which the Europeans were bringing. In the Baganda martyrs it looks as if we should recognise, that is, groups of young Baganda for whom their own interpretation of the urgent requirements of their own very profound patriotism played a very important part in enhancing their new-found religious enthusiasm to fever pitch. In the mid 1870s, and again a decade later, this involved some of them in openly courting mutilation and death. In the years which followed it led others along some rather different paths.

VII

In the immediate event, however, the unswerving loyalty which the converts gave to an ideal seems to have had a considerable impact upon the Kabaka. It is at this point that it becomes necessary to bring into focus that other main tension at the apex of Baganda society – the tension between the Kabaka and his appointed chiefs – for the alchemy of the time was compounding another whole series of developments to which we must now turn our attention.

So far as this other side was concerned the position was that by 1886–7, quite apart from everything else, Mwanga was becoming acutely aware that he could never be master in his own house so long as he looked for advice to his father's old chiefs. Yet as his mother was continually reminding him he could not rid himself of them – such was the tension which existed between the Kabaka of Buganda and his appointed chiefs – unless he could be sure that his younger contemporaries stood by his side; and he could not be sure of this if he continued to persecute them.

There was now a further consideration as well. In recent years there had been another new development in Buganda of very great importance indeed – namely the advent of guns. If any number of these were to fall into the hands of any budding overmighty subject, the consequences for the Kabaka's supremacy could well be very serious indeed. It was, therefore, vital from his own point of view that so far as possible he should monopolise their employment in his own causes.

In the months that followed the persecution of the Christians Kabaka Mwanga seems to have put all these thoughts together. At any rate he soon started to collect together the young Christians who survived (and who were now emerging from hiding) with a view to forming them up into a very largely new set of institutions – musket armed regiments (if we may call them that) of young courtiers, now scattered across the countryside, like all the pre-existing hierarchies of royalty appointed chiefs, but congregated on estates directly under his own control and near his own capital. These he sent out to raid those appointed chiefs whom he was anxious to overawe. On at least one occasion he took them upon a royal progress himself.

All this promised to bring about the final concentration of coercive power in the kingdom in the hands of the Kabaka and his immediate followers, an objective for which all Mwanga's recent predecessors had been striving and which now looked as if it was about to be secured. To this end, it seems fairly clear that Mwanga deliberately made use of the growing cohesion of the three groups of converts who were now present at his court. For one of his new regiments was officered by the leading Roman Catholic converts; a second by the leading Protestants; and a third by the leading Muslims. It is somewhat odd no doubt that these men should have been so ready to obey his orders to raid the old chiefs. But it must be remembered that the victims of the persecution were, almost by definition, those whose new religion sat more lightly upon them; for reasons we cannot go into their foreigner friends had their eyes at this time focused elsewhere; a Muganda courtier was always happiest when the Kabaka was giving him a firm lead; and it seems clear that in despoiling those of some established prominence the converts saw themselves as engaged upon destroying the old régime in the kingdom, for they took particular pride in raiding the temples of the traditional gods.

To begin with Mwanga was delighted with their performance. So successful indeed did they become that some of the older chiefs in their mounting desperation were very soon trying the expedient of putting it about that if the Kabaka did not take very good care the regiments could very well turn next against him; and to this end they were soon adding as well that unless the Kabaka were to take urgent precautions the Christians amongst them would betray him to the agents of British imperialism, now on their way up from the East African coast. This, of course, was to repeat the charge which had helped persuade the Kabaka to persecute the Christian converts back in 1886. It was just the sort of accusation to which as guardian of the kingdom's autonomy Mwanga had to listen very carefully indeed.

His position was now in any event exceedingly delicate. Nothing illustrates this more vividly than his efforts at this time to force the greatest in the land to labour with their own hands upon enlarging the royal lake alongside his palace. In the course of this palpably symbolic attempt to demonstrate his authority he brought to a head a series of conflicts with various of his courtiers – and not least with some of the Muslim leaders amongst them upon whom he had hitherto been able to rely very greatly. Fearful, moreover, lest his most carefully chosen associates should be in any mood to cast off their loyalty to him, in a number of gadfly actions in August 1888 he put to the test the worst apprehensions which were being whispered in his ear about them.

Greatly to his dismay the convert members of his newly formed regiments – no longer prepared to take their medicine quietly – openly resisted him, although at first not violently. Feeling, however, his worst fears amply confirmed Mwanga now threw all caution to the winds (as his father had been careful never to do), and took the fateful step of launching a direct frontal assault upon them. In September 1888 he attempted to maroon the leaders of his regiments on an island in the crocodile infested Lake Victoria. Such, however, was the turmoil which his impetuous authoritarianism had created at his court that his plot was quickly exposed and collapsed.

This placed him in a quite desperate position. The raids on which he had despatched his regiments and the crude treatment which he had recently meted out at his royal lake to so many of his kingdom's leading figures had lost him the support of most of his established supporters. No Mutaka at this time (no clan head) was likely to lift a finger to help a Kabaka in difficulties. By his plot against the convert leaders he had alienated the most important of his contemporaries. He was left, therefore, with no more than a rag, tag and bobtail of supporters. At first the Christian leaders remained reluctant to turn openly against him. But the Muslim leaders, who had hitherto lain quiescent for a decade past (but had recently been affronted by more than one of his actions) now insisted upon swift rebellion. The symbolism in the Kabaka's plot against the convert leaders was patent. Mwanga had clearly planned to turn them over to the tender mercies of the most important of the old gods, Mukasa, the God of the Lake, and his attendant crocodiles.

So, in the end, the Christian leaders agreed to participate. The great battle between the old order and the new, between the old gods and the new, was obviously now to be joined. The Christian leaders accordingly knelt in prayer overnight and on the morrow sallied forth with the Muslims to the assault. As leaders of the only effective military formations in the country – who alone, moreover, possessed any quantity of guns – they quickly put Mwanga to flight. As Weber would have put it, the patrimonial staff had revolted against their lord. The personal staff was now in control.[12]

VIII

We may emphasise that these events were narrowly confined to the apex of the society. Both its elaborate network of societal bonds and the pervasive influence of its inherited norms were essentially unaffected. A new prince, however, was speedily put on the throne, while the victorious leaders quickly replaced the older generation of chiefs in all the important offices of state. In these respects the events of September 1888 constituted a rebellion. There were changes of personnel, but there were no changes in the institutions of state (except that the newly formed regiments were now allowed to wither away).

In at least two other senses, however, September 1888 constituted a revolution. As we have seen one of the two or three main points of tension at the core of nineteenth century Baganda society ran between the appointed chiefs and their powerfully placed Kabaka. This tension, as Mwanga's creation of musket-armed regiments had indicated, had been steadily building up to a very high peak. If the converts' leaders had not hitherto been territorial chiefs they were nevertheless men who aspired to these positions – as their immediate appropriation of them following their victory makes very clear. As pages and junior chiefs about the court they knew very well, moreover, the acuteness of the conflict to which they would then become heirs. We may remember indeed that in recent years few people had suffered more from the Kabaka's overmightiness than they themselves and their martyred friends. So that, although the leaders of the Muslim-Christian coalition maintained the institutional framework of the state, they nevertheless now took decisive steps to carry through a major change in the locus of power within it. They carried out in effect an oligarchical revolution. They arranged that in future appointed chieftainships in Buganda should be allocated, not by the Kabaka himself as for the most part always hitherto, but by the oligarchy of senior chiefs acting in caucus. As one missionary observer put it late in 1888, 'The poor king was but a child in the hands of his Officers and Ministers. His time was chiefly occupied in giving his consent and approval to the distribution and division of the various chieftainships.'

In all this, however, there was a further revolutionary development as well. For whatever else the Christian and Muslim leaders now may have been, they were by this time millenarians as well. Thus it was that we find the same missionary observer going on to remark:

Many began to believe that the change they had been anxiously looking and longing for had been granted a beginning. . . . For a time the Baganda came about the [mission] station like a swarm of bees, from the dawn of light to the dusk of evening. . . . Many chiefs came to visit us, asking and beseeching us for Alphabet sheets that they might teach their followers and slaves. . . . As each several

Sunday came round a large number of people gathered together to hear and read the Word of God.[13]

It looked indeed as if the new religious order which had been edging its way into position at the Kabaka's court had now seized control of it. To the missionaries and the Christians there, it was as if the millenium had already dawned.

But as things turned out it very soon proved to be a false dawn. For once having let revolution loose on the apex of the kingdom, it proved exceedingly difficult to hold its disintegrating proclivities in check. Within a month indeed of the coalition's victory, the coalition itself broke into two. It split, as one might have expected, down its weakest axis. The Muslims plotted to expel the Christians, and, being first off the mark, were quickly successful; they were encouraged by the Arabs in the country, who like Mwanga and the Baganda traditionalists, did not want to see the Christians in positions of power in the kingdom, since they feared that they would use these to deliver it into the hand of the now-advancing European empire-builders. As, moreover, the turmoil deepened so fissiparous tendencies began to run right through the victorious elite. The Christians and the Muslims broke apart in 1888; by 1890 the Protestants and Roman Catholics had begun to quarrel violently amongst themselves; and thereafter at least two separate minority groups made their presence felt within (and one actually broke away from) the Protestants; while both the Catholics and the Muslims soon found themselves splitting to an even more grievous extent. Whatever else was going on here there was soon a great deal of factionalism giving itself vent, as well as a hard-fought battle for supremacy within the revolutionary elite itself. As Mutesa I seems to have feared, when the eventual crisis overtook his court it broke it apart into several sharply estranged sections.

Nevertheless the whole conflict had at the same time some very much more profound aspects to it as well. It was based, of course, on religious differences; indeed on missionary animosities. The crucial points to remember are, however, that, in the first place, for thirty years or more the forward-looking elements at the Kabaka's court had been looking for the creation of a new order: this now seemed to be beginning. But, in the second, that for the past fifteen years there had been a deep, and as yet still unresolved, difference of opinion amongst them about whether it should be based upon Islam, or upon Roman Catholicism, or upon Anglican Protestantism. This, of course, constituted an issue of quite vital importance. For if there really was to be a wholly new régime in Buganda, it was patently essential to see that its foundations were right. This was precisely the point, however, on which the adherents of the three new religions differed so greatly. As members of Mwanga's regiments they had during 1887 and 1888 already found themselves committed to fighting in the interest of larger ends within their kingdom. It is hardly to be wondered at therefore that when these deeper matters had come to the fore they should quickly have shown themselves ready to take up arms again and again. For the outcome was of immense importance to so many of the issues with which they had been concerned from their youth up.

The result was five years of turmoil and civil war. On more than one occasion the apex of the kingdom looked like falling completely apart. Sudden triumph was frequently followed by cruel disaster. Each faction had in turn to face the prospect of being excluded from the kingdom altogether. Gradually, however, the Christians managed to lay their hands on the levers of power in Buganda – though not without suffering more than one setback on the way.

IX

It was at this very moment, as it turned out, that the first British agents finally advanced into Buganda, and, as Dame Margery Perham has spelled out in her life of Lord Lugard, established their imperial control over it without coming across any concerted opposition.[14] One vital factor in their success was that, in the prevailing circumstances, it was none too difficult for them to seize the interstitial position between the warring factions at the core of the kingdom, and build up their authority upon it – very much as Baganda tradition suggests that Kintu, the first Kabaka, had done when the kingdom was originally founded. And there was a further circumstance as well, since there can be no doubt that the advent of the British was welcomed by the Christians in Buganda (and more particularly by the Protestants) because they looked like being the

best guarantors of the particular new régime which this particular section of the revolutionary elite was by this time striving
to establish. Calling in outside assistance was by no means ille-
gitimate in the kingdoms of this region. Kabaka Mwanga
himself was among those who had appealed to the British for
help. Such, however, was now the enthusiasm generated by
ideological commitments and by ideological conflict that for
many of the revolutionaries – as Mwanga and the traditionalists had all along feared – the attainment and security of the
new régime they were fashioning now clearly took precedence
over the need to maintain the autonomy of the kingdom.

The British for their part were often reluctant to take sides in
the civil war which they found erupting around them. In its
early days, when the Christians had found themselves hard up
for a prince to give traditional legitimacy to their designs they
placed their former persecutor, the exiled Kabaka Mwanga, at
their head. By the time Lugard arrived, Mwanga was back on
his throne; and to begin with Lugard showed himself anxious
to do what he could to build up his authority within the kingdom. It soon became apparent, however, that an inherently
unavoidable conflict ran between the two men. For while the
Kabaka represented the autonomy of Buganda, Lugard represented British imperialism on the offensive. The resulting
confrontation was not long delayed. It became interlocked,
however, with the rivalry between the Protestants and Catholics
in the country. For while Lugard was a countryman of the
Protestant missionaries, Mwanga during his exile at the south
end of Lake Victoria in 1888–9 had thrown in his lot with the
Catholics. When indeed the climax eventually came in February 1892, it took the form of a battle, fought in the highways and
byways of the Kabaka's capital at Mengo, in which Lugard and
the Protestants defeated Mwanga and the Catholics.

The outcome was shortly afterwards spelt out by one of the
Protestant chiefs who wrote to one of his missionary friends that,
'We hope that the Protestants will now have chief power in
Uganda, and I think the land will perhaps be at peace . . . King
Mwanga has hoisted the English flag and it is now flying
before his house.'[15]

He might have added that the oligarchical revolution had
probably been saved as well. For had the Catholics emerged

victorious in 1892 whilst Mwanga stood at their head, it is difficult to believe that he would not have made use of the very strong moral position which this would have brought to him to have secured a return of at least some of his previous authority. As things eventuated, however, he was lucky to hold on to his throne; and to this end he very soon thought it would be wise to turn Protestant.

The Catholics meanwhile took themselves off to a separate part of the country. If the Protestants had had their way they would quickly have followed after them, until one or other of them had been completely destroyed, as the year before the two of them had gone far to destroy most of the Muslims.

The British, however, were anxious for peace, not least because it would thereby be easier to secure their imperial authority. They made it their policy therefore to attempt to effect a reconciliation between the two Christian factions, while trying to find room as well, in any settlement which might be procured, for the few Muslims who remained in the country. Their chief expedient was to allot each party control over a separate portion of the kingdom. Because the Catholics, however, isolated themselves from the others in the southwestern county of Buddu this proved to begin with a not altogether effectual policy. Accordingly late in 1892, Williams, Lugard's successor, began to turn his mind to this matter, and early in 1893 managed to secure the presence of the Catholic leaders back in the capital at Mengo once again. He thereby laid the foundations for the reunification of the core of the kingdom which had up till then been in very great danger of falling apart into two or more separate sections.[16]

There were still, even so, many vicissitudes – including a further conflict with some of the Muslims in 1893, which looks as if it was precipitated by the new privileges granted to the Catholics. A working settlement, nevertheless, eventually emerged. There was an even distribution of offices of state between the Catholics and the Protestants – including the creation of a second chief ministership for the leading Catholic chief. Some Muslims were granted the leavings from the rich men's tables, in the shape (eventually) of just one county, and were happy to take them. And by 1894 it looked as if both the Catholics and the Protestants and the few remaining Muslims were beginning to think that for all the differences between them it would now be best to live and let live with each other. The personal bonds between each of the three parties and their consciousness of their common inheritance remained at once active and pervasive. In the end indeed many of those who stood at the head of the warning parties seem to have been ready and even anxious to see the apex of the kingdom coagulate once again.[17]

It looks as well as if after several years of tumult and civil war there was now some lessening of ardour upon all sides, not least when it became clear to the Protestants in particular that their British mentors did not really think it mattered very greatly after all whether Buganda became Protestant or Roman Catholic, and were quite happy to see it become a combination of the two, with Islam as a minor addendum. Some caution is necessary here. Religion still played a very considerable part in the thinking of the elite. Some of the Anglicans amongst them, for example, preferred to become ordained Anglican clergymen to becoming chiefs; while two of the most senior Protestant chiefs became both chiefs and ordained Anglican ministers. A great deal of effort, moreover, was put by the Christians in Buganda at this time into proselytising their kinsmen and their neighbours, not least in the kingdoms surrounding them. But gradually these endeavours took the place of the tumult and violence which had so engrossed these men's minds in the years which had immediately preceded.[18]

X

The resettlement amongst the ruling few of the mid-1890s was not, however, final and conclusive. It very soon became apparent indeed that there were numbers of people, not least amongst the revolutionaries themselves, who – as their renewed partiality for alcohol and for a plurality of wives served to demonstrate – were deeply dissatisfied with more than one aspect of the new régime; and in 1897 they were dramatically joined by Kabaka Mwanga himself, who fled from his capital, and raised the standard of revolt amongst them.

He quickly made it very clear that he was kicking against

almost everything which characterised the new régime. In the first place he rejected British imperial supremacy. Here he was being true both to his salt, and to all those fears to which he and his father's old chiefs had frequently given expression before 1888. He was seeking as well to overthrow the oligarchical revolution. Evidently with this very end in view he had tried in recent years on more than one occasion to wean the Catholics away from their growing association with the Protestants. But he had not succeeded; and in 1897 the event which finally precipitated his flight was a humiliating contretemps with his two Christian Chief Ministers. He was kicking as well against the Christian ascendency, as he very soon demonstrated by now turning Muslim.

As it happened the revolt which he now proceeded to lead soon became interlocked with a mutiny amongst some of the Sudanese in the country whom the British employed as mercenaries to help them maintain their pre-eminence over it. For a time indeed the British position became exceedingly precarious. But such was now the attachment of the ruling Buganda oligarchy to their oligarchical revolution and to the new régime which they had been bringing into being, that (strongly supported by their missionary mentors) they not only supported the British against the mutineers: they supported the British against their own Kabaka as well. Such, moreover, was the effectiveness of the authority of those who held control of the appointed offices of state in Buganda that they carried the bulk of the population with them. And in the event, by 1899, Kabaka Mwanga was apprehended and deported to the Seychelles (his infant son Daudi Chwa having already been placed on his throne in his place).

It was only with this that the last protest of the old order against the new was eventually concluded; and we may note that in the next twenty years the only substantial movement against it found its chief expression, not in another uprising, but in the creation of a separatist church. There seemed little point hereafter in attempting to reject the major premises of the new régime. The only feasible thing to do was turn to one's own use the models it provided.[19]

Through it all, and for all the marching and counter-marching, many of the basic features of Baganda society had remained largely unaffected. It was still an overwhelmingly rural society. Across the countryside political authority rested as before in the hands of the hierarchy of appointed Chiefs, while the rich bonds of kinship and clansmanship, and the proprieties under which men lived out their lives, remained those of their forefathers. At the apex, however, critical changes had occurred. In the last years of the century a new régime was installed at the centre, the fruit at once of long years of gestation, and of the harrowing vicissitudes of a revolutionary decade.

XI

Once the security of the new régime had been finally secured a host of readjustments within it came to be made. For a start the Christian revolutionaries now began to place an emphasis upon maintaining the remaining autonomy of their kingdom *vis-à-vis* the British to an extent they had never much troubled about before. Before very long indeed this became a major issue to which they and their successors came to pay very close attention. They may very well have been prompted to it by some realisation at the height of the crisis in 1897 that, when it came to the pinch, British supremacy in their country was as much dependent for its success upon the support which they themselves would give to it as upon the resources it could mobilise itself. But it looks as if they were prompted as well by the clear realisation that, even in their book, Mwanga's revolt had one quite valid point to it. The efforts of all their forefathers would count for nothing if they simply accepted British imperial control hereafter abjectly and completely.[20] Certainly from about 1899 onwards the Baganda oligarchy became increasingly assertive in their contacts with British officials, and increasingly insisted that there should be no further invasion of the autonomy of their kingdom. They did not establish their point here without some difficulty. Early in 1900 there was, for example, something of a crisis where Sir Harry Johnston, 'Her Majesty's Special Commissioner for the Uganda Protectorate', suddenly created the impression that he wished to abolish the indigenous chieftaincies in Buganda altogether. Such was not, as it happened, his purpose. He was anxious to see – in the phrase which later became famous – that the

Kabaka, Chiefs and People of Buganda should undertake 'to cooperate loyally with Her Majesty's Government in the organisation and administration' of the kingdom, but he had no objection to the idea that the existing structure of the Buganda 'native state' should be maintained, and he was perfectly ready to recognise that the Kabaka should be its 'native ruler'. He found himself obliged, however, to write these things into the settlement which he made at this time with the Baganda chiefs.[21]

This was embodied in the so-called Uganda Agreement of 1900 which henceforward became both the envy of Buganda's neighbours and the cornerstone of Buganda's relationship with the British for the next 55 years. For the Baganda revolutionaries it represented a compromise between the causes for which Mwanga and his father's old chiefs had worked and those which they themselves had been prepared to embrace. In a sense it exemplified the policy of the *via media* which during so much of his reign Mutesa I had striven to pursue, but which in the years that followed his death had often been lost to sight in Buganda. Things which had been rent asunder were now to be sewn together.

The fact that the external aspects of the new settlement came in this way to be arranged to the satisfaction of the Baganda leadership – and that this result had very substantially depended upon the support which some of the missionaries had given to them at a critical moment in their negotiations with Sir Harry Johnston – served to seal the existing nexus between church and state which was so central to the whole character of the new régime which the revolutionaries had been concerned to create. Although the adherence of the Baganda to the new religions was rarely again to be of the order which the martyrs had displayed in the 1870s and 1880s, there came to be a remarkable degree of adherence to them even so. Half a century later a trained foreign observer was to report that although he had found some surreptitious belief in traditional religious figures amongst the Baganda villagers whom he knew, 'I met no practitioners of indigenous religion apart from a few who had renounced Christianity for nationalistic reasons'. About fifteen per cent of the rural population had become Muslims: 'the remainder' he reported 'are Christians, mostly either Roman Catholic or Anglican'.[22] Soon after the turn of the century the Katikiro, the chief minister of Buganda, had shown himself ready to help with his own hands in the building of the Anglican cathedral. After the Anglican Bishop he had become the leading figure in the Anglican Synod. From this time forward no open session of the Lukiko, the Buganda political assembly, was to be complete unless the Anglican and Roman Catholic Bishops were personally in attendance; while the first act of the Kabaka on his return from abroad was always to be in future to attend a service of thanksgiving in the Anglican cathedral at Namirembe. The tumult of the last third of the nineteenth century had thus finally eventuated in Christianity becoming in effect the newly 'established' religion of Buganda.

XII

The alien intrusions which had so exercised the Kabaka's court in the preceding decades became in these ways assimilated to the Buganda scene. There were many purely internal readjustments, however, which were worked out as well.

In the first place the oligarchical revolution was now fully institutionalised. Hitherto the *Katikiro* or chief minister had ruled Buganda on the Kabaka's behalf. Since 1892 there had been two Katikiros – one for the Protestants, one for the Roman Catholics. In 1897 these two, and a senior Protestant chief, who was also an Anglican clergyman, had become Regents for the young Kabaka, Daudi Chwa. As a consequence of the 1900 Agreement, their roles came to be restructured. All three remained Regents; but while the Protestant Katikiro remained Katikiro, his Catholic colleague became 'Chief Justice', and the third of them 'Treasurer'. For the future these three 'Ministers' were to constitute 'the Government' of Buganda. The Lukiko, moreover, which had previously been the assembly of those who had come to pay court to the Kabaka, was now formally constituted as the 'native council' of Buganda. It was filled up with appointed chiefs who were colleagues and associates of the victorious revolutionaries; and for the future came to exercise both legislative and judicial powers of some considerable substance.

It is at the same time very intriguing that the decision which, more than any other, assuaged the wrath of the victorious chiefs at the height of their negotiations with Sir Harry Johnston early in 1900 was his agreement to address the young Kabaka, Daudi Chwa, as 'His Highness'. *Prima facie* their concern for the Kabaka's honorific title seems somewhat surprising. Had they not themselves been responsible, not once, but twice and more, for toppling a duly constituted Kabaka off his throne? Why should they now be attaching so much importance to his position? If one looks a little closer, however, their stance becomes very understandable. We may recall that the revolutionaries had persistently been careful to place someone at their head as their Kabaka – however young or however unsatisfactory they might think him to be: the extent of their revolutionary propensities was to this extent clearly limited. We may remark as well that their keen concern for the Kabakaship underlined in a paradoxical way the resounding success which their oligarchical revolution had by this time achieved. For to such an extent had the personal authority of the Kabaka been reduced by the events of the past twelve years that they no longer felt those profoundly aggressive feelings towards him which they and their predecessors had displayed in the past. They could now, it would seem, look upon him in a very much clearer and less jaundiced light.

And when they did so they appear to have seen that he was in many ways crucial to the issues which were critical for them. For, as we began by saying, every Muganda was at once a member by birth of a dispersed exogamous clan, and a subject by choice of residence of an appointed chief, and in both respects ultimately owed allegiance to the Kabaka. In structural terms the Kabaka was, that is, the one person who linked together at its apex the two patterns which ran right through Baganda society. Although the purposes of the oligarchs had patently been revolutionary – in certain respects very substantially so – they had never wanted to effect a total political revolution in their society. Their chief aim had been to establish their own control over it so they might bring about two or three important kinds of change within it. But no more than that. For the rest, having secured control of the positions of power in the kingdom, it was directly against their interest to let its society disintegrate about them. Accordingly, as the period of turmoil ended, so they appear to have become increasingly concerned to shore up its coping stone – that is, to maintain the Kabakaship. Since they were now becoming increasingly concerned to uphold the residual autonomy of their kingdom against any further encroachments by the British upon it, it was highly desirable to emphasise the institution which symbolised its unity and majesty. But what was of even more importance, if the new régime, which in so many respects they were virtually foisting upon their fellow countrymen, was to become fully acceptable to them, there was patently a great deal to be said for maintaining the existing structure of society, even while altering very markedly the allocation of power at its apex. For by such means the very considerable advantages which would flow from enlisting the sanctions of tradition in forwarding the processes of change could thereby be secured. In these respects therefore – for all the importance to them of their oligarchical revolution – the upholding of the office of the Kabakaship was now a vital matter for them.

In seizing upon this point the oligarchs were displaying their consummate political ability. They displayed it as well in several other directions. In putting into operation the new Uganda Agreement with the British they established their own control over the distribution of land in the kingdom. Provision had been made in the Agreement for a land settlement which turned out to be wholly new. Land was now to be distributed in quasi-freehold tenure. At one stroke all the tenures based either upon the claims of heads of clans to control clan lands, or of the Kabaka to distribute land to whomsoever he wished to honour, were in effect swept away. In their place there now appeared the so-called *mailo* tenure; and it did not take the oligarchs very long to seize the opportunity which the Agreement presented to them of parcelling out all the land which was at their disposal under it to their own immediate followers and to any other prominent people in the country who were prepared to accept their authority. As a consequence the ownership of land in Buganda came to be intimately linked with the preservation of the settlement of 1900; and the position of those who stood at its centre was thereby substantially buttressed. Since, moreover, land could henceforward be freely bought, sold and bequeathed in Buganda it soon began to pass into the hands of an increasing number of independent farmers. As a result such demands as subsequently emerged for a change in the land settlement found themselves having to run the gauntlet of an ever increasing number of people whose stake in the economy rested upon it. For very many years this helped to ensure that the settlement of 1900 was never (in anything more than a quite marginal way) called into question.

There were further ingenious arrangements as well. By the terms of the 1900 Agreement Buganda was divided into twenty counties, most of them based upon the old areas of territorial jurisdiction. Eleven of these county chieftainships now went to the Protestants, eight to the Catholics, and one to the Muslims – and apart from a subsequent increase of one for the Muslims at the expense of the Protestants, so it long afterwards continued. Several aspects of this distribution need to be noticed. In the first place it can be shown that of the Christians who were appointed to these county chieftainships by 1900 a substantial proportion possessed 'traditional' qualifications for chieftaincy. Over a third of them, for example, had been pages at the Kabaka's court; five more had had upbringings of a comparable kind; and at least four others were well known for their military prowess. They were thus no 'out-group', usurping the prerogatives of an 'in-group'. Rather they were those from the pre-existing 'in-group' who had successfully secured the available prizes. There was here, therefore, considerable continuity. At the same time only two of the county chiefs who were Christians had not been amongst those who had gone to Ankole when the Christians had first been driven there by the Muslims in 1888. They belonged, for the most part that is, to the original Christian cadre, and the bonds which bound them together were those which had been forged in that experience. There can be little doubt, moreover, that the two exceptions represented the two splinter factions which had emerged thereafter within the Protestant party; and it is plain that the one Muslim county chief was the key (non-royal) figure amongst those Muslims who had eventually concluded that they might be wiser to throw in their lot with the Christians rather than risk disappearance into the wilderness. As things turned out, therefore, the county chiefs of 1900 represented not just the major configurations of the victorious elite, but quite precisely all those different factions into which the revolutionary elite of the late 1880s had subsequently fragmented, but which had also eventually chosen to coalesce again. The combination of all these attributes in the leadership of the new régime naturally gave it very considerable strength.[23]

And there was a further feature to it as well. For following the 1900 Agreement four of the new county chieftaincies were given to those who had formerly held the Protestant and Catholic offices of *Mujasi* (or commander of the army) and *Gabunga* (or commander of the canoes) – which now lost all their former importance. Such realignments symbolised the fact – which came to be exemplified subsequently in a variety of other ways – that the previously existing miscellany of royally appointed chiefs was henceforth to be amalgamated into one single hierarchy. Among other things this was to mean that in future chiefly jurisdictions in Buganda were not only to be sharply delineated: they were to be free of the enclaves which they had formerly had in their midst where their writ had not run. When all this was coupled with the more general success of the oligarchical revolution, and with the strong support it enjoyed from the British, it is hardly to be wondered at that the appointed chiefs of Buganda now found themselves in a very much more powerful position than any of their predecessors. They were now indeed an exceedingly formidable combination.

The only people of consequence who were not fully incorporated into the structure of the new régime in Buganda were the Bataka, the clan heads. Some Bataka made a private deal of their own with the new order, and were often given freehold land in return. Moreover Apolo Kagwa himself – the chief of the successful Christian revolutionaries, and for thirty-seven years Katikiro of Buganda – took care to become secretary of his own clan council; and others of his ilk did likewise. They remained firmly attached, that is, to their inherited combinations.[24] But in 1912 Kagwa also proposed the establishment of an *Olukiko Lwa Bataka* (*Abakungu na Balangira*) or 'Council of Bataka (Landowners)' in Buganda, which *inter alia* looks extraordinarily like a takeover bid for the residual position of the Bataka in the country.[25] It proved unsuccessful; and some considerable separations patently remained. It was thus no coincidence that as the twentieth century unfolded some Bataka (or at all events those who made use of their symbols) should have become the leaders of the popular opposition from amongst the peasantry of Buganda which eventually emerged to challenge the oligarchs and their successors. For all the readjustments which had been brought about, one long standing tension persisted, essentially unaltered and unrelieved, to wrack the new régime in the decades ahead.

XIII

Yet for all the success of the revolutionaries in seizing control of all the appointed offices of state, nothing was henceforward to be of greater importance to their role in Buganda than their leadership of those quite new institutions, the religio-political parties, which were to be so immensely important for more than half a century ahead.

Despite the splintering from which each of these had suffered there were in the end only three of them – the Protestants, the Catholics and the Muslims. Their origins went back to those small clusters of personal friends who first opted in the 1860s, 1870s and 1880s, to attach themselves as groups to one or other of the foreign teachers of the new religions. During the ensuing persecutions their original loyalties became deeply entrenched. By 1887 the institutions which were crucial to their growing cohesion were Mwanga's musket armed 'regiments'. Thereafter they constituted the extended clientages of the Protestant and Catholic and Muslim oligarchs – to whom their attachments were riveted by the tribulations of exile, by the bitter experience of the battles which followed, and by all the pressing uncertainties of a revolutionary decade. As the original revolutionaries – or, in the case of the Catholics, and more particularly the Muslims, some of them at any rate – attained political success, and as the new ideologies which they championed won an increasing number of converts; as more particularly the Christian missionaries and the Baganda evangelists added to the ranks of the Christian baptised, so their size grew. No correlation of any consequence had so far been shown between any one clan and any one political party. But that is scarcely to be wondered at. For these religio-political parties were ultimately the offspring, not of the localised clans, but of the circumstances which ensued upon the dispersal of clans.

They soon came to display, moreover, new forms of cohesion. They tended to be endogamous. More important, although during the 1880s and 1890s there seems to have been some distribution of brothers in elite families amongst the different warring factions[26] – partly no doubt because of the conflict which was inherent between brothers in a society where there were no fixed orders of succession, but partly too, one may assume, to ensure that in a period of grievous uncertainty a prominent family should not lose out completely – from 1900 onwards families seem to have adhered fairly steadily to the religious party of their father. What was more, although clan membership was still important for such things as the choice of one's marriage partner and for the determination of one's inheritance, it was henceforward the religious party – to which in the next generation one belonged in the first place by birth rather than by choice – which, through baptism or circumcision provided one's symbolic entrance into the new régime in Buganda; through its associated network of schools, set one on the road to a future career; and thereafter, through its labyrinth of personal linkages, became the vehicle for one's political administrative, ecclesiastical or educational promotion. In the lists of chiefs that survive from around 1900 a man's clan is usually given in addition to his chieftaincy and his name: these were the three symbols which still identified his person, his allegiance and his hereditary connections. At the same time it is very striking indeed that in the first extant list of members of Buganda's newly reconstituted 'native council', the Lukiko, which dates from 1902, each member should have been primarily designated as either 'P', 'C', or 'I' – Protestant, Catholic, or *Islaimu*.[27] These designations were now indigenous to Buganda. They had become indeed established as amongst the most important which men possessed.

It should not be thought, however, that the political activities of these parties were in every respect their most important. For a start, the network of churches, mosques and schools which they established were of outstanding importance. Furthermore, they each had their quota of men and women of profound spirituality. The Anglican clergyman, Canon Apolo Kivebulaya, for example, is only the most remarked upon of these.[28] Half a century later, moreover, no political pronouncement was to be of greater significance than the *Pastoral Letter on Church and State* issued in November 1961 by the Muganda Catholic Archbishop Kiwanuka. In a remarkably precise manner it exemplified the combination in these parties of their religious as well as their political concerns.[29] If the new régime was not quite therefore what its protagonists had originally thought it might be there cannot be much doubt that its ramifications in Buganda society taken as a whole turned out in the end to be both very profound and very far reaching.

It looks as if there were two special reasons why the parties at its core became so significant. First and foremost, they provided the new structures which were the institutional expression of the new political and ideological régime which had now been superimposed on Buganda. In a very exact manner they were its organisational corollary, and the vehicles for its maintenance in Baganda society. Secondly, they expressed within themselves (and accordingly to a quite unusual extent within one and the same institution) important characteristics of both of those two patterns – the Bataka pattern and the Bakungu pattern – which we have seen permeating Baganda society. On the one hand they comprised a dispersed but clear-cut hereditary sub-community within the total society, with which were associated designated office holders who were recognised guides to religious and familial norms. At the same time they were dependent at their core upon the authority of the hierarchy of appointed chiefs. Their mesh with Baganda proclivities was thus extraordinarily close.

Nothing was more striking about these parties, however, or about the settlement of 1900 with which classically they were connected, than the quite remarkable balance to be seen in their relationship with each other between cohesion and conflict. The leaders of the two main parties, and in effect their Muslim associates as well, were agreed upon the need to preserve Buganda's ordered society; upon the need to preserve its residual autonomy (and their own supremacy, of course, within it); as well as upon the desirability of advancing the new cultural complex of which they had made themselves the champions. At the same time they were clearly divided into their three separate camps; they were very careful to see that members of rival parties did not secure more than their allocated share of the spoils which were going; and they were in some considerable measure of very real difference over religion. As regards, therefore, both the operative structures in society and the distribution of power and their own continuing concern for the lights by which it should live, there was an astonishingly even balance in their relationship between cohesion and conflict. In the last analysis it was these things, we may suggest, which during the ensuing half century gave the new régime they headed not only its very considerable strength, but its very considerable resilience as well.

XIV

So to sum up. Within the double-knit social order of Buganda's society as it mounted to its apex, discernible tensions had existed. In the last decades of the nineteenth century two of the most important had eventuated, in association with a variety of extraneous forces, in a religious upheaval at the centre on the one hand, and in a great political upheaval there as well. During the period of revolutionary turmoil which ensued, the one gave birth to a 'Christian' revolution, the other to an oligarchical one. Since at the critical moment in the late 1880s the two upheavals had converged, their respective *dénouements* thereafter conjoined. The one involved a close association with European missionaries; the other became linked to a bilateral political connection with British imperial administrators. The changes they entailed introduced a new régime at the apex of Buganda's society in both religious and political respects. It was coupled at one and the same time, both with the careful maintenance of almost every other characteristic aspect of the society and with the development of some new over-arching institutions. The latter gave structural expression to the new order, but incorporated cardinal features of Buganda's society as it persisted throughout.

The fact that the connections between the first of the tensions we have discussed – that between the ruler and the clan heads – and the religious upheavals which ensued, did not have the symmetry which marked the connection between the second

tension – that between the ruler and his appointed chiefs –
and the consequential political upheaval, meant that in the
period of resolution which followed the first tension was in the
event no more than marginally relieved. It therefore persisted.
It came to operate thereafter in ways which related not to the
tensions which operated within the new régime (though these
were real enough), but to those which its imposition upon the
rest of society generated in Buganda's society taken as a whole.
For those who participated in them successfully the linked
revolutions in the two decades before the turn of the nineteenth
century represented a release of quite epic proportions for their
kingdom's *élan*. Many of them thereafter looked back to this
time as to an heroic period. What was more they set the tone
for the elite of Buganda's society for many decades to come, and
indeed for the elite of many other societies surrounding.

The photograph facing page 148 of this book epitomises the
outcome. It was taken on the steps of Namirembe Cathedral,
the Anglican cathedral overlooking the Kabaka's palace at
Mengo, after a service held to commemorate the coronation in
1902 of the British King, Edward VII. It was taken, that is,
just half a century after the first Zanzibari traders had arrived
in Buganda, just forty years after the first white man had set
foot in the kingdom, and just twenty-five years after the first
Christian missionary had arrived. Clearly there have been some
considerable changes in the interim. The small boys standing
in the front are the young Kabaka, Daudi Chwa, and his two
young brothers; and the tall figure, the second from the right,
is the Katikiro, Apolo Kagwa. Evidently the offices of Kabaka
and Katikiro, and all which they stood for, were very much
therefore still intact. The fact, however, that their holders had
been attending a service in honour of a British coronation indicates something of the degree to which the leaders of the
kingdom had now become associated with the British. The key
positions in the photograph, moreover, of the Anglican Archdeacon – in the centre – another Anglican missionary – on the
far left – and an African clergyman – on the far right (the Reverend Henry Wright Duta Kitakule, one of the early Christian
converts who had become a clergyman rather than a chief)
indicates the important role which was now occupied by the
new religion. Although the Arab influence is patent – in the

clothes both the Kabaka and his brothers, and Apolo Kagwa, are wearing – so, at this level, is the British, and the Anglican – the Kabaka wears a 'western' waistcoat and a watchchain, and Kitakule appears in the fully fledged robes of an Anglican clergyman. In symbolic form one can even see the oligarchical revolution: how the ample figure of Apolo Kagwa towers above his young Kabaka! In a more straightforward way one can see as well, both the 'protectorate' status to which Bugunda had now been subjected, and the formal recognition of its (albeit reduced) autonomy by the British. The British Commissioner is not in the picture. The British tutor to the Kabaka, however, stands at his elbow; yet he only stands in the back row,while the Kabaka and Katikiro dominate the foreground.

Two more features of the *dénouement* are symbolised as well. Buganda is evidently at peace. But two of the major points of tension which remained at its apex are vividly exemplified. Buganda is being officially represented; but there is no Catholic or Muslim to be seen in the picture, let alone a clan head.

NOTES

1. Major sources for all that follows are Apolo Kagwa, *Basekabaka be Buganda*, London, 1927; B. M. Zimbe, *Buganda ne Kabaka*, Mengo, 1939; H. Mukasa, *Simuda Nyuma*, 2 vols., London, 1938 and 1942; J. Miti, 'A Short History of Buganda', Unpublished Mss. in the Makerere Library; J. Roscoe, *The Baganda*, London, 1911; L. A. Fallers (ed.), *The King's Men*, London, 1964.

2. Max Weber, *The Theory of Social and Economic Organisation*, translated edition, New York, 1947, contains the classic statements.

3. The main essentials of all this analysis derive from the conclusions of Father Gorju following his researches into oral tradition in Buganda during the first two decades of the twentieth century, J. Gorju, *Entre le Victoria, L'Albert et L'Edouard*, Rennes, 1920. See also A. H. Cox, 'The Growth and Expansion of Buganda', *Uganda Journal*, XIV (1950), pp. 153–9.

4. See, more especially, J. V. Taylor, *The Growth of the Church in Buganda*, London, 1958.

5. E.g. Roscoe, *The Baganda*, Ch. 10.

6. Colonel Long's account in *Provinces of the Equator. Summary of Letters and Reports of H.E. the Governor General, Part I, Year 1874*, Egyptian General Staff, Cairo, 1877, pp. 61–2.

7. E. E. Evans-Pritchard, *Nuer Religion*, Oxford, 1958, pp. 116, 308–10, 319.

8. Ahmed Katumba and F. B. Welbourn, 'Muslim Martyrs of Buganda', *Uganda Journal*, XXVIII, 2 (1964).
9. H. M. Stanley, *Through the Dark Continent*, new ed., London, 1890, p. 206.
10. This and the next four sections are based more especially on a detailed investigation of the Uganda mission archives of the Church Missionary Society in London. I hope to give details elsewhere.
11. The most substantial account is in J. F. Faupel, *African Holocaust*, London, 1962.
12. See also C. C. Wrigley, 'The Christian Revolution in Buganda', *Comparative Studies in Society and History*, II, 1 (1959), pp. 33–48, and M. Southwold, 'Bureaucracy and Chiefship in Buganda', *East African Studies*, No. 14, Kampala (1961).
13. E. C. Gordon to H. W. Lang, 7 November 1888, Church Missionary Society Archives, G3 A5/05.
14. M. Perham, *Lugard, The Years of Adventure*, London, 1956; M. Perham and M. Bull, *The Diaries of Lord Lugard*, London, 1959; F. D. Lugard, *The Rise of our East African Empire*, London, 1893.
15. Kitakule to a missionary in Zanzibar, 5 April 1892, Zanzibar Secretariat Archives.
16. E.g. Williams' memorandum, 11 January 1893, Entebbe Secretariat Archives, A2/1.
17. E.g. Jackson to Hill, 20 April 1895, Public Record Office, London, Foreign Office, 2/92.
18. For this whole subject see Louise M. M. Pirouet, 'The Expansion of the Church of Uganda (N.A.C.) from Buganda into Northern and Western Uganda between 1891 and 1914 with Special Reference to the Work of African Teachers and Evangelists', University of East Africa Ph.D. thesis, 1968.
19. F. B. Welbourn, *East African Rebels*, London, 1961.
20. E.g. Wilson to Lugard, 22 March 1899, Lugard Papers, Rhodes House, Oxford.
21. Much of the detail for this and the next section will be found in D. A. Low and R. C. Pratt, *Buganda and British Overrule: 1900–1955*, London, 1960, Part I.
22. M. Southwold, 'The Ganda of Uganda', in J. L. Gibbs (ed.), *Peoples of Africa*, New York, 1965.
23. For the details here see D. A. Low, 'Religion and Society in Buganda, 1875–1900', *East African Studies No. 8*, Kampala, n.d., especially pp. 13–14.
24. Cf. the following very helpful comments: 'The continued existence of clan systems, with the same vague functions, during the following century suggests [that] the very vagueness of its functions may have permitted the clan to become a symbol of important values. A clan system stood to the people as a recurrent reminder of the basic verities of their heritage and of their membership in some larger community. It symbolized the importance of descent, the obligations of kinship, the interdependence of kinship groups which had to rely upon one

another for marriage partners. In a sense the clan could represent the common concerns of all men. The clan names, easily remembered, the clan slogans, dramatic to recite, served to place people in a wider social context and to remind them of their manifold responsibilities to one another'; Elizabeth Colson, 'African Society at the Time of the Scramble', in L. H. Gann and Peter Duignan, *Colonialism in Africa, 1870–1960*, Volume I, Cambridge, 1969, p. 55.

25. Michael Twaddle, 'The *Bakungu* Chiefs of Buganda under British Colonial Rule, 1900–1930', *Journal of African History*, X, 2 (1969), pp. 309–322.

26. E.g. see the account in Ansorge to Colvile, 16 November 1894, Entebbe Secretariat Archives, A2/3.

27. D. A. Low, 'The Composition of the Buganda Lukiko in 1902', *Uganda Journal*, XXIII (1959), pp. 64–8.

28. A. Luck, *African Saint*, London, 1963.

29. *Pastoral Letter of the Most Rev. Archbishop Joseph Kiwanuka, D.D., Archbishop of Rubaga (Uganda), Church and State, Guiding Principles*, Kisubi, 1961. For an Anglican counterpart (written by the then Principal of the Anglican theological college in Buganda with his Baganda friends very much in mind) see J. V. Taylor, *Christianity and Politics in Africa*, Harmondsworth, 1957.

2

British Public Opinion and 'The Uganda Question': October–December 1892

At the end of 1886 the British and the Germans made their first agreement partitioning East Africa. Germany obtained the lion's share, but Great Britain gained control of Mombasa, the best harbour on the coast. By an exchange of notes in 1887 the British and German Governments agreed to the so-called hinterland doctrine, whereby he who held a stretch of coastline had a pre-emptive right to the interior lying behind. On 3 September 1888 the Imperial British East Africa Company received a Royal Charter from Lord Salisbury's Government. The Chairman was Sir William Mackinnon, already Chairman of the British India Steam Navigation Company. Shortly afterwards it began operations at Mombasa. By 1890 the scramble for the area of the Great Lakes was leading to a crisis (when Peters and Jackson raced each other for Uganda) that might have created a 'Fashoda' incident eight years before Fashoda. But diplomacy disposed of the conflict, and by the Anglo-German Agreement of 1890 Germany recognised *inter alia* a British sphere of influence which included Buganda.

When the Agreement was signed in July the Chartered Company's operations, apart from Jackson's expedition, were practically confined to the coast, but the British Government had been doing its utmost to persuade the company to send a full scale expedition to occupy Buganda for some months past. Eventually the Company dispatched Captain Lugard, who in December 1890, marched into Buganda.

For some years the Baganda had been consciously opposed to European entry into their country, but by 1890 they were broken up into three or four mutually hostile parties, not one of which was in a position to keep the Europeans out, two of which were prepared to let them in. Yet it was one thing to

55

allow European agents to come in: it was another to acknowledge their control. Lugard stayed in Uganda for some twenty months during which the crucial question between him and Kabaka Mwanga was, who was overlord? This and the hostility between the two dominant, Christian parties was at the root of all the confusion – the inaptly called 'religious wars' – which so fully occupied Lugard's time. Because of this he could do no trade and his operations became increasingly costly, with the result that the Company soon decided that it could not maintain him and his force in Uganda any longer, and sent him orders to withdraw. These he received in December 1891 just when the situation was leading up to a crisis, and he was naturally taken aback.

But meanwhile the Company had told Bishop Tucker and the Church Missionary Society what it planned to do, and they were equally disconcerted. Tucker then made an arrangement with Mackinnon of the Company whereby it agreed to maintain its agents in Buganda for a further year, if Tucker could find £15,000 to help cover the cost. The CMS were not in a position to hand money over to a commercial company, but Tucker made a remarkable appeal to the friends of the CMS, and starting with an anonymous gift of £5,000, he had collected more than he needed within ten days. He then tried to extend his fund to cover the cost of a lake steamer for the Company, but he was severely criticised for this in evangelical circles in Britain, and the fund remained at around £16,500. That was enough however to enable the Company to remain in Uganda for a further year.

Mackinnon made it clear that at the end of 1892 the Company would certainly have to withdraw from Uganda. It was unlikely that Tucker would be able to repeat his appeal with comparable success, and the unfortunate company was unlikely to attract more capital. The year's interval was therefore to be used to persuade the British Government to take over Uganda and pay for British operations there from Treasury funds.

For this there was not much support in either political camp in Britain. The classic British policy for the scramble for Africa had been to carve out by diplomacy a sphere of influence and then authorise a chartered company to take up the burden, thus relieving the British taxpayer of the cost. This had been successful for some years and (with the exception of Nyasaland where there were special circumstances) there had been no declaration of a direct imperial protectorate in Africa since early on in the scramble, in 1885, when rather reluctantly a British Protectorate had been declared over Bechuanaland. But here in Uganda the classic policy was breaking down. What was the Government going to do?

It had to find another policy. Salisbury, who was Britain's Prime Minister till August 1892, and also Foreign Secretary, in which capacity he dealt with East Africa, had long since decided that his policy would be to help the Company to build a railway, which by cheapening the otherwise extremely costly communications would keep the Company afloat.

But this was a half measure which overlooked the already dire financial straits in which the Company found itself – and the situation in Buganda itself, which had so perturbed the minds of Bishop Tucker and the CMS in the previous autumn. For though a railway would help in the long run, what was to happen in the interval between the withdrawal of the Company from the interior, and its return on the tracks of the railway a few years later? Salisbury scarcely seems to have been aware that a hiatus might be disastrous; if he was, he postponed making any further decision until after the General Election of July 1892, at which, as it happened, he was defeated. So for seven months of 1892 no further step was taken by the Government than the fulfilment of their promise to pay for a railway survey.

Buganda was three months journey from the East African coast, which meant that, if British agents were to be retained there some decision had to be made by 1 October 1892. There was no discussion of the Uganda question during the election. It was too delicate, and Ireland occupied the whole arena. Once it was over everything had to wait for the entry into office of the new Liberal government, Gladstone's fourth and last, which did not take place until 15 August. That left only six weeks of breathing space. Lord Rosebery became Foreign Secretary, but for a month nothing was done. On 13 September the CMS became desperate and its General Committee passed a resolution appointing a deputation to wait on Lord Rosebery at the Foreign Office.[1] He saw them on 23 September.

The year's delay had scarcely improved the situation in Buganda. Lugard and both Christian parties had been involved in the battle of Mengo in the previous January, and though Lugard had 'pacified' the country by April, he had only succeeded in doing so by dividing the country unevenly between the three religious parties. These only agreed to the settlement, and refrained from flying at each other's throats, because he had shown that his maxims were more effective than their antiquated muzzle loaders. From the available evidence – and it is sufficiently diverse – there need be little doubt that the CMS were right in saying that the Company's withdrawal at this juncture would have led to warfare and bloodshed in Buganda. All this and much more was clearly put forward by the CMS deputation, and Lord Rosebery promised to lay their views before his colleagues.[2]

He had already laid before them the views of Sir Percy Anderson, the head of the Slave Trade Department of the British Foreign Office. Anderson suggested that on the company's withdrawal, the Government should annex the whole area up to Lake Albert in order to forestall French and Congo control of the Upper Nile which would threaten the British position in Egypt. This led to an immediate and trenchant outburst from Sir William Harcourt, the new Chancellor of the Exchequer, against what he called this 'Jingo' memorandum. Few were as downright as Harcourt, but his view was shared in general by Gladstone and most of the Cabinet, and not even Rosebery was prepared to defend Anderson's proposals. The fact was that the majority of the Cabinet was opposed to any kind of extension of the British empire, and in particular to the extension of direct imperial responsibility: they argued that the empire was large enough already. There 'the Uganda question' might have ended, despite the CMS who after all were interested parties.

But even before the CMS saw Lord Rosebery, he had received a cable from his Consul-General in Zanzibar, Sir Gerald Portal. Portal had been to Mombasa and had there met Lugard who had come down to the coast on his way to England where he planned to tell the British public about the situation in Buganda. After talking to Lugard and to some others. Portal solemnly warned Rosebery by cable that there would be anarchy and bloodshed in Buganda if the Company withdrew. This altered the situation in the British Cabinet. Rosebery fought an apparently hopeless fight there with great skill and persistence, and on 30 September, with not a day to spare, the Cabinet 'adhered to the acceptance by their predecessors of the principle of evacuation', but agreed to pay the Company to remain in Uganda for a further three months, ostensibly to allow evacuation to be more carefully organised, but in fact to give the Cabinet three more months in which to make up its mind on a matter over which it was hopelessly divided. Rosebery was not satisfied and entered a caveat, but he told the Queen that among other things the three months delay would give time 'to elicit the real feeling of the country, which, is, he is certain, against evacuation'.[3]

By this time – the end of September 1892 – the press in Britain had taken up the question. But like the Cabinet, it was divided, with Conservative papers and *The Times* in favour of annexation, and Liberal papers opposed. In a leading article, one of the latter, *The Globe*, argued that 'great as our reserves are, they might easily be strained to the breaking point were England to accept the responsibility of establishing law and order in all parts of the Dark Continent where anarchy prevails. She has made, and is still making, enormous sacrifices on that altar but her people may be pardoned if they look askance at this new demand.'[4] The *Manchester Guardian* went further. 'For our part' a leader said, 'we hope the Government will decide absolutely against interference of the kind suggested.'[5] On the other side was *The Times* which on 1 October declaimed against 'the cowardly and disgraceful nature of the 'scuttle' we are asked to effect, in order to save at the outside £40,000 a year until Administration becomes, as it probably soon would, self-supporting'.

The three months grace was not very long and *The Times* had already made the point that 'at the present time the question of Uganda suffers, in common with most others, from the political apathy following a general election.' Parliament had met in August to turn Salisbury out of office; it had then adjourned till January. Even the Cabinet dispersed and had to be recalled from as far away as Austria and the north end of Scotland. It was not therefore possible to launch a Parliamentary campaign. Accordingly *The Times* in that same leader went on to say that 'Everything must depend . . . upon the way in which the time of grace is used by those – and we believe their number is very great – who would deplore the abandonment of Uganda.'[6] The hint was taken – and *The Times* itself was soon to the fore, with a series of leading articles calling unmistakably for the 'retention' of Uganda.[6] It was upon this simple point that public opinion in Britain now concentrated.

Lugard wrote a long letter to *The Times* on 6 October, soon after his arrival in England.[7] He wrote again ten days later. By that time there was a spate of letters in the papers about Uganda, particularly in *The Times*. They were mostly in the same vein; 'I am not an explorer' one correspondent wrote to *The Standard* on 4 October, 'nor a shareholder in the East African Company, but like thousands of my countrymen, I am deeply interested in the fate of Uganda.' Stanley the explorer delivered an oration about Uganda on the 3rd, when he received the Freedom of Swansea.[8] On the 11th the CMS passed a long resolution insisting that 'a grave responsibility lies on the nation'.[9] On the 20th a deputation 120 strong, organised by the Anti-Slavery Society, was received by Lord Rosebery at the Foreign Office.[10] On 25 October the *Morning Post* reported 'the growing disaffection caused in the country by the proposal to abandon Uganda'. This was a little premature, but on 7 November *The Times* could say with some accuracy that 'evidence of the true sentiment of the nation upon the question of Uganda is accumulating with satisfactory rapidity'. It is not without point that on that same day the Cabinet decided to send a British Commissioner to Uganda 'to report his opinion whether any and what measures ought to be adopted with respect to it after its evacuation by the East Africa Company'.[11]

The decision however remained secret while Rosebery tried to secure the Company's assistance in providing for the Commissioner's safety. A Press Association report on the 12th stated that the Government had decided to continue the possession of Uganda, but the official announcement about the appointment of a Commissioner was not made until 23 November. Meanwhile, ignorant of the Cabinet's discussions, British opinion had been stirred into protest, and before the end of of October, the movement for the retention of Uganda had switched from the columns of the newspapers to the platforms of the country.

Early in November the Conservative politician Balfour spoke in favour of the retention of Uganda at a great gathering of the National Union of Conservative Associations in Scotland.[12] Four days later Salisbury spoke similarly to the Nonconformist Unionist Association.[13] Throughout November, Lugard toured England and Scotland speaking to geographical societies, chambers of commerce and public meetings.[14] Stanley and Bishop Smythies of Zanzibar were also campaigning, though rather less systematically.

But even Lugard's campaign was only part of a much wider movement of public opinion expressed through the large number of resolutions, petitions and memorials which were soon reaching the Foreign Office from meetings up and down the country. These were mostly agreed to unanimously, and over 100 meetings were specially summoned to discuss Uganda. There were, it is certain, a few Uganda meetings that did not send resolutions to the Foreign Office, but all the available information about them merely confirms the evidence of the Foreign Office collection. An analysis of this reveals the nature and extent of a very remarkable movement of Victorian public opinion during those autumn months of 1892.[15]

The earliest of the resolutions in the Foreign Office collection is dated 13 October, but taking them all in all it appears that the movement reached its height in the first half of November. It is a little difficult to be absolutely precise with the figures, as in some instances only the date on which the resolutions were forwarded to the Foreign Office is available, but with this reservation they are otherwise clear enough. With the exception of the third week in November, there were, for five weeks, from the last week in October to the end of the fourth week in November, at least twenty meetings (of all kinds) in each week discussing 'the Uganda question'.

The meetings really began in the third week in October when there were six; in the fourth there were twenty. During the first week of November there were thirty-three; in the second thirty-two. By the third week the number was down to seventeen, but the next week – during which the Government announced its intention to send a Commissioner to Uganda –

the number was up again to twenty-five. The following week it was down to ten. During the week ending 10 December there were eight, but in the next only four. By then it was over. It was thus a short, sharp campaign.

The resolutions forwarded from a single county, say Yorkshire (even allowing that it is the largest), give some idea of the range of organizations from which the resolutions came. There were twenty meetings in Yorkshire which sent petitions or resolutions. These included Ruridecanal chapters, large public meetings in town halls, chambers of commerce, an Anglican diocesan conference, 'Friends of Missions', branches of the CMS, village and parish meetings, a Conservative organisation, and a Ruridecanal conference.

Taking the country as a whole there were 147 sets of Resolutions, 11 memorials and 16 petitions. Seventeen sets of resolutions and one memorial came from various branch meetings of the Church Missionary Society; seven from branch meetings of the Society for the Propagation of the Gospel, a missionary society of High Church, perhaps Anglo-Catholic, views (an indication from the start of the diversification of support), and two from large meetings of 'Friends of Missions'. Seventeen sets of resolutions and two memorials came from village or parish meetings, many of them convened by the Vicar, but not all. Fourteen petitions also came from parishes, some of them originating in yet more parish meetings. One petition, one resolution and two memorials came from Presbyterian churches, and one resolution from a Wesleyan Methodist meeting. Two resolutions came from clerical societies and fifteen from Rural Deanery chapters – in other words, from small gatherings of Anglican clergymen. Four sets of resolutions, a petition and a memorial came from Ruridecanal conferences, and one resolution from an Archidiaconal conference. Seventeen resolutions came from diocesan conferences or synods, one from the Commission of the General Assembly of the Free Church of Scotland; and there was a remarkable memorial signed by the heads of all the separated Presbyterian Churches of Scotland. More than a hundred approaches therefore (that is more than half) came from the churches.[16]

But these were not necessarily the most significant. For though there were occasionally large meetings, as at St John's,

Kennington, where '400 men and women of all political opinions' were present, and though several others were 'largely
attended', many of them must have been like the Dalton
clerical meeting – with its 'twenty-five persons'. So that apart
from the diocesan conferences, these expressions from religious
organisations were probably from small gatherings, which
would not have had the same influence as the larger meetings.

Five more sets of resolutions came from a miscellaneous group
of Mutual Improvement Societies and YMCA 'Parliaments'.
Six political organisations – only one Liberal – sent resolutions.[17]
But then there were eleven sets of resolutions and one memorial
from town and county councils, nineteen sets of resolutions and
one memorial from large public meetings, many of which were
held in town halls, and finally twenty-one sets of resolutions
and two memorials from chambers of commerce.

Can one gain an impression of what all this meant in detail?
At Dorchester early in December, a public meeting presided
over by Colonel Robert Williams, a strong supporter of the
CMS, was called to discuss the Uganda question: it was
'numerously attended by persons from all parts of the country'.
Two resolutions were moved and 'in the end carried *nemine
contradicente*'. A proposal in favour of waiting for further information was made, but not seconded. Such slight departures
from unanimity were unusual. Greenock Chamber of Commerce sent a memorial: 'Your memorialists number', it said,
'over two hundred members, and represent Importers of
Produce, Exporters of Goods, Sugar Refiners, Shipbuilders,
Shipowners, Makers of Machinery and others.'

The village of South Creake in Norfolk sent a petition from
its Vicar, churchwardens and parishioners. It was signed by
104 people – ten of them were illiterate, and simply put their
marks. The list is headed by the Vicar (a Spencer Compton –
possibly a relation of the Liberal Unionist leader, the Duke of
Devonshire) but it was also signed by the Congregational minister, so it would not seem to have been a denominational affair.
Three people named Cook from the 'Manor House' signed.
Among the villagers' names there were five Waseys, five
Vipans and five Cousinses, so that here was support for the
cause from a typical English village, which in fact probably
knew very little about Uganda.

In Cambridge, where Lugard spoke on 25 November, there was a 'largely attended Public Meeting' in the Guildhall. The Vice-Chancellor, Dr John Reile, Master of Christ's, was in the Chair. The resolution was proposed by the Regius Professor of Greek, Sir Richard Jebb, who was also one of the MP's for the University. He was seconded by the Master of Trinity, and as Dr Reile reported, the meeting was attended by a 'large proportion of the Heads of Colleges and Professors as well as other graduates of the University'. They desired 'respectfully to urge upon Her Majesty's Government the importance of maintaining British influence in Uganda'.

In Bristol there was a local campaign all on its own, with twelve meetings in the town and others nearby in Somerset and Gloucestershire. On 11 October, Sir Michael Hicks-Beach who sat for the local constituency of Bristol West spoke about Uganda at the annual meeting of the Bristol Conservative Working Men's Association. 'He most earnestly trusted that before any final steps were taken in this matter the whole circumstances and facts might be put before the people of this country for their opinion, that Parliament might have an opportunity of expressing its judgement upon it and that the result might be beneficial, not merely to the interests of this country, but to humanity and the progress of the world (cheers).'[18] This passing reference may have set the Bristol campaign off to an early start, though on 3 October, 'a working man' from Bristol had written to the CMS, saying that 'a great crime will be committed' and suggesting that 1,800 people should be asked to pay £1 a year for three years towards the cost of Uganda.[19] At all events on 17 October there was one of the earliest meetings in the whole country in St Silas' School, Bristol. In forwarding the ensuing resolutions the Vicar, the Reverend G. A. Sowter wrote a letter to Lord Rosebery which was typical of many to come.

I have the honour [he said] to lay before your Lordship a copy of two resolutions adopted unanimously at a well-attended meeting in St Silas' School, Bristol, last night. I do so with the greater pleasure because I believe your Lordship is keenly alive to the terrible results which will not improbably follow the withdrawal of the representatives of the Imperial British East Africa Company from that country. I recognise the fact that the exact course to pursue must be left to those in responsible positions in the state who are better informed of all the circumstances of the case, and in so difficult a matter as this, your Lordship has the fullest sympathy of many. But there can be little doubt that the evacuation of Uganda in March next will retard the civilization of that important country, perhaps for centuries, besides imperilling the lives of many native Christians and giving a fresh impetus to the slave trade now largely held in check.

Mr Sowter wrote on 18 October. On the 17th the annual meeting of the CMS Union of Younger Clergy for Bristol, Clifton and neighbourhood had also passed a resolution. On the 21st there was a parish meeting at Long Ashton and a meeting of the friends and supporters of the CMS in the Victoria Rooms, and they passed more resolutions. A few days later there was a parish meeting at St Luke's; on the 28th a meeting of the Israel's Identification Association at Clifton, and a day or two later of the Bristol Protestant League. On 2, 4 and 7 November, there were three further parish meetings, and on the 8th a meeting of the Bristol Presbytery of the Presbyterian Church of England. That evening came the climax – a crowded meeting in the Bristol Guildhall with the Mayor in the Chair. Bristol was quick off the mark and made up its mind early. With the exception of the Guildhall meeting (and Hicks-Beach's), all the meetings were religious and Protestant – there was no move by the Town Council or the Chamber of Commerce – but then Bristol had long been a Protestant stronghold, and its early connection with the slave trade had given it an interest in succouring its potential victims.

Norwich took longer, but its reaction was similar. The county is, after all, Buxton country. A CMS meeting was held on 4 November at King's Lynn near the Buxton home, but despite the meeting of the Rockland Ruridecanal Chapter on 23 October, and the petition from South Creake on 12 November, the campaign was late in starting. On 24 November there was a CMS meeting convened by a Mr Gurney (doubtless a member of the anti-slavery family) who was CMS Group Secretary for the Norwich district. It was possibly at this meeting that arrangements were made to collect signatures for parish petitions to the Foreign Office. These were drawn up in copper plate by some enthusiast from a printed draft petition which was also used by six other parishes in other parts of the country. There was a good deal of signature collecting in the parishes of North and South Heigham, 129 from the latter, 142 from the former including 5 Laceys from No. 11 and 5 Hineses from No. 40 Adelaide Street. But interest flagged. St Giles' Parish, Norwich only produced 50 signatories, St Margaret's and St Swithin's 33, St Mark's Lekenham 21, and Old Catton only 11 – there it had probably been forgotten as it was not sent to the Foreign Office till 22 December, and this was a month after it was known that the Government had decided to send a Commissioner to Uganda. Even so, this was not the full measure of Norwich's support for the cause, for Lugard was invited down, and spoke at two very large meetings, held in St Andrew's Hall, Norwich, on Monday, 12 December – in the afternoon for the county, with the Bishop in the chair, and in the evening for the town, presided over by the Mayor. Identical resolutions were sent to the Foreign Office. As in Bristol – and in many other towns – the movement reached its climax with large meetings open to the public.

Even so, in Bristol and Norwich, the interest was almost entirely religious. This was true elsewhere. In Oswestry in Shropshire the Chapter of the Rural Deanery, presided over (unusually) by the Bishop of St Asaph, passed a 'Uganda' resolution on 4 November, and the annual meeting of the local branch of the SPG on the 8th. Both sets of resolutions were forwarded by Mr Stanley Leighton, from Sweeney Hall.

But this was by no means the whole story. Southampton shows how complex the campaign had become. On 2 November the annual meeting of the Southampton Branch of the SPG (High Church) passed a resolution: on the 10th at Gosport the Hampshire Church Missionary Prayer Union (evangelical) passed another: by the fourth week the established Ruri-decanal Council had added its voice, and they had already been joined on the 21st by the chamber of commerce.

Swansea was classic: the town council passed a Uganda resolution on 19 October, Llandaff Diocesan Conference on the 27th, the Parish of St Simon's, Swansea, on 24 November, and the chamber of commerce on the 25th. Perhaps they were specially moved by Stanley's appeal when he received the freedom of the borough on 3 October.

66

But Worcester was similar – though there was a local variant in the unusually specific support of the Conservatives. On 27 October the William lodge at Kempsay, near Worcester, of the National Conservative League passed a resolution: on 2 November the Diocesan Conference; on 9 November the city council; on 7 December the chamber of commerce, and on 19 December the Worcester 'Beaconsfield' lodge of the National Conservative League.

What was true of the south of England was true of the north. In Hull the interest was religious. There were only three meetings which sent resolutions – the Rural Deanery Chapter, the local branch of the CMS, and the CMS Junior Clerical Society – a small circle in which the Bishop, a suffragan of York and the Rural Dean, were active.

Leeds was more complex. There was a meeting in St Andrew's Parish School on 7 November. On the 14th a large meeting in the town hall, presided over by the Bishop of Ripon (he had already presided over his diocesan conference when it passed a resolution in October). To cap all the chamber of commerce passed a resolution on 30 November.

On Tyneside the Newcastle Diocesan conference passed a resolution on 25 October, and the Wearmouth Deanery Conference two days later. There was a large public meeting of the Sunderland ratepayers under the chairmanship of the mayor on 24 November, and on Monday 28 November a great meeting in Newcastle at which Lugard spoke.[20] On Teesside the Rural Deanery chapter of Middlesbrough passed a resolution on 10 November; there was a public meeting at Stockton on the 24th; on the 29th the Stockton Chamber of Commerce held a special meeting, and they were followed by the Middlesbrough Chamber the next day.

Birmingham – Chamberlain's Birmingham – gives as good a picture of the movement as any. Chamberlain himself wrote a letter (published 27 October) to the Anti-Slavery Society regretting that he could not take part in meetings, as he was going abroad, but strongly supporting the movement for the retention of Uganda. In Birmingham it opened with a quaint meeting on 1 November of the Birmingham Ladies Negro's Friend Society in the Temperance Institute: there were gentlemen present, for a canon proposed and a councillor seconded the resolution which declared that the Mayor should be invited to convene a town hall meeting. According to *The Times* a convening committee met in the middle of the month, but the chairman, Mr F. B. Goodman, said that it was believed 'the pressure already brought upon the Government had induced them to modify their views, and that at the present time their intention of evacuating Uganda had been abandoned. In these circumstances the committee considered it would be inexpedient to hold a town's meeting at present'. However, on 3 November the Blackheath, Dudley, branch and on the 7th the Birmingham branch of the CMS met, and forwarded resolutions to the Foreign Office. The chamber of commerce followed on the 16th, and were soon joined by the Walsall and District chamber. On Monday 21 November, the Dalton clerical meeting at Wolverhampton passed a resolution. And then Lugard was invited down and the Birmingham chamber held a special second meeting on 2 December, and that evening there was, after all, a 'crowded and enthusiastic meeting' in the town hall.

On a smaller scale, the same pattern was being reproduced north of the border. Two presbyteries, one at each end of Scotland, at Dumfries and Fordyce, held meetings at the end of November: Fordyce had already sent a petition to the Foreign Office on 1 November. The Duns Mutual Improvement Society sent a resolution, while the town council of Linlithgow sent a memorial incorporating resolutions. On 10 December the Commission of the General Assembly of the Free Church of Scotland passed a resolution, and the diocesan conference of the two Episcopal dioceses of Edinburgh and of Glasgow and Galloway joined their Presbyterian countrymen at the same time. But if these were isolated cases, the voice of the churches of Scotland was quite unmistakably expressed in a memorial sent to Lord Rosebery by Mr J. Cowan as early as 3 November. This stated that the facts of the Uganda situation 'forbid withdrawal'. It was signed by the Moderators, and by all the convenors and secretaries of the Foreign Missions Committee of the three Presbyterian Churches – the Church of Scotland, the Free Church of Scotland and the United Presbyterian Church of Scotland. It was also signed by the general secretary of the Alliance of Reformed Churches holding the Presbyterian System, the chairman and secretary of the Livingstonia Mission Committee of Glasgow, and by Dr Robert Laws – Laws of Livingstonia – the senior Scots missionary in British Central Africa who happened to be on furlough – a formidable army with which, three years earlier, Lord Salisbury had successfully frightened the Portuguese when they had threatened British claims to Nyasaland. During November these church leaders were joined by five of the most important chambers of commerce, Glasgow, Edinburgh, Leith, Greenock and Dundee. In Scotland therefore religion and trade had joined hands: there was no need for any further indication of what Scottish opinion wanted.

Apart from a large meeting of the Friends of Foreign Missions in Belfast on 2 November, Ireland was not stirred. In October Archbishop Lord Plunket presided over the conference of his three dioceses of Dublin, Glendalough and Kildare and all three passed resolutions in favour of the retention of Uganda. But besides these the only resolution which was sent from Ireland to the Foreign Office came from the Protestant parish of Powerscourt in County Wicklow, from which there was also a petition: but these were obviously inspired by Archdeacon Henry Galbraith who had long been interested in Uganda.[21]

Taking the movement all in all, though it varied from say, the 'influential and largely attended public meeting' at Stockton-on-Tees, to the small parish 'Declaration of Opinion' from the village of Icomb near Stow on the Wold 'representative of a small but vigorous community, sincerely interested in foreign missions' (as the Vicar put it), resolutions, memorials or petitions came from some part or other of thirty-five out of the forty-two English counties (Oxford, Suffolk, Northampton, Buckingham, Huntingdon, Westmorland and Rutland comprising the unrepresented remainder), so that, though there were certainly pockets of enthusiasm, it was still a country-wide movement, with resolutions reaching the Foreign Office from north and west, from town and country, from market town and manufacturing town, and from the metropolis itself. It was truly nation-wide.

There are one or two minor features of the campaign which are worth noting. There was only one meeting on a Sunday, and that was of the chapter of the Rural Deanery of Luton on

27 October – hardly a breach of the Sabbath. Without doubt sermons were preached (it would be valuable to know when and how many – though political sermons were not very common – and on what text). Prayers were certainly said, and the pious could certainly claim their efficacy. Strangely enough Saturday seems to have been an unusual day for meetings – the favourite was Thursday. For the first three of the five busiest weeks there were more meetings on a Thursday than on any other day – sometimes twice as many. Thursday, 3 November and Thursday, 10 November held the record with nine on each day.

Another feature – a notable feature of English life – was the way in which mayors and bishops presided over meetings other than their own town councils and diocesan conferences. Mayors presided over most of the public meetings and on 23 November the Mayor of Guildford presided over the parish meeting at the village of Stoke-next-Guildford up on the Hogsback in Surrey. The Bishops of London, Manchester, Liverpool, Norwich, Worcester, Ripon, St Asaph, Hull and Lichfield all presided over meetings at which Uganda was discussed. The Bishop of Chester, Dr Jayne, seems to have been as active in the movement as anyone. He presided over the Wirral and Birkenhead branch of the SPG on Thursday, 18 October, when they passed a resolution. He took the chair at a meeting of the Birkenhead branch of the CMS on Monday 31st when they passed another one. On 3 November, his Diocesan Conference passed a resolution, and that same evening he seconded Judge Hughes' resolution, at the public meeting in Chester convened by the mayor. It seems that public meetings became respectable if the mayor could be persuaded to preside and that bishops were local figures of importance who could give prominence to public meetings at which they were in the chair.

Taking the larger meetings, as presumably being the most influential, the Anglican diocesan conferences seem to have made up the earliest important series. Carlisle on 13 October, Dublin on 24 October, Newcastle, Liverpool, and Glendalough in Ireland on 25th, Kildare on the 26th, Llandaff and Chichester on the 27th (where the resolution was proposed by the brother of the murdered Bishop Hannington, and the

70

Bishop of Chichester told the conference that the cost of administering Uganda would be 'about the cost of a single picture in the National Gallery').[22] Truro followed the next day, and Ripon at about the same time. Worcester followed on 2 November, Edinburgh, Chester and Hereford on the 3rd, Glasgow on the 10th, Rochester on the 15th, and finally Southwell on 5 December. In most cases this was the normal time for diocesan conferences – they can hardly have been specially summoned – but the opportunity of their meeting certainly seems to have been taken to proclaim the Church's attitude.

The chambers of commerce seem in general to have been specially called to consider the Uganda question. Blackburn was the first on 31 October. Glasgow, Leith and London met in the first week of November; Greenock and Newport in the second; Manchester, Edinburgh, Birmingham, Dewsbury and Gloucestershire in the third. By the end of November, the chambers of Walsall, Southampton, Dundee, Swansea, Stockton, Exeter, Leeds and Middlesbrough had passed Uganda resolutions. By 12 December, when the last of this series – Rochdale – passed a resolution, Liverpool and Worcester had also met, and Birmingham for the second time. The chambers of commerce mostly followed the diocesan conferences and their meetings were spread out during November and early December. The same was true of the town and city council meetings and the great public meetings in town halls.

It was of course still the heyday of the British public meeting, and in the absence of other forms of mass entertainment and more sophisticated instruments of propaganda, it was still a weapon which could be wielded to considerable effect. Indeed, with the extension of the franchise, politicians had found that if they were to be masters of their craft they had to be equally at home in two very different atmospheres, the House of Commons, and the public meeting, and this remained true until, with the expansion of the electorate, the voters to be wooed quite exceeded the seating capacity of the local town hall, and until broadcasting enabled an eminent personality to be heard in several places at once. But in 1892 these changes lay in the future, and the weapon that had been forged by extra-parliamentary movements from 1780 onwards was still available to any new movement that desired to influence British policy. The large public meetings about Uganda were therefore of the first importance.

So, of course, were some of those of the chambers of commerce, particularly those which Lugard addressed – London, Edinburgh, Dundee, Manchester, Birmingham and Liverpool. But these were not open to the public, and though widely reported, they only represented one interest. It seems necessary however to include among the large public meetings two possibly doubtful cases: one was the meeting at Stockton-on-Tees under the auspices of the chamber of commerce, for this was a public meeting in the Public Hall under the chairmanship of the mayor, who happened also to be president of the chamber; the other was the SPG meeting at Reading since this was also open to the public and presided over by the mayor.

The public meetings then began on 31 October with one at Leamington in Warwickshire. On 2 November this was followed by a meeting at Durham, with the mayor in the chair and the dean moving the resolution. On the 3 November there was the meeting at Chester, convened by the mayor at which the bishop seconded the motion. On the 7th the Mayor of Wells in Somerset presided over a meeting in the Public Hall. On the 8th was the great meeting at Bristol, on the 10th one at Woking (which seems to have led to the subsequent petition from Woking) and that night the largest of the public meetings in London – in Kensington Town Hall – with speeches by Lugard and the local MPs and an overflow meeting nearby. On the 14th there was the large meeting presided over by the Bishop of Ripon in Leeds Town Hall; on the 18th another in London at Woolwich; on the following Monday – the 21st – a crowded public meeting (the mayor presiding) in Tunbridge Wells; a meeting at Malvern two days later; with one at Sunderland and the one at Stockton-on-Tees on the 24th. The next day saw the Cambridge meeting, the 28th the Reading one (and the one at Newcastle[23]). On 2 December there was the 'large and enthusiastic' meeting at Birmingham; another at Cheltenham on 7 December; in the same week the county meeting at Dorchester in Dorset, and last of all the two meetings in St Andrew's Hall, Norwich, on 12 December, and a meeting at Richmond, with the Liberal mayor in the chair, on 16 December.

It might have been possible to discount the views of the interested parties expressed through diocesan conferences and chambers of commerce. But these crowded, enthusiastic and unanimous meetings could not be ignored. In the absence of more exact calculations, these public meetings provided a guide, of which politicians made use, to the strength of British public opinion on a particular issue, so that of all the meetings on Uganda, these public meetings were probably the decisive ones.

Decisive moreover because like many of the smaller meetings they were widely representative. This point is specially brought out in several of the letters forwarding the resolutions. One vicar wrote of a parish meeting 'The room was quite full, and a large number of working men were present'. To this another vicar could add 'our meeting was numerously attended by men widely differing in social position and political opinion'. The Mayor of Tunbridge Wells wrote that his meeting was 'representative of all classes of the inhabitants and of all shades of religious and political opinions' and the Bishop of Ripon reported that the meeting in Leeds Town Hall 'was largely composed of the working classes, and was very enthusiastic. There were representatives of various religious bodies present. The meeting was in no wise political in tone or composition, and it was supported by many influential persons' – which only means that it was a truly national affair.

Critics in the House of Commons subsequently tried to argue that the movement did not have the support of the Liberals in the country. It is true that only one Liberal organisation – the City of London Association – sent a resolution to the Foreign Office, and that it was non-committal (the only one, it should be said, in the whole collection), and that five other political organisations which sent resolutions to the Foreign Office were all Conservative. It is also true that only Conservative or Liberal Unionist politicians – Hicks-Beach, Chamberlain, Balfour and Salisbury – publicly expressed their support for the retention of Uganda, and that at least one Liberal MP, Sir Wilfred Lawson, spoke against it.

But this is inconclusive, and further evidence, as for instance from Woking, indicates that 'both Liberals and Conservatives' were supporters of the movement. The evening meeting in Norwich was 'attended *and addressed* by persons of all shades of political opinion'. There were Liberals among the MPs who attended Lugard's meeting with the London Chamber of Commerce. Mr H. F. Brooks forwarded a 'largely signed petition by men of both parties' in his constituency. The Mayor of Richmond, writing 'as a humble supporter of the present Government' forwarded a resolution strongly in favour of the retention of Uganda, while the chairman of a meeting in Hornsey wrote, 'the bulk of the people here are strong Liberals, but at the same time they feel most deeply that to evacuate Uganda is a mistake.'

Perhaps the most striking instance is the support given to the Uganda retention campaign by John Cowan of Beeslack. He was a noted philanthropist and a vice-president of the Royal Scottish Geographical Society. He was also, and had long been, the chairman of Gladstone's election committee in Midlothian, and became a baronet when his name appeared in the short list of honours which Gladstone secured upon his final resignation from office in March 1894. Yet it was Cowan who organised the memorial from all the leaders of the Presbyterian Churches in Scotland. His support was a sign of the times. The Liberal critics were almost certainly mistaken, for the evidence suggests that the movement cut across the normal political alignments.

Odd as it may seem there were only very meagre attempts to organise the campaign. The CMS were pressed to go in for 'agitation', but studiously avoided doing much more than making their position clear whenever there was an opportunity – though there can be little doubt that their supporters were well to the fore in the movement in the country. There was of course Lugard's tour, which grew as it went. There was also the decision on 25 October of the Swansea Town Council to send a copy of their resolution of 19 October to (probably) every town council in England and Wales. Nine of them used the Swansea formula, which leaves only two town councils which devised their own. Here was a measure of organisation, but not a very effective one. The Swansea formula was also used by the Newport (Mon.) Chamber of Commerce on 11 November, and their secretary was instructed to send copies to all the chambers of commerce in the country. But the twenty-three other chambers that sent resolutions, with the exception of Leeds, were all independent enough to devise their own. In addition to the Swansea resolution, there was also a draft 'petition' going the rounds, which was used in twelve of the seventeen petitions, but the only other duplications that can be traced are between the memorial of the great public meeting in the Guildhall in Bristol and the memorial of the inhabitants of Blaby in Leicestershire, and between the resolution of the meeting in Woking and the resolution of the meeting in Chester. But these prototypes account for less than 30 out of 174[24] which comprise the Foreign Office collection. There were certainly organising committees in individual towns but there was no central organising campaign committee or anything in lieu of one.

In most of the resolutions the order and subject matter varied considerably. All manner of combination can be found which suggests that most of them were drawn up individually. It is only possible to give three or four examples at random.

The Halifax Friends of Missions were brief. Resolved, they said, 'That this meeting, in view of the great and various interests involved, desires to urge upon the Government the importance of maintaining British influence in Uganda.' That was on 6 November. A month later, the Liverpool Chamber of Commerce, to take another example, resolved (copy to Mr Gladstone) 'That in view of the important geographical position and natural resources of Uganda, the Council of this Chamber urges upon Her Majesty's Government the expediency of placing that country under direct Imperial control so that peace and order may be maintained and opportunity be afforded for the spread of civilisation and commerce among the inhabitants.' Statutory church organisations were busy, and the Southampton Ruridecanal Council, for instance, resolved

That we contemplate with the greater anxiety the withdrawal of British Authority from Uganda, believing, that the result will be disastrous to the missionary converts in that country; will endanger the lives of British subjects; will stop the advance of civilisation in Central Africa; will close a promising field for the trade of this country; and will bring dishonour upon England as a Christian nation, in whose power and faithfulness the natives have learned to trust: Your memorialists therefore pray [etc.]

75

And to take one of the occasional prototypes, as used in Chester, the public meeting there resolved

> That this Meeting of the Citizens of Chester believing that the Slave Trade would be grievously promoted and that the cause of Christ as well as lawful commerce and national honour would be injured by the evacuation of Uganda, earnestly request Her Majesty's Government to maintain the just influence of England within that territory in Africa which was assigned to this country by the treaty of 1889.

The treaty was in fact signed in 1890, but that was a minor point.

The main point is that these last two resolutions from Southampton and Chester show very clearly how inextricably the religious and commercial arguments were intermingled.

Nonetheless, though there were few standard texts, the same phrases and the same arguments constantly recurred, and an analysis of the number of times each occurs in the 174 instances available gives perhaps the best indication of what that ephemeral figure 'the British Public' had in mind.[25]

As one might expect, the interests of trade and commerce were mentioned frequently – seventy-five times in fact – and there are seven or eight further references to the fruitful and promising field whose resources would now be opened to development. This was clearly important. Continental markets were closing and hostile tariffs were being evolved everywhere. It was therefore necessary for the British to look to the future when their existing markets would be more and more restricted and when they would be glad of every available new one. But it was not annexation with a view to immediate exploitation that was in mind: it was merely annexation in case of need of new markets.

The appearance of economic arguments however is not the most striking feature of the campaign. The most striking fact of all is that in 104 cases out of 174, there is some mention of slavery or the slave trade – the need for its abolition and the danger of its resurgence unless the British Government maintained the British position in Uganda. The British public knew very little about Africa, but the preachings of Wilberforce, Buxton and Livingstone had sunk deep into the national mind, and any reverse in Africa instantly recalled the horror of slavery which was the one thing that most of them knew about Africa. Buganda had suffered a great deal less from the ravages of the slave trade than many other areas, but public opinion was not concerned with such fine distinctions as this: it went for the broad fact. It would not be going too far to say that a fear for the revival of the slave trade was the most important single factor in persuading British public opinion to insist on Britain's retention of Uganda.

But fear of the slave trade did not stand alone. The dangers of civil war and massacre, 'barbarism' and grave disaster, anarchy and bloodshed, were mentioned in the resolutions more than fifty times: and the need for peace, order and good government about a further twenty. This reveals a more telling assessment, probably garnered from the newspapers, of the real issue.

From the newspapers too there came, no doubt, the fears for the Christian mission: the plight of the Christian converts was mentioned thirty-eight times, there were ten references to the plight of mission work, twenty to the plight of the native races or native inhabitants, and twenty-eight to that of the missionaries.

In addition the call of national duty also played its part. The fact that 'the natives' had placed their trust in the British was mentioned five times. There were thirteen references to the distrust in the British that would be engendered if withdrawal took place. There were eight or nine references to Britain's 'moral policy' or 'moral' or 'legitimate influence'. There were seven examples of the notion that Britain had a responsibility to discharge, and thirty-one of the importance of upholding British prestige and the British position in Africa. And then thirty-eight of the resolutions and petitions referred to the honour of England and the iniquity of a breach of faith.

Certain stock phrases were liberally used – 'philanthropy' however only four times, but 'humanity' over twenty, 'civilisation' thirty-nine times, and Christianity (or Religion, which at the time was a synonym for Christianity) over fifty times.

This is not, of course, a guide to the rarified thoughts of the political speech makers, but an indication of the sentiments of the groundlings. What these resolutions reveal is the ubiquity of the Victorian thought-connection between Africa and the slave trade, and the fact that people in Britain were still ready to make an effort to see that the slave trade was suppressed. They show as well that there was a profound concern about the fate of Buganda – its people, its Christian converts and its Christian missionaries. But no less important were the interests of trade and commerce – 'peaceful' and 'legitimate' commerce as it was called. While super-imposed on everything was 'the call of national duty', and the proud confidence that Britain, having, it was said, found the means to raise herself above all other 'civilised' nations, was well placed to impart the benefits of Christianity and civilisation, for which she had striven and to which she was the heir, to others. As Chamberlain put it succinctly from a platform in 1894, 'What is wanted for Uganda, is what Birmingham has got – an improvement scheme.'

What had happened was that some ideas, deep-seated in the national character, had been profoundly stirred. In this case, a Christian horror of slavery; fears for the passing of free trade; memories of Gordon and Khartoum, and confidence that the keys to progress had been found and could easily be transferred to Africa. They may be strange bedfellows, and very different from the precise problem in Buganda (which was simply to prevent the collapse of the delicate balance between three hostile parties within a single state); very different also from the British Foreign Office's primary concern (with gaining control of the headwaters of the Nile to prevent any other power upsetting the delicate British position in Egypt). But clearly enough public opinion is quite capable of having its own reasons, irrespective of what might be called 'real' or 'adequate' or 'well-informed' reasons.

Part of the strength of the movement lay in its assortment of allies, not of course so strangely mixed for the Victorians as for a later day. Only a year previously the CMS had campaigned for money for the Company and for a steamer to be shared between the Company and the Mission: but their success had only been partial, because they had worked alone. Shortly afterwards Mounteney-Jephson, who had been with Stanley on the Emin Pasha Relief Expedition, went the round of the chambers of commerce[26] urging the commercial value of

Uganda, and several of the Chambers had sent memorials to the Foreign Office, but with no noticeable effect on Government policy. Two years later, in 1894 over the Bechuanaland question, the missionaries and the empire builders were on different sides, with the result that neither got their way. Rhodes got his railway strip (from which he launched the Jameson Raid) yet gained no control over the bulk of the tribal lands. But in 1892 in this Uganda campaign the churches, the chambers of commerce and the empire builders for once worked together for the same object and at the same time: for the object they were after was quite straightforward – the retention of British influence in Uganda.

Of the resolutions and petitions ninety-five per cent were seen and initialled by Lord Rosebery in the Foreign Office, but judging by the minuted dates, by the time he wrote his decisive memorandum for the Cabinet on 3 November, though he had probably heard of some of the more recent public meetings, he cannot have seen more than twelve of the resolutions and petitions and there were over 160 more before the movement had finished. By 7 November, when the cabinet made its decision to send a Commissioner to Uganda, he had seen fourteen more, but there were still 148 to come. It is doubtful therefore whether the movement had much influence on the Cabinet when they reversed their decision of 30 September.

To some this second decision – to send a Commissioner to Uganda – was sufficient. It was 'cordially' welcomed by a public meeting in the quaint old market town of Wooler in Northumberland, and by a crowded audience at Godalming 'with intense satisfaction'. But there were other views. A CMS meeting at Bedford 'while expressing its earnest thanks to Almighty God for the evident answer to prayer, which the present concession of the Government respecting Uganda indicates ... would most urgently press upon the Government the necessity of maintaining an active control over that land'. St Simon's, Swansea was a little more downright: 'We regret that the decision of the Government so far appears to be somewhat temporising.' The Vicar of Kirkby Wharfe called it 'apparently provisional' and he was right. On the face of it there had been a compromise which left a way out, for the Commissioner could still recommend evacuation, and

Gladstone and Sir Edward Grey in the debate on the Address in the House of Commons in the following January, when the question was raised by the Little Englanders, promised that no final decision would be taken until the Commissioner's report was received.

But already Rosebery had made up his mind that there was no way out. Writing to Portal, after he had telegraphed to him confirming his appointment as British Commissioner in Uganda, Rosebery told him that his formal instructions would follow,

but I consider it as settled that your main duty will be to arrange the best means of administering Uganda ... There may, of course, be indicated to you the possibility that should the difficulty of retention be found insuperable, or at any rate too vast, you should so report. But as a rather one horse company has been able to administer I suppose the empire will be equal to it, and therefore that saving clause is mainly one of form.

Writing again a week later a covering note to the official instructions he said that he had little to add, 'but I may say this as my confident though not my official opinion, that public sentiment here will expect and support the maintenance of the British sphere of influence'.[27] Both these letters were private and confidential – presumably from his colleagues; and they provide a striking example of the occasional emptiness of official instructions and of the importance of confidential ones.

But here was the success of the campaign, that as early as the first week in December it was quite clear that British public opinion would not tolerate withdrawal, and that behind the back of the still-hesitant Cabinet, Portal was instructed accordingly. The final decision was not taken till Portal's Report had been received, but for fourteen months it had been almost a foregone conclusion.

Almost but not quite. As *The Times* wrote on 8 December:

What the Government is now doing in the matter of Uganda is satisfactory enough as far as it goes, and if Lord Rosebery had a free hand we have no doubt that it would be made more satisfactory still. But it is still only by a decided expression of public opinion that he has been enabled to do anything, and it must not be forgotten that energetic prosecution of the policy now sanctioned cannot be expected unless the pressure of public opinion can be maintained.

The spate of meetings, however, could not be maintained, and public attention turned to Egypt and to Gladstone's Home Rule Bill. Moreover, by the beginning of 1893 the opponents of retention had raised their voices in the reviews; chief among them Sir Charles Dilke; most effectively the Reverend J. Guinness Rogers. But before the end of the year Lugard's two handsome volumes on *The Rise of Our East African Empire* appeared, as did the Company's apologia *British East Africa, or IBEA*, compiled by its Secretary P. L. McDermott. The Company also published pamphlets. R. Bosworth Smith published his three letters to *The Times*. The CMS printed booklets, one of which had sold 25,000 copies even before the end of 1892. The newspapers continued their support and all this was sufficient to prevent the effect of the 1892 campaign from wearing off.

Reporting a speech at the morning meeting of the 94th anniversary of the Church Missionary Society on 1 May 1893, the *Church Missionary Gleaner* said that 'so far as anyone can forecast the picture Sir John Kennaway (the President) feels that the retention of Uganda is now secured'.[28] On 12 December 1893 at a meeting of the Royal Colonial Institute, Lugard said, 'I hope we may now assume that East Africa and Uganda are saved from the chaos and anarchy which abandonment would involve, and that the nation will not now have to face the shame which would be ours if we were to withdraw.'[29] Two months later, Rosebery in circulating his comments on Portal's report to the Cabinet said 'I believe the country has made up its mind.' There was a delay while Gladstone resigned (over the Naval estimates), and Rosebery succeeded, as Prime Minister. There was one last fracas in the Cabinet on 7 April 1894[30] but the decision to retain Uganda was taken and announced in both Houses of Parliament on 12 April[31] – in the Commons by Sir William Harcourt, its most formidable opponent at the outset.

Such was the result of that brief, spontaneous, countrywide, strangely compounded but truly national movement of British public opinion in the late autumn of 1892.

In Buganda it was scarcely noticed, for the Company Protectorate was merged into the Imperial Protectorate without the hiatus which had been expected. But in England it marked not merely a change in policy towards Uganda (in the words of a notable article,[32] the last step in the advance from 'informal' to 'formal' empire), but it also heralded the beginning of the end of that mid-Victorian anti-imperialism which had on most occasions fought against the creation of 'formal' empire. When Gladstone came into office he had hoped to be able to evacuate British forces from Egypt. Egypt was still under British occupation when he resigned eighteen months later, and none of the projected withdrawals were carried out as he would have wished. By the time the Conservatives succeeded to office in 1895, any withdrawal was out of the question, and the Liberals had actually agreed to the building of the Uganda railway, though they had hounded Salisbury for the suggestion that he should do so less than four years before. The movement for the retention of Uganda had therefore an importance transcending the immediate issue. Its details emphasise, however, the need for the reconsideration of 'imperialism' which are now being made.

NOTES

1. Church Missionary Society Archives M.C. LVI p. 632.
2. *Manchester Guardian*, 24 September 1892.
3. Rosebery to the Queen. *Letters of Queen Victoria*, 3rd Series, vol. II (London 1931). p. 159.
4. 4 October 1892.
5. 24 September 1892.
6. 30 September 1892.
7. *The Times* 8 October 1892.
8. *Western Mail*, 4 October 1892.
9. Church Missionary Society Archives, M.C. LVI, pp. 670–4.
10. *The Times*, 21 October 1892.
11. Gladstone to the Queen, 7 October 1892. *Letters of Queen Victoria*, 3rd Series, vol II p. 178.
12. *The Times*, 9 November 1892.
13. *Daily News*, 24 October 1892.
14. See M. F. Perham, *Lugard: The Years of Adventure* London, 1956.
15. The collection will be found in the Public Record Office, London, Foreign Office 84/2192 upon which the text of this chapter is based except where other references are specifically made.
16. There were none from Roman Catholic sources. This is not to say that they were opposed to the retention of Uganda but they were more concerned at this time with the rights and wrongs of the events in Buganda earlier in the year.

17. The National Union of Conservative Associations of Scotland passed a resolution on 8 November (*The Times*).
18. *The Times*, 12 October 1892.
19. A Working Man to (Wigram), 3 October 1892, Church Missionary Society Archives, packet 418.
20. *The Times*, 29 November 1892. No resolution reached the Foreign Office.
21. I have counted this as a memorial.
22. *Daily News*, 2 October 1892.
23. This did not send a resolution to the Foreign Office.
24. A few of the resolutions, etc. were forwarded twice. I have naturally only counted them once. But I have distinguished between the afternoon and evening meeting at Norwich on 12 December, though their resolutions were forwarded together.
25. Slight variations in the figures must be allowed for, owing to occasional variations in the precise wording of the oft-repeated phrases.
26. E.g. 22 December 1891. Joint Meeting, Edinburgh Chamber of Commerce and Royal Scottish Geographical Society. A. J. Mounteney-Jephson. 'Trade Prospects in Uganda,' *Scottish Geographical Magazine* VIII (1892), 93.
27. Rosebery to Portal. 1 December and 9 December 1892. Portal Papers, Rhodes House, Oxford.
28. *C. M. Gleaner*, XX (1893) 85.
29. *Proceedings of the Royal Colonial Institute*, XXV (1893–4), 120–1.
30. Rosebery to the Queen, 7 April 1894. *Letters of Queen Victoria*, 3rd Series, vol. II, p. 389.
31. *Hansard*, 4th Series, vol. XXIII, pp. 180–1, 223.
32. J. Gallagher and R. Robinson. 'The Imperialism of Free Trade,' *Economic History Review*, 2nd Series, VI (1953), pp. 1–15.

3

The British and the Baganda

I

One of the marked tendencies of the colonial powers in their day was to overlook one crucial strand in their connection with the peoples who were subject to them. Their own predilection was to describe the relationship with them in legal or administrative terms. Periodically there were some valuable attempts by one of their number – especially when there were sizeable alien communities to sharpen the issues – at describing the relationship in social terms; while 'economic exploitation' regularly provided their critics with a fourth frame of reference. Often, however, because there was no adequate history, save for the face-saving paragraphs in an annual report, the critical importance of a developing political relationship over time was ignored. On two occasions, in 1892 and 1954, British public opinion was keenly stirred over an issue concerning Britain's relationship with the Baganda. But the unfolding relationship between the two parties over the best part of three-quarters of a century was rarely given even passing consideration. Its pattern, however, seems relatively plain.

II

In the first half of the twentieth century Buganda owed its size and preponderance, as much as anything else, to the fact that, during the period from 1875 to 1900, it alone of all the lacustrine kingdoms provided a fairly permanent abode for the Europeans who began to move into the area at that time. These first Europeans came (as to a good many other parts of Africa) upon invitation. The Baganda seem to have been impressed with the success which the Egyptians were enjoying in the 1860s and 1870s once they had secured Europeans –

Sir Samuel Baker and Colonel Gordon – as allies for their imperialist thrust southwards. They therefore began to look around for some European allies of their own as a counterpoise. Their neighbours in the kingdom of Bunyoro were faced more immediately by the threat from the north which the Egyptian enterprise represented; but, unlike Buganda, they determined to keep the Europeans out after some unfortunate experiences with them. If Buganda had lain farther south, she would very likely have obtained assistance for her dual attempt to emulate the Egyptians while securing external assistance against them from European traders from South Africa. But, being so far distant from any already established European base, the only Europeans who would come to the country to settle were missionaries, and they proved to be of little use as political (let alone as military) allies. These first attempts to procure an external alliance proved in the event therefore to be largely abortive.[1]

But their failure did not prove disastrous, for with bankruptcy in Egypt and the revolt of the Mahdi in the Sudan, the threat from the north receded. And as it happened the missionaries were allowed to remain. This was to have immensely important consequences. The ruler, Kabaka Mutesa I, his chiefs and his pages, soon showed a keen interest in their teaching, and by the early eighteen-eighties the first conversions to Christianity in Buganda had occurred.

By the middle eighteen-eighties a new threat had developed, this time from the east, where, following an agreement to partition East Africa between them, British and German elements had begun to move inland from the coast. Fearing that their invasion was upon him and that the missionary bishop, James Hannington, was a pioneering imperialist agent, Kabaka Mwanga had him murdered. For the missionaries who remained in the country the period which followed was extremely precarious. Their converts were persecuted; some of them were put to death. As it happened, however, these converts were drawn from the rising generation at the Kabaka's court. They were thus amongst the 'new' men of their time. By 1888 those that survived the persecution had renewed cause to fear for their future at Mwanga's hands. They accordingly joined in a revolt against him in that year, and helped to turn him off the throne. Within a month, however, they themselves, and the missionaries associated with them, had been expelled by a coalition of Arabs and Muslim Baganda who now took over control of the country.

Thereafter there was for a while no secure European foothold remaining in the equatorial lakes region. The Imperial British East Africa Company, which was working inland from Mombasa, planned at first to make its up-country headquarters, not in Buganda, but with the remnant of Egypt's crumbling Equatoria Province, north of Lake Albert. Had this project come to fruition, the subsequent British position in the interior of East Africa would very likely have been based within that region; and there could very easily have been a substantial war between the British and the Baganda, of the kind which further south was soon to lead to the destruction of the Ndebele kingdom.

But much to their surprise the British suddenly found that the door into Buganda stood open before them. For, the missionaries' converts, having acquired arms from one of the few European traders now in the area, had, after some anxious moments, re-conquered their country (with, as it chanced – such were the confusions of the time – their former persecutor Kabaka Mwanga at their head). So precarious, however, was their position that they were soon sending to the British Company's agent for help. In effect this meant that they called the British empire-builders into their country. In December 1890 Captain Lugard of the IBEA Company marched into Buganda, and was soon making a treaty with Kabaka Mwanga by which British 'protection' was proclaimed over his kingdom.

There followed a complex passage and a tragic one. The Christian Baganda were by now divided into Protestant and Roman Catholic parties, and by 1892 these were showing themselves ready to fight each other for control of their country. At the same time Lugard found himself increasingly at odds with Kabaka Mwanga over who was to be ultimately supreme in the country. Following the Battle of Mengo in 1892, when Lugard and the Protestants defeated Mwanga and the Catholics, Lugard decided to divide up the country between its leading factions. He gave the Protestants the largest share. And for the first time the Kabaka was forced to fly the British flag in front of his palace in recognition of his submission to it.[2]

From this beginning there emerged the special relationship between the British and the Baganda which was to prevail for the next sixty years – as well as the strange contradictions at its core. For while the British had defeated the Kabaka, and had imposed their own settlement on the country, they had in the first place been deliberately invited into the country, and had not defeated its dominant party. This party, moreover, owed the security of its position to its alliance with the British. At the same time the British position in the country rested primarily upon their association with it.

Both sides found the alliance extremely valuable. In 1893, they joined together for instance in successfully fighting their mutual enemies the Muslim Baganda. Between 1894 and 1899, the Baganda Christians helped the British against the Banyoro (who continued to resist the British advance as no doubt the Baganda would have done but for the Christian revolutions) and, following the British conquest, found themselves presented with the transfer to Buganda of a large slice of Bunyoro as a reward. The alliance therefore was not without its benefits. Its most remarkable proof came in 1897 when Kabaka Mwanga revolted against it, but the Christian chiefs preferred alliance with the British to support for their own Kabaka. The seal was eventually set upon it by Sir Harry Johnston's Uganda Agreement of 1900 – which the Christian chiefs accepted, despite some significant protests, because they feared that a breach with their British allies might thrust them back into the period when all was at stake once again, and not least their future as chiefs. Buganda was thus firmly settled under British control, and so were the chiefs in power. The British had joined with the 'new' men who had come to power in the previous decade. Apolo Kagwa, who had been appointed Katikiro or Chief Minister of Buganda in 1889, was to remain at his post for a full thirty-seven years.[3]

III

The alliance continued to be remarkably effective. While the chiefs lost their old pre-eminence as leaders of an independent kingdom, they gained a new pre-eminence as a result of their cultural leadership (which flowed from their close association with the European missionaries), a basis for a striking economic predominance (stemming from their ownership of land under terms of the 1900 Agreement) and an unprecedented political supremacy inside their kingdom. By contrast to the Kabaka's power, their power was substantially enhanced. During the first decade of the twentieth century, for example, they were able with almost effortless authority to enforce the rigid regulations of Sir Hesketh Bell, the first British Governor, both when he took strong measures to safeguard the quality of the embryonic Uganda cotton crop, and when he had the whole of the Victoria lakeshore cleared of population during a successful campaign against sleeping sickness. The British were naturally delighted with such performances. Their alliance with the Baganda leaders was now extended beyond Buganda into most parts of the expanding Uganda Protectorate. Wherever the British went they took Baganda with them as subordinate administrators. This of course enhanced the status of the Baganda above all their neighbours; and, moreover, provided openings for those Baganda who could not be readily accommodated within the chiefly hierarchy in Buganda itself. It also gave the Protectorate a certain unity.

As early as 1911, however, there were already beginning to be some signs of sharp friction. In that year a young British official felt constrained to lecture Sir Apolo Kagwa, the Katikiro, on Article 6 of the 1900 Agreement, in which it was laid down that the Baganda were to cooperate loyally with the British Administration in the organisation and administration of the kingdom. The Katikiro openly resented it. The Baganda leaders were already feeling themselves more secure than they had been in 1900, and were more ready than they might have been before to express their resentment at a tactless lecture from a comparative newcomer. The British, it seems, conceived of their position primarily in terms of sovereignty and control. To the Baganda leaders, however, the compact between them represented at bottom an agreement between equals. In the next fifteen years – despite British concessions over such things as rents and forced labour – the incipient rift along these lines widened, and by the nineteen-twenties the Buganda Assembly, the Great Lukiko, seems to have become decidedly independent-minded.[4]

The differences in the interpretation which the two sides placed upon the association between them, and of the Agreement at its core, became obscured, however, by the events of the nineteen-twenties. In 1919 a Young Baganda Association was formed in opposition to the chiefs in power. In 1921 an organisation calling itself the Federation of the Bataka was created to champion the rights of the heads of clans to own the traditional clan burial grounds – rights which they claimed had been ignored when the land allocation had been made by Kagwa and his associates under the 1900 Agreement. For a time the Federation provided a focus for the discontent of the peasants whose rents were being increased by the chiefly landowners as cash crop production expanded. That the protests against the land settlement were not louder was probably due to the relative ease with which peasant Baganda could acquire the quasi freehold *mailo* land.

With much of this complex of discontents the British administration had considerable sympathy. They were now indeed preaching the rights of the peasants against the interests of their still extant chiefly allies of twenty years before. Though they could not bring themselves to make any substantial change in the allocation of land, they did secure a remarkable rent restriction act, the Busulu and Nvujjo Law of 1927.[5]

By then the old alliance, badly strained, had collapsed. The British had become anxious to carry through what they considered to be long overdue reforms in the workings of the Buganda Government – particularly in its financial administration (following a scandal over some misappropriation of Buganda Government funds in 1924, when the Treasurer had been sent to prison). They had already therefore begun to ease out some of the older chiefs, several of whom had been in office since 1900 or earlier. The climax came in 1926, when Kagwa, the Katikiro appointed in 1889, clashed with the Provincial Commissioner. He appealed in mitigation both to his special status and to his long years of loyal association with the British. But he was roundly rebuked by the Governor. Control, not alliance, it was asserted, must predominate. Kagwa thus finally found himself forced to resign after an unedifying dispute over beer permits in the capital.[6]

This could have been disastrous to the association between

the British and the Baganda had not the line taken by the British accorded with popular feeling. There had been a significant occasion before his resignation when Kagwa had bid for British support against the young Kabaka Daudi Chwa (1897–1939), and had been sharply rebuffed. Instead of backing the old men against the new, the British backed the new men against the old – as in effect they had done on the previous occasion in the 1890s. They thereby replaced in a disarmingly successful way the old alliance between British administrators and Bagada chiefs by a new association between new administrators and new chiefs. They retained the best of the existing middle-aged chiefs – Martin Luther Nsibirwa, who subsequently became Katikiro, being the most prominent – and then brought in a new generation of more educated chiefs, some of whom had been involved in the recent opposition movements: the most outstanding of these was Serwano Kulubya, who became Treasurer of Buganda in 1928. Reforms (particularly financial reforms) were then carried through, and the new men were given – and soon showed themselves quick to take – their chance. Buganda enhanced its reputation in British circles as a flourishing African kingdom. So well pleased indeed were the British with their success that in the early nineteen-thirties they offered neighbouring Bunyoro and Busoga Agreements similar in intention to that enjoyed by the Baganda. The alliance, was, moreover, subsequently confirmed by the response of the Baganda leaders to the Administration's evident interest in, for example, African education, and by the abandonment of the plans for an East African Federation which were afoot at the time – plans which to the Baganda, then as later, implied the rule of European settlers from Nairobi.[7]

IV

The nineteen-thirties, however, did not see a mere repetition of the ingredients of the earlier period. It was a more peaceful era, so that the alliance for the new Baganda leaders was not the dire necessity it had been for their predecessors. A new wind was blowing. The younger chiefs owed their position with their people, not so much, like their predecessors, to great politico-religious followings, but rather to their place within the politico-administrative hierarchy; and, as the 1920s had demonstrated, these were not to be assured immutably. The younger chiefs, moreover, were soon not so young, and as a consequence of the rapid expansion of education, were soon being overtaken in their cultural and educational leadership by yet another generation of 'new' men. What was more, chiefs no longer enjoyed any special economic pre-eminence. For there were soon sons of former chiefs and other beneficiaries of the 1900 Agreement, who were not chiefs themselves but were heirs to their father's freehold estates made under the 1900 Agreement, who in many cases were very much wealthier. Given, moreover, that landownership implied the status of chief, even where it did not explicitly carry the formal power and function of a chief, many such men considered themselves to be the equal of the chiefs. All this created a quite new situation. At the same time, in accord with the persistent tendency of the court in Buganda to be a centre for fervent intrigue, there was, by the end of the nineteen thirties, first a quarrel between the Kabaka and his court on the one hand, and the Ministers and the Lukiko on the other, over the cost to the Buganda revenue of the Kabaka's household, which led to a threat of abdication by the Kabaka; and then in 1941 much controversy over the re-marriage, contrary to custom, of Kabaka Daudi Chwa's widow to a commoner, which led to the resignation of the now elderly Nsibirwa from the Katikiroship, and of Hamu Mukasa, once the greatest of the county chiefs, from the Lukiko.

Sir Philip Mitchell who became Governor in 1935 was aware that something was wrong, and divined, to his credit, that there was something especially unsatisfactory about the structuring of the relationship between the Protectorate Government and the Buganda Government. The oversight which the British exercised over Buganda was organised on a territorial basis; for the purposes of British administration Buganda was divided into several districts each under the aegis of a British District Commissioner. Mitchell decided that it would be better to exercise British control solely from the top through a Resident, and sketched out a plan by which the functions of the two governments were to be functionally interrelated, instead of being confusingly duplicated as hitherto. These proposals were welcomed by the Baganda leaders, even though they only touched part of the problem. They were only, however, very thoughtlessly applied by his successor, who aimed at extending the autonomy of Buganda as far as possible, while ignoring both the need to fit Buganda into the wider Uganda, and the more urgent need to see that the chiefly hierarchy was not left isolated as the paid agents of an alien régime. A substantial crisis followed in 1945.[8]

An essential problem by this time stemmed from the fact that the further generation of new men who had come forward in the nineteen-thirties had found that the very success of their predecessors had blocked the road for similar swift advancement for themselves. With the growth, moreover, by this time of an indigenous western-educated chieftainship in the areas outside Buganda there were no longer additional openings for aspirant Baganda in the rest of the Protectorate as once there had been. It was all too evident, moreover, that not all the rising literate class in Buganda could become chiefs; and although there were unofficial members in the Lukiko these were still in a minority and nominated by the hierarchy in power. Some of the most outstanding of the new men accordingly took to other careers such as schoolmastering. But in 1942 in a seminal affair at the premier mission school, King's College, Budo, a number of the most prominent of them clashed with the English headmaster, and left. Once the Second World War began there had (owing to the rise in the world prices of primary products) been a little more money around, and many of the rising generation thereafter took to founding limited liability companies.[9] For a year or two indeed there was a regular 'South Sea Bubble' around Kampala. But one by one, owing to lack of capital, lack of expertise and the smallness of the market, these companies went bankrupt. There was soon, moreover, some rather more general economic discontent, partly because, as the war dragged on, a shortage of goods occurred, but also because a real drop in the value of the price which the British administration was prepared to accord to the primary products grown by the peasantry came to be felt by very large numbers of them. When all these things were coupled both with distillation of the ideals for which the free world fought, and with the frustrated maturity of the increased class of men raised above the bottom levels of ignorance and poverty, new political demands were not unnaturally generated. This coincided both with renewed fears for the expropriation of land; and with a now chronic intrigue within the chiefly hierarchy itself for the premier position within it.

The result was the riots of 1945, in which, it was significant, the chief single object of rioters was to secure the resignation of Serwano Kulubya, the Treasurer appointed in 1928. In this their success was dramatic. At the height of the rioting Kulubya resigned. Shortly afterwards, however, the British deported Wamala, the Katikiro who had succeeded Nsibirwa in 1941, for his part in the affair; and replaced him by none other than Nsibirwa himself.[10] But this time the transition was by no means as smooth as it had been twenty years previously. Nsibirwa was killed in a political murder on the steps of the Anglican cathedral at Namirembe a few months later.

The crucial point for our present purposes in this further period of crisis seems very plain. The British reversed the policy they had pursued in the two former periods. Previously they had backed the new men against the old. This time they backed the old men against the new.

Given the general state of the imperial mind on African policy at this time that was probably inevitable. On the first occasion the British had been glad of the help of the new men in establishing their power. On the second they had wanted to reform the Buganda Government. But to have backed the new men on this third occasion would have hastened the diminution of their power before they were in any mind to contemplate this at all. Furthermore this time not all the old men were all that old; indeed so far as the British were concerned the best of them were fulfilling their functions admirably.

But the result was that the Administration lost contact with the Baganda. The reforms which were advanced, such as the Co-operative Societies Ordinance, and the increasing introduction of elected unofficial members in the Lukiko, did not meet the situation. The Registrar of Co-operative Societies became almost a dictator, and the unofficial members in the Lukiko remained in a minority. There was, moreover, considerable feeling against the controlled price for cotton, and against Nsibirwa's successor as Katikiro, Apolo Kagwa's imperious son, Kawalya Kagwa. There was as well a rising atavism in the so-called Bataka party, which came to prominence at this time. Accordingly further riots occurred in 1949.[11]

Both in 1945 and in 1949 the British administration made much of the activities of 'agitators', to the detriment of a clearer view of the basic issues, and the men identified were soon deported. Much more significant, however, was the fact that the tentacles of the Protectorate police were now for the first time in its history extended into the Buganda countryside so as to reinforce the now slender bonds of the old association between the British and the Baganda. In the end indeed the British administration's control over the country only survived because of an unheralded improvement in the economic position of the peasantry, and the support of a few key individuals in the Buganda Government.

V

The Buganda Government, was, however, in a very vulnerable position.[12] The most serious incidents in the riots of 1945 and 1949 had taken place at the gates of the palace of the Kabaka – by this time the young Mutesa II – and the British had only somewhat tardily come to his support. These facts seem to have loomed large in the mind of Mutesa II when he entered into his major controversy with the British Governor of Uganda, Sir Andrew Cohen, in 1953. For the reforms which the two men jointly announced in March of that year had sought to introduce an unofficial majority into the Lukiko. In the circumstances of the time that could very easily have placed the Kabaka and his Government at the mercy of the populace. When there was a stir over the possibility, once again, of the creation of an East African Federation, the Kabaka seems to have thought that the time had come for him at all events to call in the new men. Certainly in his dispute with Sir Andrew Cohen in the autumn of 1953 he turned to some of the younger figures who appeared to have popular support, and ignored those who were renowned for their association with the British. To the British this made his threat to oppose them publicly on the policy which they announced at this time of creating a unitary state in Uganda a most serious matter. There had been a number of previous occasions when the association had worn very thin. It could very easily now have been submerged in a violent conflict. That was avoided by the Kabaka's deportation by the British in November 1953. But the effect of so desperate a step was traumatic. The absence of any attempt to resolve the contradictions in the alliance between the British and the Baganda in any really substantial way had left the Baganda firm in the notion that in the end the British were still fundamentally their teachers, protectors and friends. Now it was starkly apparent that they were their masters.

It was part of Sir Keith Hancock's subsequent achievement on his constitutional mission to Buganda in 1954 to have begun the re-creation of a broken association. The damage which had been done by the events of ten years and more was, however, vividly illustrated by the subsequent repudiation of the Hancock Committee by the Lukiko; and in the relations between the Protectorate and Buganda Governments frankness and formality thereafter did battle. The Kabaka had, however, jumped just in time to emerge as a popular hero. The change which his move had effected is very well illustrated by the contrast between 1897, when the Baganda supported the British against their own Kabaka, and 1954, when the Baganda supported the Kabaka against the British.

There were of course various other aspects to the crisis which erupted. To begin with there was the position of the Kabaka himself. The 1900 Agreement had declared that he was the 'Native Ruler' of the kingdom. In practice, owing to the long regency at the outset of Kabaka Daudi Chwa's reign at the beginning of the century, power was concentrated in the hands of the Katikiro, who traditionally had ruled Buganda for the Kabaka, and two other Buganda Ministers; and in practice British officials dealt directly with the Ministers and the Chiefs. From time to time there were objections to this procedure from various Baganda, and from time to time Kabaka Daudi Chwa had ventured to take things into his own hands. On their side the British had veered between a policy of relying on the Kabaka's personal responsibility, and insisting that his rule should be democratically exercised. In due course Kabaka Mutesa II played this game back at them. In his dispute with the Governor in 1953, he began by taking the discussions into

95

his own hands, and ended by claiming that he was personally responsible to his Lukiko – a course of action which the British thought to be intolerable for a hereditary monarch to pursue.

Simultaneously there was another thread as well. By the nineteen-twenties the Baganda agents were being withdrawn from the other Districts of the Protectorate and indigenous chiefs were taking their place. The first bonds which linked the Protectorate together were thereby loosed. A Legislative Council for the whole Protectorate of Uganda had met for the first time in 1921. But by 1931 – and there had been earlier protests – Buganda's recently appointed Treasurer, Serwano Kulubya, was telling the British Parliament's Joint Select Committee on Closer Union in East Africa that the Baganda did not wish to participate in any central legislative body for Uganda since they had their own legislature, the Lukiko, whose importance they feared might be diminished if they participated in any other such body.[13] The Baganda maintained their opposition for the next quarter of a century, and in 1953 the Kabaka, pressed by the Lukiko, told the Governor that he would not even nominate Baganda members to the Uganda Legislative Council.

Behind all this lay the sequence of three distinguishable British policies. At the outset the British had begun by treating the Baganda as associates in the rule of other peoples; Buganda was deemed to be of special importance because it provided the British administration with its only firm base. When such considerations were no longer paramount, Buganda was treated as a special native kingdom – in close association with the Protectorate Government – and for the most part the emphasis (which the Baganda welcomed, and which was based upon the superiority of their Agreement) was upon their relative autonomy. But after the 1945 war it soon appeared that British policy had changed once again, and that the Buganda Government was now being thought of simply as a local government subordinated to a central government for the whole of Uganda which was to derive its power from an all-embracing Uganda Legislative Council (the earlier idea of an interim central native council having been dropped). In this Council the Baganda were expected to share with some representatives of the alien communities who had come to Uganda, but with whom they never felt any sense of association, and with their former subordinates in the rest of Uganda. Despite some verbal formularies, Buganda's only substantial speciality lay in its larger size. In pressing this new policy upon the Baganda the British now started to place an emphasis upon the clause in the 1900 Agreement which stated that Buganda was to be but one province of the wider Protectorate. Kabaka Mutesa's reaction to such suggestions was to press in 1953 for the separated independence of his kingdom from the rest of the Protectorate. He soon found himself deported from his country for his pains.

VI

After protracted negotiations, the crisis of 1953–5 was eventually resolved. Kabaka Mutesa was restored to his country, while the Protectorate Government succeeded in securing elected Baganda members in Uganda's Legislative Council for the first time. Much now depended, however, on the creation of a new understanding – not now between new administrator and new chief, but between expatriate civil servant and African political leader. In 1955 five members of the Uganda National Congress (the premier political party, formed in 1952) became members of Uganda's Legislative Council, and the Governor appointed one of them, Mr A. K. Kironde (Sir Apolo Kagwa's grandson) as Assistant Minister for Social Services in the central Uganda Government, with a seat on its Executive Council (he had headed the poll in the recent Buganda elections). The new Kabaka's Government in Buganda now derived its mandate from a Lukiko with a substantial unofficial majority, and the British Resident told them that henceforward it was his duty merely to 'advise'. For the time being the British administration retained an official majority in both the central executive and the central legislature of Uganda as a whole, as well as the right to give 'formal advice' to the Kabaka's Government in Buganda. Nevertheless, in more than one way it now made a deliberate attempt once again to associate itself with yet another new generation of new men, though on a basis obviously different from anything in the past. Patently in the years immediately preceding self-government, no nationalist politician could afford to be in the old sense an 'ally' or an 'associate' of the British, and the best that could be hoped for was a political deal. Some, however, of the elements of that existed, if only because the Protectorate Government still had the sole ability to disburse funds and facilities for social and economic development, and because in giving up its power it could on occasion provide some of those angling for the succession with a critical advantage.

The political deal proved, even so, far from easy to sustain. For with the return of Kabaka Mutesa ii in 1955 the control of the British masters in Buganda was severely weakened, and it was now the Buganda Government which, in an atmosphere of traditional intrigue, set the conditions of the association. The Protectorate Government found itself having to pay a very high price for the estrangement of the previous ten years in the suspicion with which its actions were now almost invariably received by the great majority of Baganda. The choices no doubt for British policy had been very uninviting. If ten years previously the brake had not been applied the diminution of power would have begun before they would have felt that anything was ready; but there would also have been less of the subsequent estrangement, with all its manifold consequences.

In the mid-1950s, the confusion in the constitutional relations between the central government and Buganda was in some respects improved. But it remained even so ultimately unresolved. It was usually considered in terms of the conflict between 'federal' and 'unitary' conceptions for the future of Uganda as a whole – both having their protagonists, not least amongst Africans. It was questionable, however, whether these were the most apposite terms in which the problem needed to be considered. Here the past offers its clues. For one aspect of the continuing ambiguities in the relations between the British and the Baganda lay in the fact that the British were never at all clear whether their relations with the Buganda Government (within, of course, the colonial context) were fundamentally administrative, or fundamentally politico-diplomatic.[14] Sir Philip Mitchell had tried to disentangle the threads, but had not stayed on long enough to carry through his own proposals effectively. An acute susceptibility to this uncertainty had long since led the Baganda to demand that, in effect, they should be treated by the central government politico-diplomatically. To begin with this was not necessarily a demand that a federal relationship should obtain, at least if this implies that there was a demand for further transfers of function. It is notable that there was never much demand by the Baganda for any increase in the functions of their own Government. The devolution of services which was carried out in the 1950s was made entirely upon the initiative of the Protectorate Government, and the reason for such incipient demands for change as did occur stemmed primarily from the fact that the Buganda Government was African, the central government still predominately European. The motives, that is, were as much 'tribalist' or 'nationalist' as 'federalist'. For essentially what the Buganda Government disliked was being administratively subordinated to the central government. It wished to be master in its own house. Its remarkably successful struggle with the British on this issue over nearly three quarters of a century – in the context of its leaders' alliance with the British through most of that period – had strengthened its resolve to this end to a quite astonishing degree. By the time the British Protectorate came to an end in 1962 that resolve remained both unchecked and unabated.

NOTES

1. J. M. Gray, 'Mutesa of Buganda', *Uganda Journal*, I, pp. 22–49, is still the most authoritative account.
2. Oxford *History of East Africa*, Vol. I, Ch. 11.
3. Low and Pratt, *Buganda and British Overrule*, Part 1.
4. Oxford *History of East Africa*, Vol. II, Ch. 3.
5. R. L. Buell, *The Native Problem in Africa*, New York 1928, Vol. 1, Section VI; H. B. Thomas, 'An Experiment in African Native Land Settlement', *Journal of the African Society*, XXVII (April 1928), pp. 234–48.
6. J. R. Postlethwaite, *I Look Back*, London, 1947, p. 106.
7. For this and the next two sections see in general Low and Pratt, Part II, and D. E. Apter *The Political Kingdom in Uganda*, Princeton, 1961.
8. See also Sir Philip Mitchell, *African Afterthoughts*, London, 1954, Ch. 9; Sir Charles Dundas, *African Crossroads*, London, 1955, Ch. 13; Margery Perham, *Colonial Sequence 1930–1949*, London, 1967, pp. 169–173.
9. A. B. Mukwaya wrote a very interesting note on this when he was a member of the East African Institute of Social Research in the 1950s. It since seems to have been lost.

99

10. Reference may be made but with caution to the *Report of the Commission of Inquiry into the Disturbances Which Occurred in Uganda during January 1945*, Entebbe, 1945.

11. Cautious reference may be made to the *Report of the Commission of Inquiry into the Disturbances in Uganda during April 1949*, Entebbe, 1950. See also A. B. Mukwaya, 'The Rise of the Uganda African Farmers' Union in Buganda, 1947–1949', Conference papers, *East African Institute of Social Research, June 1957.*

12. For the details of this and the next section see Chapters 4 and 6 and the references cited there.

13. House of Commons, *Joint Committee on Closer Union in East Africa*, 156, 1931, Vol. II, Minutes of Evidence, pp. 549–580.

14. Low and Pratt, op. cit., Ch. 6.

4

The Namirembe Conferences 1954

I

In the early 1960s self-governing African régimes secured control of well over half the African continent. In West Africa the movement towards independence was not obliged to establish the principle that non-western peoples subject to western imperial domination ought to have their political independence. That had already been conceded by the British in India. It was necessary rather to ensure that what had already been secured on the banks of the Ganges should apply on the banks of the Volta and the Niger as well: and much skilful effort went into seeing that it applied there rather more speedily.

But the successes of the Indian and of the West African movements for independence were not of themselves decisive for East and Central Africa. For here in the areas subject to British imperial control there was a great confrontation, of a kind which India and West Africa never saw, between two conflicting sets of now widely established doctrines of British imperial policy, each of which had its origins in the same historical quarter – in North America during the late eighteenth and early nineteenth century, and more particularly in Lord Durham's *Report*[1] on Canada of 1839. On the one hand there was the doctrine that British settler communities scattered across the globe should have responsible government along the lines which Durham had adumbrated; and on the other – following the application of Durham's doctrine to India by the Montagu declaration of 1917[2] – the doctrine that non-western peoples within the British Empire had a right to self-government in due course as well.

In the British territories in East and Central Africa there were not only European settler communities but large African populations as well. Already the first doctrine stemming from Durham had been applied to South Africa and Southern Rhodesia, to the benefit of their European communities.[3] Had there not been sustained campaigns against federation in East and Central Africa and against the establishment of further 'settler' régimes in those areas in the 1920s and 1930s responsible government for settler communities would very probably long since have been established further north as well. By the early 1950s, however, no decisive step had been taken to determine the long-term future of the territories between the Zambezi and the headwaters of the Nile; and the two doctrines, both stemming from Durham, now faced each other there in glowering opposition.[4]

Britain's imperial policy makers were well aware of the depths of the doctrinal confrontation, and during the 1950s they pressed vigorously for their proposed resolution of it. At the beginning of the decade British policy for the British colonial territories in East and Central Africa was directed, as James Griffiths, the Labour Secretary of State for the Colonies, himself asserted, towards the establishment of a 'partnership' between the races.[5] The humanitarian thrust of this doctrine was emphasised to the detriment of the exclusivist features of the other two, and in its classical political form it regularly found expression in those balancing formulae for the representation of the different races which were so central a part of the constitutions of their legislative and executive councils. In the four eastern territories there were Asians as well as Europeans and Africans. The fact, however, that the ratios applied bore little or no relation to the relative numerical size of the races involved – indeed in several instances ran in diametrically opposite directions[6] – soon made it clear to Africans that they were even less of a bulwark against the advance of the first of the doctrines deriving ultimately from Durham than had been the delaying tactics of the opponents of settler régimes between the Wars. The most disturbing development in this direction came in the opening years of the 1950s when, in association with some miserably insubstantial efforts to insert some shreds of a balancing formula into its constitution, a European dominated Central African Federation was formed; and one British colonial secretary clearly let the thought cross his mind (as we shall see) that something similar might be effected in the East African territories as well.[7]

No doubt there were political and economic arguments in favour of a closer union between the East African territories – as indeed successor African governments have periodically recognised.[8] But during the 1950s Africans saw very clearly the depth of the implications which the primarily political and constitutional arrangements bore. For much of the decade, and in most of the territories, 'partnership' formulae presented to them a cover for the continued predominance of local European influence over the fashioning of society;[9] even in their most idealistic form[10] they promised a non-African orientation of a kind which the overwhelming majority of articulate Africans rejected. The struggles over constitutional formulae which ensued thus raised fundamental issues about the shape of the society, and about the culture of the lands, which, fortified by history and by the population figures, Africans felt to be in every respect primarily theirs.

In the Kingdom of Buganda in the British protectorate of Uganda there was between 1953 and 1955 a serious political crisis in which these issues played a central role. Its outcome represented a crucial step in the process of their resolution.[11]

II

By the so-called Uganda Agreement of 1900 – in fact the *Buganda*[12] Agreement – Buganda secured a remarkably privileged position as compared with its neighbours. Under the terms of the Agreement much of the available land was guaranteed to African hands, while the constitutional relationship between the British protectorate government and the government of the Kingdom was set out at some length. Its central clause ran as follows:

So long as the Kabaka, chiefs and people of Uganda (sc. Buganda) [Article 6 of the Agreement declared] shall conform to the laws and regulations instituted for their governance by Her Majesty's Government, and shall co-operate loyally with Her Majesty's Government in the organisation and administration of the said Kingdom of Uganda, Her Majesty's Government agrees to recognise the Kabaka of Uganda as the native ruler of the province of Uganda under Her Majesty's protection and overrule.

The ninth article had the effect of recognising as well the county chiefs of Buganda – Saza chiefs as they were called – but gave the British ultimate control over their appointment and dismissal. By Article 10 the Kabaka was allocated three Ministers to assist him in the government of the Kingdom (the *Katikiro*, or Chief Minister; the *Omulamuzi*, or Chief Justice; the *Omuwanika* or Treasurer); while Article 11 set out the constitution of 'the *lukiko*, or native council', which, in addition to the three Ministers, was henceforward to consist of the twenty Saza chiefs, three 'notables' selected by the Kabaka for each county, and 'six other persons of importance' (who came to be known as the Kabaka's representatives). So constituted, the Lukiko was empowered to pass resolutions concerning 'the native administration of Uganda' (sc. Buganda) for forwarding to the Kabaka; but before giving effect to them it was ordained that he was both to consult with and 'in this matter, explicitly follow the advice of Her Majesty's representative'.[13]

Such arrangements did not always make for easy relations; but for over half a century this formal recognition by the British of formally promulgated constitutional arrangements for the kingdom provided a bulwark against any further invasions of its political integrity. They made Buganda the envy of all its neighbours, not just in Uganda itself, but in the surrounding territories as well.

The 1948 census found that Buganda had a population or 1,296,000.[14] The racial figures for the whole of the Uganda Protectorate were as follows:[15]

Africans	5,286,000
Asians	47,400
Europeans	6,600
Others	2,900
Total	5,342,900

By mid-century Buganda had a considerable cash crop economy, based on the production for export of cotton, and increasingly of coffee too.[16] It comprised about one quarter of the total area of the Uganda Protectorate, the rest of which was divided into a number of small Kingdoms and districts, each of which was never more than a third its size. Kampala, the Protectorate's capital and chief commercial and educational centre (together with so much that goes with these things) stood within its borders, and *vis-à-vis* its neighbours it saw itself with some justification as superior.

Its ruler, Kabaka Mutesa II, had in 1939 succeeded his father at the age of fifteen. During the 1940s he spent three to four years in Britain as an undergraduate at Cambridge and as an officer in the Grenadier Guards.[17] Twice during the 1940s – in 1945 and 1949 – there were disturbances in his kingdom,[18] in which his Government, and thus to a degree he himself, became the main butt of the rioters' political and economic protests. Although in the short run the riots were contained, their implications remained to trouble the rulers of the country in the years that followed.

In 1952 Uganda had a new British Governor, Sir Andrew Cohen, aged forty-two.[19] He was not a career colonial administrator, but the former head of the Africa Department of the British Colonial Office. There he had had a great deal to do both with the very considerable recent constitutional developments in the Gold Coast (now Ghana) and Nigeria, and with the preliminary negotiations over the establishment of the Central African Federation. Upon his arrival he took a close look at the political and constitutional position in the country, and upon the basis of an enquiry into local government [20] formulated the crucial doctrine:

that the future of Uganda must lie in a unitary form of central Government on parliamentary lines covering the whole country with the component parts ... developing within it according to their special characteristics and, where they exist, according to the Agreements ... The Protectorate is too small to grow into a series of separate units of government, even if these are federated together. The different parts of the country have not the size, nor will they have the resources, to develop even in federation with each other the administrative organs which modern government requires. This can only be done by a central Government of the Protectorate as a whole with no part of the country dominating any other part but all working together for the good of the whole Protectorate and the progress of its people.[21]

Because (among other things) of the resilience of 'kingdom' politics in Buganda, and their replication in the other smaller kingdoms and districts of the Uganda Protectorate, 'nationalist' politics in Uganda were scarcely yet in being.[22] (The embryonic Uganda National Congress was only formed in March 1952 two months after Cohen's arrival in January.) The riots in the 1940s, and the rumblings in their aftermath, suggested, however, that it was high time to move towards the greater democratisation of Buganda. Moreover as a firm believer in African advancement – which he fostered on a number of fronts, only some of which can be discussed here – Cohen was clearly unhappy with the existing paucity of African representation in Uganda's Legislative Council (a body formed in 1921 for the whole Protectorate) as well as its total absence from the Governor's Executive Council. He soon therefore decided that changes here should not await the flowering of modern-style political parties. Accordingly in July 1952 he brought six unofficials – two Africans, two Europeans and two Asians – on to this Executive Council. In March 1953 moreover after private negotiation with Kabaka Mutesa II, he published with him joint proposals for constitutional reform in Buganda.[23]

The chief item of the latter was the proposal that all, and not as latterly only some, of the sixty seats in the Lukiko for 'notables' should be thrown open to election – which had the effect of giving the Lukiko an elected majority for the first time. Hitherto the range of the Buganda Government's executive functions had been relatively limited: it was now proposed that the Buganda Government should take over responsibility for the first time from the Protectorate Government for primary and junior secondary education, and for most health and agricultural services; and to this end it was proposed that three new Buganda ministries should be created. It was also proposed that a delegation of twelve or sixteen members of the Lukiko should consult with the Kabaka about the people to be appointed to all the available ministerial positions, and that once the Governor's approval for the Kabaka's eventual choice had been secured, the Lukiko would have the opportunity to vote 'without debate' for or against it. The two men declared as well that 'the Uganda Protectorate has been and will continue to be developed as a unitary state' with the Kingdom of Buganda 'under the government of His Highness the Kabaka' as 'a component part' of it. The Kabaka thus committed himself to the doctrine that the Protectorate should be developed as a unitary state which Cohen had formulated. There were issues here to which we must return shortly; but these reforms, particularly those for an elected majority in the Lukiko, were well received, and arrangements were made for an election to the Lukiko in the manner proposed in November of that same year, 1953.

In the meanwhile Cohen proceeded in August 1953 to announce changes in the Protectorate's Legislative Council.[24] Hitherto this had had sixteen official members on the Government side and sixteen unofficial on the Representative side, eight of them Africans, four of them Asians and four Europeans. He now announced that there would be an increase in the numbers on each side of the Council to twenty-eight. About eight of these on the Government side were to be nominated to support it on matters of confidence but would otherwise be free to act as they chose; while on the unofficial Representative side the African members were henceforth not to be nominated by the Governor, but to be elected by the councils of the kingdoms and districts into which the Uganda Protectorate was divided. The proportional distribution of seats between the races on the Representative side was, however, to remain as before; there were, that is, to be seven Europeans, seven Asians and fourteen Africans (while the corresponding allocation of seats for the unofficials of the three races on the Executive Council was to remain as from the previous year – at two each).

Before these further changes could be put into effect a major crisis had overtaken the Protectorate in Buganda. In it eight issues came to the fore:

1. The whole question of the political and socio-cultural future of the peoples of Uganda (of whom the Baganda saw themselves to be the chief) in an era of 'partnership' policies and their symbolically structured constitutional formulae.
2. The question of whether or not a federation was to be imposed against their will upon the African peoples of the East African territories, as one was currently being imposed in Central Africa.
3. The issue of the relationship between the Kabaka and his Government, and the Buganda Lukiko.
4. The position of the Kabaka and his Government situated as they were to be between a Lukiko with an elected majority and a

Protectorate Government whose 'advice' under the 1900 Agreement they were required to 'explicitly follow'.
5. The manner in which the British were to exercise the responsibility they claimed to be theirs of directing Uganda towards a viable independence.
6. The precise relationship between the kingdom of Buganda and the larger country of Uganda which had grown up around it.
7. The distribution of power between what the 1900 Agreement called 'the Kabaka, Chiefs and People' of Buganda.
8. The extent to which the British could respond sympathetically to the disposition and apprehensions of the peoples of their colonies.

The last two points require just a brief comment here. The 1953–5 crisis became the occasion for the first major redistribution of political power in the kingdom since the end of the last century. This issue stands somewhat outside the others to be considered; it has been discussed elsewhere and will only be incidentally touched on here.[25] The importance of the last item for what followed will appear very soon below.

III

The Buganda crisis had its launching with a speech in London on 30 June 1953 in which Oliver Lyttelton, the Conservative Secretary of State for the Colonies, referred (at a time when a European dominated federation was being imposed on the Central African territories) to the possibility 'as time goes on of still larger measures of unification and possibly still larger measures of federation of the whole East African territories'.[26] For thirty years Buganda's leaders had been actively opposed to the creation of an East African Federation. They and their British liberal allies had eventually checked the idea in the 1930's. But their protests in the 1940's had not succeeded in halting the formation of the East African High Commission[27] – which linked together a number of East African 'common services' in a kind of embryonic federation – and the prominence given by the main European newspaper in Kenya to Lyttelton's statement in 1953 immediately brought a protest (in the absence of the Kabaka in London) from the Buganda Ministers.

There were soon other protests as well, and on 11 August
1953 – the day on which Cohen announced his proposals for
the reform of the Protectorate's Legislative Council – he gave
prominence as well to an official announcement stating that
the fear which had been expressed that the British Government were considering creating an East African Federation
was 'groundless'. Although the future could not be precisely
foretold, he went on, any possible future developments would
'take local public opinion fully into account'.[28] This reply gave
some satisfaction. But already on 6 August 1953, the Kabaka
had sent the Governor a long and carefully argued letter
attacking the inadequacy of an interim private reply which
had been sent in response to the protest from his Ministers.
In this he asked that the responsibility for the affairs of
Buganda in London should be transferred from the British
Colonial Office to the British Foreign Office and that a timetable for the independence of his country should be put into
operation.[29]

There need be little doubt that the Kabaka was giving expression to the profound concern he felt as accredited head of
his kingdom about the direction in which it seemed British
colonial policy was taking it. In doing so he was being true – to
an extent that those who know only constitutional monarchy
can all too readily overlook – to his role in the Buganda polity.
The ruler was its spokesman and bore the chief responsibility
for its well-being.[30] When he had talked that summer with the
Permanent Under-Secretary at the Colonial Office in London
he had been given a clear impression that the ultimate political
destiny of Uganda was in many critical respects still undecided.
Large-scale federal schemes were in the air. The doctrine of
partnership as exemplified in the formulae prevailing within
the Protectorate's central constitutional organs (even as reformed by Sir Andrew Cohen) clearly ran counter to the situation in his own kingdom as it had hitherto been secured under
British 'overrule';[31] and as early as this he saw quite clearly
that if independence did come to Uganda in the shape Cohen
had adumbrated, the prospect was that Buganda would at
best simply be part of a unitary state along with its neighbours –
a future which was far from pleasing to those Baganda (and
that was most of them) who were fearful of how they might

fare in a larger polity in which their hitherto lesser neighbours might be able to line up against them. Like his grandfather Kabaka Mwanga (Kabaka 1894–7), Mutesa II was somewhat prone personally to adopt a defensive and recalcitrant posture, in place of the adventurous and daring stance so typical of his great grandfather Mutesa I,[32] and periodically of his father, Daudi Chwa;[33] and as it chanced he and Sir Andrew Cohen seem to have found their personal relations difficult.

The two men now entered into a series of six private meetings at the Governor's residence at Entebbe[34] during which it quickly became apparent that a crisis lay before them. Cohen in due course satisfied the Kabaka with renewed assurances against the arbitrary creation of an East African Federation; but he resisted him on his further demands. For the plain implications of the second of these – which the first meeting at Entebbe clearly brought out – was that the Kabaka was asking for the separation of his kingdom from the rest of Uganda. It was not just that such a proposal contravened both the 1900 Agreement and the recent joint declaration of March 1953. It was a frontal assault on the doctrine of the unitary state. It would have involved wrenching the central area of the whole country away from the rest of the Protectorate (which would have been rather like separating England from the United Kingdom). At this stage in the history of the country – and more particularly in a period before strong nationalist parties had developed – Cohen could not in good conscience agree to this. The Kabaka, however, had his demands endorsed by the outgoing Lukiko (the Lukiko soon reinforced indeed – on 27 October 1953 – its earlier refusal to elect Baganda members to the Uganda Legislative Council by asking the Kabaka not to nominate them either): at the same time Mutesa mobilised his fellow rulers of the smaller neighbouring kingdoms in his support; and established contact with the embryonic Uganda National Congress. Having on two previous occasions of political tension – during the riots in 1945 and 1949 – stood with the British, he was evidently now busily engaged – with his eyes clearly focused on the changing constitutional and political scene – in building up his own personal position as the champion of his own people against the colonial government.[35]

Cohen saw there a disruptive confrontation, and if it should spill out into the open, a dangerous one as well. There had been leaks on the Baganda side to the vigorous Luganda press, some parts of which were making increasingly strident demands for early independence.[36] The Kabaka's basic concerns were real enough, but his proposed solutions – not to mention the ways in which he sought to secure them – were clumsy and crude. Cohen on his side was so clear about the correctness of his own formulations that he made little attempt to whittle out the hard core of anxiety which lay beneath the Kabaka's demands. From his point of view Mutesa's campaign looked to be completely destructive. With the concurrence of the Colonial Secretary in London he accordingly moved to secure, in line with the 1900 Agreement, the Kabaka's acceptance of the policy of the British Government. In particular he required the Kabaka to assure him specifically that he would not in any way publicly oppose the Government either on account of its assurances about Federation or over its policy for the development of Uganda as a unitary state.[37]

The Kabaka now found himself in a trap. He had kept the details of his campaign against the Protectorate Government from all but a small circle of confidants; but enough people knew of his conflict with it to have constituted a dire threat to his standing with his own people if, after having mounted the assault on the Protectorate Government, he had at the end weakly crumpled before them. He told the Governor that he could not give the assurances sought from him without consulting the Lukiko. He had, however, not consulted the Lukiko before sending his considered demands to the Governor on 6 August, and the Government insisted that what mattered was what he would say to the Lukiko when he did consult them. In the end he was given a final weekend for further consideration, but he stuck to his refusal to give the assurances for which he had been asked and at the conclusion of a last meeting at Government House, Entebbe, on 30 November 1953, Cohen signed a declaration withdrawing British recognition from Mutesa 'as Native Ruler of Buganda under Clause 6 of the 1900 Agreement.'[38] Fearful, moreover, of the possibility of physical disturbances resulting, Cohen declared at the same time a State of Emergency, and deported Mutesa by air to Britain. By the time an announcement of what had occurred had been made publicly, troops were already patrolling Mengo, the Kabaka's capital, and the adjacent commercial city of Kampala.[39] Their swift deployment defused the violent potentialities in the situation, and in the event Cohen's urgent precautions almost certainly saved lives. There was certainly no repetition of the disturbances of 1945 and 1949.

IV

This was to be of great importance. The Baganda were clearly thunderstruck. The Kabaka's chief sister when she heard the news of his deportation collapsed and died. Her funeral two days later was a peculiarly tense moment.[40] The thunderclap was quite unexpected. A profound sense of shock overwhelmed the Baganda people. It was made all the more severe because, of all the African peoples of East, Central or Southern Africa, no one had hitherto been accorded more respect by Europeans than the Kabaka of Buganda. Now he had been bundled from his country in a military aircraft, after what had all the marks of a carefully prepared *coup*. The reaction of the Baganda could so easily have been sharp and violent: it is some measure of the circumstances prevailing that the Kabaka should have gone armed to his last meeting with the Governor and should have allowed the thought to cross his mind that he would shoot the police officer detailed to arrest him.[41]

But it was not to be: Cohen's deliberate precautions had checked the explosive potential. And when the Lukiko which had been elected two days before[42] the deportation held its first meeting two days after, the opportunity to take a different course of action just lay open.

The opportunity was seized by a very small group of young professional men, who had had as much western education (some of it overseas) as almost anyone in Buganda, several of whom had just been elected to the Lukiko for the first time. They proposed that a delegation should go to London to see the Colonial Secretary to make an appeal for the Kabaka's return. This was quickly agreed;[43] and on their arrival in Britain they soon found a good deal of support in 'Africanist' circles, in the churches, the press, the universities and the Labour Party, for their cause.

This too was to be of first importance. There was dismay here at the drastic nature of Cohen's action, particularly since he had been widely regarded as one of the ablest and certainly the most liberal minded of Britain's Governors. In such circles there was little or no disposition to credit him with either having withstood a demand whose concession would have been grievously disruptive of Uganda as it had developed over the past half century, or with having had a security problem to face.[44] These circles were primarily concerned with the manner in which the Buganda crisis seemed to be yet one more disturbing episode in the recently very disturbing course of British colonial history – a history which included the suspension of the constitution in British Guiana, the Malayan emergency, the imposition of a settler dominated Federation in Central Africa, and the Mau Mau conflict in Kenya. It is notable that the Buganda crisis became the occasion for the moving of a motion of censure by the opposition Labour Party against the whole course of recent Conservative colonial policy.[45] There can be little doubt, moreover, that but for the close personal links which bound the former Colonial Secretary, Griffiths, to his own appointee Cohen, the storm in England on the Kabaka's behalf would have been very much greater.[46]

As it was, the Colonial Secretary, Oliver Lyttelton, defended the withdrawal of recognition and the Kabaka's deportation most adroitly.[47] What was more, in the debate on the deportation in the House of Commons on 2 December 1953 he made a seminal statement. Asked by a Labour member, Mrs Eirene White, for a clear declaration of the goal towards which Uganda was to move, Lyttelton said that Uganda's future would be as 'primarily an African country, with proper safeguards for minorities'.[48] This represented Sir Andrew Cohen's thinking. It was only, however, the pressure of critical parliamentary probing that secured its endorsement by the Colonial Secretary. It marked the first crucial breach in the 'partnership' line which the Colonial Office was seeking to hold in East and Central Africa.[49]

Shortly afterwards Lyttelton saw the Lukiko's delegation. Despite, however, a declaration by the Kabaka that he would now give the assurances previously sought from him – a declaration which the Government now felt to be insufficient –

Lyttelton announced that Kabaka Mutesa would not be allowed to return to his country.

The Protectorate Government would have liked the Lukiko to elect a new Kabaka.[50] Mutesa's supporters, and they were very numerous, claimed that this was unthinkable. At the least they were being unhistorical: Baganda had themselves replaced Kabakas on several occasions in the past,[51] and there is no doubt that some highly placed Baganda would have been prepared to find and support a new Kabaka from amongst Mutesa's kin if they had had any real encouragement.[52] But they would have needed extremely strong support from the Protectorate Government; and Cohen was much too humane a man to complete his coup d'état by riding roughshod over the Baganda a second time. The absence of disturbances, and the steadiness of the Baganda in their dismay, had now won widespread respect in British unofficial circles, and in all the manifold circumstances of the time the liberal lobby in Britain would pretty certainly have revolted at any second draconian move.

In any case Cohen himself – though adamant that Mutesa could not be allowed to return – felt very strongly that the deeper causes of the crisis needed the fullest consideration; and when Margery Perham, the *doyenne* of British Africanists wrote to *The Times* in February 1954[53] suggesting that a constitutional mission should go out to Buganda, she was largely expressing the views which Cohen himself had formed. His idea was that a representative group of Baganda, with such independent help as could be secured, should think through their own problems in preparation for some subsequent discussions which he would be prepared to hold with them.[54]

V

Independent outside help meant independent expert assistance. Several senior British academics had already played an important part in constitutional discussions in Africa, particularly in East and Central Africa.[55] Since the Buganda case needed to be differentiated from these, someone new had to be found. Back in 1942 Sir Keith Hancock had been asked to go out as Reforms Commissioner to India. Since he could not bring himself to leave Britain when the war was still at its height, he had on that occasion declined. Now his name was suggested once again. He consulted his friends: and discussed the purport of a possible mission to Buganda with Cohen in London. He did not, however, accept the proposal to go out to Buganda as an independent constitutional expert until he had discussed the idea with the Lukiko delegation in London, and it was not until he was assured of their support that he told Cohen he would go.[56]

Hancock was at this time Professor of British Commonwealth Affairs, and Director of the Institute of Commonwealth Studies, in the University of London. He was a particularly apt choice. As editor of the British civil histories of the war he knew his way around Whitehall. He was also the foremost Commonwealth historian of the day. His first book had been about Italian nationalism, and one of his two major works had involved substantial studies of Africa. Through his teaching of colonial administrators who had come on 'Devonshire' courses to the University of London he had come into close touch with some of the younger officials – of more than one race – from the colonies. He already had an enviable reputation as a seminar chairman. He could, as well, *listen*. Furthermore he was an Australian – a fact which helped to underline his personal independence of the British colonial government.

Although his appointment was welcomed by the Lukiko delegation in London, there was now much reluctance in Buganda to accept anything short of the immediate return of Kabaka Mutesa – and any direct consideration of this was deliberately omitted from Hancock's brief. At a Lukiko meeting on 23 March 1954 the delegates to London argued that Hancock's visit would be a step towards the return of the Kabaka and successfully prevailed upon the Lukiko to elect a committee to meet him. Two of those nominated to this were Dr Ralph Bunche, of the United Nations, and Dr Kalibala, a Muganda long resident in the United States who was now serving with the United Nations.[57] On the grounds, however, that the committee should be conversant with the situation and resident in Buganda, Cohen vetoed these two appointments, and upbraided the delegates to London for saying that Hancock's visit would be a step towards the return of the Kabaka.[58] Eridadi Mulira, Thomas Makumbi and Apolo

Kironde, the three key members of the delegation to London who had been among those elected to the new committee, thereupon resigned from it in protest against the Governor's riposte;[59] and the Hancock mission looked as if it might be over before it had even begun.

At this moment Hancock made his first key interventions. Early in May he wrote to Cohen explaining how he proposed to go to work once he had arrived in Buganda. His aim, he said, would be to produce 'an agreed memorandum between the Governor and the representatives of Buganda' on all the issues in dispute. Although he was bound by his terms of reference to exclude from formal consideration the personal position of Mutesa II he affirmed that he 'must naturally bear these events in mind in so far as they illustrate a basic constitutional problem'. He did not think he would be creating a constitution for a self-governing Uganda. That would be a later task for another hand. But he made it plain that he attached considerable importance to Lyttelton's December statement that the British objectives for Uganda were to make it a primarily African and self-governing state; and voicing the convictions of the circle from which he sprang he remarked as well:

I feel bound to add that the mission will not in my view make sense unless it does something immediate and practical to open the road towards their realisation and to strengthen confidence among the Baganda and others that they will in fact be progressively realised.

If he and the Baganda committee could not come to any agreement they would each, he concluded, write their own separate reports.[60]

In response to this approach Cohen on 20 May saw Makumbi and Kironde (the third member, Mulira, was in London seeing Hancock, among others). It was a seminal encounter – the first between a British Governor of Uganda and some locally elected legislators on a major issue of public policy. Hancock by this time had written to Cohen again. Whilst not pressing him to rescind his veto on Dr Bunche – who would probably not have been available in any case – he asked him to withdraw his veto on Kalibala, in exchange for the return to the proposed committee of the three members who had resigned. Both sides accepted his suggestion. The mission was still to take place, and Hancock had already demonstrated his strength as a mediator.[61]

He could not make himself available, however, until his academic year in London was over. In the interval, the patience of some Baganda began to wear thin, and there was in fact a fair amount of intimidation in the rural areas against those who were not thought by their fellow countrymen to be loyal enough to Mutesa II: after some strong talk by the members of the new Uganda Legislative Council the original State of Emergency, which had gradually been lifted in March, was reimposed on 31 May.[62] But the delay gave Hancock – despite his academic preoccupations – a little time to prepare himself. He read a great deal about Buganda, and talked privately with a wide range of people. He held, moreover, a series of six private meetings at his own Institute in London at which a group of academic colleagues who were knowledgeable about Buganda were joined by some specialist experts from the Colonial Office. And he eventually compiled a splendidly idiosyncratic document called – following Bishop Berkeley's eighteenth-century proto-type – 'The Buganda Querist'.[63] This contained 249 questions in an archaic style designed to test whether he had become seized of all the issues which were at stake, while exploring in a tentative way the various alternatives which might henceforth be available. He procured comments on this from a variety of sources in Britain to help him on his way.

He left London for Uganda by air on 21 June 1953, taking with him Lady Hancock (an able and perceptive observer if ever there was one), his confidential secretary Miss Marjorie Eyre (who was to be heavily worked in the next three months) and Stanley de Smith, shortly to become Reader in English Law at the London School of Economics.[64] Hancock had wanted an assistant whose skills would complement his own. De Smith was already one of the three or four most knowledgeable men on the law and constitutions of the British colonial territories. He had, moreover, a superb command of the English language, and his minutes of the fifty meetings in Buganda which ensued are a model of their kind.[65]

VI

The day after his arrival, Hancock addressed the Lukiko, his slight build and shock of white hair standing out sharply against the ample girth and dark hues of the senior chiefs between whose ranks he was escorted to the dais beside the Kabaka's empty throne.

I have been called [he said] an independent expert. I do not like the word 'expert'. It implies that I know all the answers. But I do very much like the word 'independent', for it means that I am not in anybody's pocket. I have come here by my own choice as a free man to do certain work which I myself have defined. If the Government should attempt to take away my freedom I would not permit it. If the Lukiko committee should attempt to take away my freedom I would not permit it.

It was a classic mediator's declaration *urbi et orbi*. Amid applause he then declared:

To me it seems that the Baganda in their relations with the protectorate, and to some extent, in their internal affairs, have lost the main road ... Your committee and I may not travel a great distance together, but I hope and I believe that we shall at any rate find the main road.[66]

The language of the Baganda, Luganda, has no 'H'. 'Hancock' accordingly became Wancock, or rather Wankoko, meaning a chicken! The pun was widely enjoyed, and provided some welcome relief whenever his mission came to be discussed.

The Committee he faced was not typical of the membership of the Lukiko; and the absence from it of Amos Sempa, the exceptionally adroit Secretary of the Lukiko, was an indication that it had been formed with a view to its being, if necessary, easily repudiated. The Lukiko's chief concern had been to marshal a western-educated group of Baganda who would know enough about the Europeans' ways to be able to probe their weakest spots (the lack of any direct representative of the Uganda National Congress was deplored by the Congress leaders, but was not by many others felt to be serious).[67] The Committee consisted as all such things had done in Buganda for half a century past of roughly half Catholics and half Anglicans with just one more of the latter than the former. The Catholics comprised a Bishop, Kiwanuka, and two priests, Kasule and Masagazi (all three of whom had been at some time educated in Rome), together with two senior chiefs, Mugwanya, the Omulamuzi (Chief Justice), and Musoke, the Kyambalango (a Saza Chief). Significantly there were no priests or senior chiefs amongst the Anglicans: but a lawyer, Kironde, a journalist, Mulira, two schoolmasters, Makumbi and Sengendo Zake, a University lecturer, Lule, a Ph.D. from Yale, Kalibala, and an older elected unofficial member of the Lukiko, Kyaze. Two missionary bodies – one Roman Catholic, one Anglican – had worked in the same society for the same length of time: in accordance with their different educational policies (and behind that their differing theological emphases) they had, it seems, produced two substantially different elites.[68]

It had long been thought – not least by Cohen – that it would be undesirable for the Committee to meet in Government buildings. The site chosen was Namirembe hill, the Anglican headquarters. There the Hancocks lived – and the Committee worked – in some buildings adjacent to the Anglican Bishop's House, with views out over the green, tree-dotted hills of Kampala and the surrounding countryside. The tropical greens and the red murram soil of Buganda could never be far from their consciousness.

VII

At its first meeting the Committee elected Hancock as its chairman and decided to keep its discussions confidential.[69] Not long afterwards the question was raised whether its meetings should not begin with prayers (since this was a widespread practice in Buganda). The religious divide presented problems. But a compromise was effected. Every plenary session of this constitutional conference thereafter began with a period for silent prayer. There were to begin with four such sessions each week – on every Tuesday to Friday morning. Periodically a steering committee met in the afternoon; and whenever time allowed both Hancock and Lady Hancock made it their business to see privately outside the conference room as many other individuals as they possibly could. Once they even went for a tour of Katwe, the suburb of Kampala where the vernacular newspapers and embryonic political parties had their offices: Hancock made a couple of effective speeches to several hundred people.[70]

The second meeting of the Committee (on Friday 25 June) was unminuted. Hancock asked the members to express their feelings as fully as they could. There seems to have been a forceful expression of distress and horror at the deportation of Mutesa and at the unwarranted hostility which the British had thereby displayed against Buganda – the formerly sovereign state which had voluntarily accepted British protection. The Committee seems to have emphatically demonstrated, moreover, that while they felt the Buganda Government to be, as it was put, 'ours', the Protectorate Government was 'theirs'; and much criticism was directed in particular at the Protectorate Government's agents in Buganda, the British Resident and Assistant Residents of Buganda. It was a vital morning. Feelings that would otherwise have been dangerously bottled up were given full vent. Thereafter Hancock and de Smith could have no illusions at all about the profundity of the issues with which they were dealing. At the same time, however, agreement was reached that afternoon on the agenda for the next week's meeting.

Hancock opened the detailed discussions on the following Tuesday with a long statement explaining what he had meant by telling the Lukiko that Buganda had lost the main road. There were tensions, he said, between head and heart; between the desire to belong to the future and the yearning for the past. The ensuing strain between Buganda and the Protectorate had fallen on one man – the Kabaka. The way ahead would involve two principles – participation in the Government of Uganda, and modernisation of the Government of Buganda. At the same time he emphasised that, since he would have to be back in London on 27 September for his University term, there would have to be a timetable for the discussions. They should, therefore, try to clear their minds within the next four weeks, and then open discussions with the Governor. The pressure of the timetable clearly concentrated discussion.

Very quickly, moreover, the Baganda members put generalities behind them, and began to concentrate upon constitutional details – three members of the Committee who had been on the delegations to London, Mugwanya, Mulira, and Kironde to begin with making the running. A number of points were discussed – the exclusion of Saza chiefs from the Lukiko; the appointment of Permanent Secretaries to all the Buganda ministries, with a view to turning the Ministers into purely political figures. There was a good deal of discussion about 'constitutionalising' the Kabakaship, and about the difficulties of doing so. And within the first few sessions the switch to the hard task of constitution-making was clearly effected.

At the steering committee's instance Hancock made another opening statement at the beginning of the next week, this time on relations between Buganda and the Protectorate – a central part of the issues in dispute. Since he already felt the ground hardening beneath his feet, he pulled no punches. It was his longest intervention. A new settlement, he said, was obviously required. There were three extreme courses which were conceivable: the maintenance of the *status quo* (including the continued boycott by the Baganda of the Uganda Legislative Council, while the other peoples of Uganda went ahead within it); or the disintegration of the Protectorate (and the end, he argued, of economic advance); or the disappearance of Buganda as a political entity (somewhat as Ashanti had been totally submerged in the Gold Coast – although the Baganda, he felt, would probably not like that). If none of these were favoured, then, he said, a choice between two other courses remained: 'the building of a fence' (the technical term, he said, for this was federation), or what he called 'devolution'. A federal constitution for the country would be more definite and precise. But he warned that

if the Protectorate Government found itself obliged to agree to the erection of a fence beyond which it could not pass, it would doubtless have to keep most of the land on its own side of the fence, leaving only a restricted area for Buganda to cultivate without the possibility of interference.

'Devolution' had its risks, of course: but these, he argued, would reduce as moves were made towards filling out the Colonial Secretary's pledge that Uganda would in due course

be a primarily African self-governing state with proper safeguards for minorities. That could not be finally achieved as yet.
But he believed there could, and should, be a firm step in that
direction without further ado. The outline of a final settlement
was obviously already shaping in his mind.

For the moment, however, the Committee sidestepped the
extremely delicate points which were at issue here, and spent
several more days discussing further changes within the
governing structure of Buganda. By this time most members
of the Committee were making substantial contributions, and
agreement was in the offing upon a series of further reforms, by
which, in particular, the Buganda ministers would become
responsible to the Lukiko instead of to the Kabaka.

When, however, the Committee returned to the question
of a federal constitution for the country a great debate ensued.
The tide flowed strongly in favour of a federal solution and
against the line which Hancock (following Cohen with whom
after much careful consideration he very much agreed) had
patently been pursuing. Lule, an Education Lecturer at
Makerere University College – now emerging as one of the
Committee's most influential members – gave as one reason
why he preferred the federal idea the fact as he saw it that the
Protectorate Government's educational policy was hampering
educational advancement in Buganda; a Buganda Government
with full powers here would very quickly, he believed, put such
things to rights.

For the moment no conclusion was reached and for the
moment the Committee turned aside once again. A lot of other
ground was covered in the next fortnight. The Committee
discussed the role of the Residency in Buganda, and safeguards
against an imposed federation of the East African territories.
At one point Mulira produced some initial proposals for a
restructuring of the Protectorate's Legislative and Executive
Councils. But the Committee obviously felt that unless they
secured some federal[71] arrangements, there was no chance
whatsoever of persuading the Lukiko that any Baganda should
participate in these. For the most part Hancock made himself
sit silently and listen. But when the Committee took up yet
again the proposal for a federal 'fence' around Buganda, he
intervened powerfully on more than one occasion. He argued

for an adventurous against a defensive posture, and emphasised the economic issues which would have to be taken into account. Bishop Kiwanuka, however, expressed the general attitude of the Committee when he riposted that the difficult problems would be solved very quickly once it was recognised that Buganda was a political nation. He and others made it emphatically clear that despite Hancock they wanted a 'fence' around Buganda. The closest, however, that Hancock would come towards them was to concede that a 'special relationship' between Buganda and Uganda might just be feasible.

It was a vehement debate, with the Baganda sticking staunchly to their case. Thanks, however, to Hancock's resourcefulness and courtesy there was no breakdown. Already arrangements had been made to hold meetings with the Governor towards the end of July, and this procedural commitment probably helped to keep the discussions in being. Yet it is clear that Hancock was now very gloomy about the outcome of the discussions,[72] particularly if Cohen were to be – or found himself required to be – inflexible. With a view to the later discussions, and in accordance with the independence which he had asserted and which the Committee had accepted, he was now in touch with Cohen and revealing his mind to him.

VIII

Hitherto Hancock had been presiding over the Buganda Constitutional Committee. With the Governor's advent the meetings were now transformed into 'the Namirembe Conference' proper.[73] In preparation for it Hancock and de Smith drew up 86 'Propositions' for discussion. On a number of points these constituted a first approximation to a definite conclusion: on others – and particularly on the federal question – they left the issue open. The style of Hancock's private opening document, 'The Buganda Querist', periodically reared its head. After six weeks of discussions, queries had, however, been transformed into propositions: and the confidence of the Buganda Committee in both Hancock and de Smith – together with their sensitivity to the Committee's point of view – was now such that, for all the outstanding difficulties, their drafts were quickly accepted as the agenda for the ensuing negotiations.

The Namirembe Conference opened on Friday 30 July 1954. Cohen came to it accompanied by two members of his Executive Council, Serwano Kulubya (who had been Omuwanika, Treasurer, of Buganda between 1928 and 1945) and the Resident of Buganda, J. P. Birch. It is difficult to think of any other occasion on which a British Governor sat down with a locally elected committee under an independent chairman to discuss constitutional reforms in his territory. What followed constituted a *tour de force*.

At the Committee's suggestion Cohen addressed them on the first day at considerable length. Instead of basing his approach on the need to resolve the troubles concerning Buganda, he took his stand on the Colonial Secretary's December statement declaring that Uganda would for the future be primarily an African state. A positive move in this direction would, he said, be much the best step they could take. He prefaced his detailed discussion, moreover, with his own personal apologia: 'he had come to the country,' he said, 'with but one basic object: to put its African inhabitants firmly on the road towards eventual responsible government, both politically and economically.' He raised a multitude of issues. On the points which had been made about amending the constitution of Buganda he found himself in general agreement. But he made no bones about his impression that so far as the relations between Buganda and Uganda were concerned there was likely to be a substantial difference of opinion between them. For him the heart of the matter was this:

He did not think anything should be done in devising a relationship between Buganda and the Protectorate which either weakened the unity of Uganda as a whole or the power of the Centre to develop the country towards self-government and to do the things which were necessary for political and economic welfare. He felt that if they were to compromise the unity of the country they might be getting an apparent short-term advantage while sacrificing the long-term aim of self-government ... If the Protectorate Government's power to guide and advise were taken away, Buganda might well lose its lead over other parts of the Protectorate which would continue to have the benefit of that guidance and advice.

It is some measure of the total impact of this opening statement that after some discussion of it the Conference went on to deal immediately with all but seven of the first thirty Propositions before them. Early in the following week they agreed, moreover, to meet members of the Uganda Legislative Council, and on 4 August Mulira set out detailed proposals for the reform of the Protectorate's central institutions, the practical effect of which would have been to give Africans twenty-one seats on its Representative side and the immigrant communities seven. This was to go much farther than Cohen could contemplate; he said so, and it was a cold douche on the talks. But at the same time he sketched out for the first time in the history of Uganda the possibility of a ministerial system at the centre, in which – a quite crucial point – Africans would from the outset hold a substantial majority of the ministerial appointments. The full list of Propositions, moreover, lay on the table to be discussed. Cohen contributed positively to their discussion at a very great number of points, and the Committee obviously saw no point as yet in throwing in their hands; they even modified Mulira's proposals; and the outlook began to brighten.

They went on indeed to deal in some detail with the reforms within Buganda itself, where there were wide areas of agreement; and when they came back to Buganda-Uganda relations, Cohen produced a crucial paper setting out how the Buganda Government might have a defined field of operation; how (as originally suggested by Kironde) consultative committees of the two Governments might operate to resolve differences between them; and how the Protectorate Government's right to give formal advice to the Buganda Government might be carefully circumscribed. It was a formidable *démarche* against the federal idea; and it was reinforced by an offer from the non-African members of the Legislative Council, whom the Committee met on 11 August, to give up one European and one Asian representative seat upon it. The consequence came the next day when, speaking very clearly for the main body of his colleagues, one of the Baganda members said:

that the composition of the Protectorate institutions had been the main factor influencing the attitude of the Committee towards the federal solution. They had wanted to protect the affairs of Buganda from control by a Legislative Council they did not trust. However in view of the attitude that His Excellency had shown in the recent discussions, he thought that the question of erecting a constitutional fence no longer arose.

It was now 12 August. Cohen was booked to fly to London the next day to explore the views of the new Colonial Secretary, Alan Lennox-Boyd.[74] But with one contentious issue now out of the way, a second threatened to bring the talks to a halt. In proposing that a ministerial system should be introduced into the government of Uganda, Cohen had said all along that one of the ministers would be a European and one an Asian. The thought of an Asian minister in the Uganda Government was more than the Baganda members could stomach. They said so vehemently. In particular they were concerned about how they could persuade the Lukiko to accept a settlement which included any such provision, for it was all too symbolic of that whole concept of a political order for their country against which their deepest political and cultural instincts revolted. Cohen, however, urged 'that the question was not whether an Asian should be given a Ministry but whether his [i.e. the Governor's] discretionary power to allocate a portfolio to a non-African should be fettered to the exclusion of a particular class'. The next day the Committee told him roundly that the appointment of an Asian minister did not have their support. Nevertheless they accepted his point that it would be wrong to fetter the Governor's discretion: he made it clear that, if they did not, he would not proceed with his proposals for a ministerial system at the centre; and that they were not now prepared to throw away.

The Conference then adjourned for twelve days whilst Cohen went to consult the Colonial Office in London. In the interval Hancock visited the three western kingdoms of Ankole, Toro and Bunyoro (where in a variety of ways constitutional changes were afoot, and where very briefly indeed he was able to lend a hand in their resolution).[75] Meanwhile de Smith transcribed the Conference's amended Propositions into Draft Articles of Agreement: and the formulation which had begun with the 'Querist' now took a shape which was close to its final result.

On his return from London Cohen reported that the new Secretary of State was agreeable to the general outlines of the

Conference's proposals for turning Buganda into a constitutional monarchy. Lennox-Boyd had also agreed, he reported, to the introduction of a ministerial system at the centre. Furthermore, by the inclusion of Africans in various capacities on the Government side of the Legislative Council, one-half of all its members would in future be Africans, while on the Representative side the proportions would be sixteen Africans, six Europeans, and six Asians.

Now came the crunch. The 16:6:6 formula was unacceptable to the Baganda members. In the next week twenty-nine of de Smith's Draft Articles – for which Hancock took full responsibility – were discussed, and for the most part accepted after minor amendments. But on 1 September, Sengendo Zake mounted a full-scale attack on the proposed Legislative Council ratios which Cohen had been authorised to put forward by the Colonial Office. At the first encounter Cohen had shown that he was ready to move from 16:6:6 to 18:6:6 (the increase in the African seats from the existing 14 to 16 had allowed for an increase of two seats for Buganda: the next two would be for districts outside Buganda). But the nearest the Committee would come to this was 20:5:5.

The battle of the symbolic formulae was now joined. Cohen stuck to 18:6:6, and all he would offer as a sweetener was a concession elsewhere. He had originally proposed that there should be a review of the new constitution after ten years. Prompted by the Omulamuzi, Mugwanya, who asked for 'not less than five, and not more than ten', Cohen said he would accept this if the Committee would accept his proposed membership ratios. But they declined. Kironde, moreover, then led a second assault, while Makumbi urged the difficulties which the Committee would encounter in securing the agreement of the Lukiko to anything like the 18:6:6 formula. Cohen riposted with an offer of a review of the constitution after seven years. But after the weekend's adjournment Mulira announced on Monday 6 September that the most the Committee could possibly accept was 20:6:6. For Cohen this was still out of the question; but if, he said, they would agree to his 18:6:6 – a simple formula still – he would agree to a review of the constitution after *six* years. But the Baganda resisted still.

In such circumstances Hancock's policy was always to turn

aside to the less contentious issues, and in the days that followed he saw that a great deal of hard labour went into settling such issues as the role of the Residency in Buganda, the allocation of financial resources to Buganda, the future procedure for British recognition of a Kabaka, and the precise title of the Buganda Government (Kabaka's Government?). So many detailed points were in fact settled satisfactorily that by the time the Conference came back to the issue of the Legislative Council ratios on 10 September the Baganda members saw it in a different light and announced that while they still emphatically opposed the principle, they would accept Cohen's 18 : 6 : 6 ratio, so long as it was coupled to his last offer of a review of the Constitution after six years. To this he quickly assented.

But no sooner was this agreed than the Conference ran into what proved to be yet one more conflict – a conflict, moreover, whose outcome was to have substantial consequences. The Baganda wanted the Governor to give up his discretionary power over the appointment and dismissal of the Saza chiefs – those seniormost chiefs in Buganda who held sway over each of its twenty counties. Cohen was very hesitant here: in his view the Saza chiefs played a vital role in the maintenance of law and order. Yet with so much already secured he was clearly under very great pressure to make a concession. He twice suggested modifications to the existing position. But the Committee would have none of them. Kulubya, Cohen's Executive Councillor and a Muganda himself, now came out in support of the Committee, and argued that the safeguards already agreed upon ought to suffice. The Governor was to have the right to approve Buganda's Ministers. He was also to have the right to approve the members of the Buganda Appointments Board which was to be set up as a 'non-political' body to handle the appointment of chiefs and other officials in Buganda. Cohen acknowledged that there were possibilities of an accommodation here, but he wanted to ensure that the safeguards were sufficient. Under intense pressure he accepted in the end a formula by which the regulations of the Appointments Board were to be agreed between the Buganda and Uganda Governments, with any apparent infringement of them being referred by either Government to a committee of investigation.

IX

With this the final corner was turned, and on 15 September 1954 forty-nine Articles of the *Agreed Recommendations of the Namirembe Conference*,[76] together with an appendix establishing a Council of Clan Elders, and a *Statement by the Governor*, were signed by all of those attending. Article 1 declared that Buganda should continue to be 'an integral part of the Protectorate of Uganda'. There were careful statements in Articles 4 and 5 which were aimed to secure the dignity of the Kabaka (and, let it be added, satisfy Baganda loyalist opinion and British liberal opinion). Article 8, however, stated that 'the conduct of the affairs of the Kabaka's Government shall be the responsibility of Ministers', while Article 13 provided elaborately (and necessarily in the still continued infancy of political parties in the country) for the election of Buganda's Ministers by the Lukiko. Articles 32, 33, 37 and 38 laid down procedures for the resolution of disputes between the Uganda and Buganda Governments, while Article 16 secured the Governor-in-Council's right to give the Buganda Ministers 'formal advice' and dismiss them from office if necessary.

Apart from Article 1, Cohen's great triumph was Article 43 which recommended that the Lukiko – for the first time – should agree to elected Baganda participation in the Uganda Legislative Council, a step which, fearful of itself being thereby submerged, it had hitherto, for a quarter of a century, consistently rejected. No one said so out aloud, but the concept of a unitary state for which Cohen had so vehemently striven was thus underwritten. The *quid pro quo* here was spelt out in the attached *Statement by the Governor*. In the first place this laid down that half the total membership of the Uganda Legislative Council was to be African. Secondly, it announced that there was to be a ministerial system at the centre which was to include 'seven members of the public, of whom five would be Africans'.

Here in the formation of the new central Executive the old, simple, balancing formula – which for the time being was still to apply on the representative side of the Uganda Legislative Council – was discarded. It constituted the most notable shift in the whole settlement. In Cohen's initial reforms of his Executive Council in 1952 the ratios between the races in Uganda, for all their actual numerical disproportion in the country, had been 2 : 2 : 2 – two Africans, two Europeans, two Asians. At Namirembe in 1954 they became 5 : 1 : 1. This change had patently Cohen's strong personal support. It provided one way of symbolically resolving one of the main issues which had exercised the Kabaka in 1953, and it fulfilled Hancock's early hope that 'something immediate and practical' should be done to meet Baganda anxieties about the shape which their political future would take. Even allowing for the 'proper safeguards for minorities', the 'primary African state' was clearly now in the offing. Although the Colonial Office held the line on a simple, balancing formula – and thus on the 'partnership' concept which this embodied – on the Representative side of the central Uganda Legislative Council (it was not finally broken until the Wild Committee of 1959[77]) in two other crucial respects it had now given way. Both so far as the non-official membership of the Executive was concerned, and as regards the *total* composition of the Legislative Council – taking the Government *and* the Representative sides together there was to be an overall African majority – a substantial African dominance had now been conceded in Uganda. It was a seminal moment in the history of East and Central Africa. Montagu's adaptation of the earlier Durham doctrine had achieved it first triumph on the last battleground of empire. Five and a half years later Macmillan's 'Winds of Change' speech delivered the *coup de grâce* so far as British policy was concerned.[78]

Formulas for the resolution of all of the issues which had been raised by the crisis and which were susceptible of constitutional settlement had thus been achieved.[79] The notion of a primary African state had for the first time been given constitutional specificity. Firmer safeguards against an imposed East African Federation had been fashioned.[80] The principles of a securer role for the Kabaka *vis à vis* the now mainly elected Lukiko had been adumbrated. Machinery for governing the resolution of disputes between the Uganda and Buganda governments had now been worked out as never before: it included provision for British guidance in those matters which the British administration as the protecting power still felt to lie within its responsibility in the years before independence. At the same time the separation of the Baganda Ministers, who were henceforth to be the political executive dependent on the Lukiko, from the Baganda Chiefs, who were to be subject to the authority of an administrative Appointments Board, had been formulated.[81]

Above all, the terms of a relationship between the Kingdom of Buganda and the wider country of Uganda which had grown up around it had been given shape within the framework of a unitary constitution to the satisfaction of an official Baganda committee; and upon both the personal and the political front Hancock, Cohen and their associates had shown that, even in the immediate aftermath of a bitter dispute, accredited representatives of British colonial authority could respond sympathetically to the concerns of the accredited representatives of a colonial people. The Namirembe settlement had, in outline at least, covered all of the items in dispute.

X

News of the agreements at Namirembe – though not their details – was published on 16 September.[82] Hancock received numerous congratulations. Reconciliation between the British and the Baganda had been his objective. So far as the Constitutional Committee was concerned he had triumphantly succeeded: on the purely personal level – which humanly speaking was after all very important – his relations with the individual Baganda upon it had now become unusually warm.

As things transpired, however, the *Agreed Recommendations* could not be published immediately. They had first to be translated into Luganda, and in the event that meant they could not be made public until after a major case testing the validity of the Government's right to withdraw recognition from the Kabaka had been heard in the Uganda High Court. In giving his judgment on this the Chief Justice found that, although the Government possessed this right in that they had carried out an Act of State that was perfectly valid within a Protectorate, in so far as they relied (as they said they had) on Article 6 of the Agreement they had erred; for he found that its very particular provisions had not all been breached.[83]

This legalistic rebuff weakened the Government's posture and increased the pressure upon it to make sure of the Hancock settlement by allowing Mutesa II to return to his country. Cohen was now clear that this could not be avoided, and after some high-level tussles in London, he was instructed to tell the Lukiko on 16 November 1954 that the Government would agree to this happening, once the Hancock reforms had been in operation for a settling-in period of nine months.[84]

Yet because throughout the confidential discussions of the Committee at Namirembe – as the memoranda it received made abundantly clear – public opinion in Buganda had only been interested in the Kabaka's return, it felt itself grievously thwarted by the condition here; and in the disgruntled mood which ensued, the Lukiko set up a second committee to review the Namirembe recommendations from top to toe. In the event, however, this second committee concurred in all essentials with the conclusions of the first,[85] and these were eventually accepted by the Lukiko on 9 May 1955.[86] A new Agreement was then laboriously drafted in London. Early in September the Uganda Legislative and Executive Councils were reconstituted, with elected Baganda members in the first, and elected Africans in the second, for the first time;[87] and eventually on 18 October, following the Kabaka's return amid tumultuous rejoicing the day before, Cohen and Mutesa signed the new Buganda Agreement 1955 in a specially erected pavilion outside the gates of the Kabaka's palace at Mengo.[88]

These events and the year's delay[89] removed the shine from the Hancock settlement, and, for all its seminal importance for the transfer of power in east and central Africa, large parts of it were soon draining away into the sand. Under the pressure of the last stages of drafting in London – Hancock himself had been out of the running for nearly a year – the Government had relinquished its control to the Kabaka over the membership of the Buganda Appointments Board. This enabled Mutesa and his associates upon his return to bring pressure upon 'disloyal' chiefs to resign and so allow them to appoint 'loyal' ones in their place: despite the formal constitutional situation effective political control of the kingdom thus remained in his hands – as the years which followed were to show. (Had the Governor retained control at Namirembe over the appointment of Saza chiefs this would have been more difficult.) Since, moreover, Mutesa and those associated with him had not been parties to the education in the workings of constitutional monarchy which had taken place at Namirembe, they did little upon his return to put it into operation, and the coercive authority of the Protectorate Government had been so reduced as a result of the circumstances surrounding the return that it could do little to expedite the process.

What was more, whatever may have happened at Namirembe, Mutesa himself and very large numbers of his people saw in the final outcome of the crisis not reconciliation with the British but his own triumph over them. Even so it was Sir Frederick Crawford, Cohen's successor as Governor, who threw away the greatest gains of the Namirembe achievement when in 1957 he provided some Baganda members of the reconstituted Legislative Council with some very plausible excuses for resigning their membership of it.[90] For in the aftermath the federal unitary state argument came to be reopened all over again. The political conflict of the last years of the Uganda Protectorate and the first years of Uganda's independence resulted.[91]

For all this the Hancock settlement had four very considerable achievements to its credit. In the first place, for the first time in the history of East and Central Africa it blocked out the concept of the primary African state: within ten years this was to prevail in the whole of the area southwards to the Zambezi. Secondly, by so doing, it resolved the major issue between the British and the peoples of Uganda, to which *inter alia* the Kabaka had attempted to draw attention (although not very skilfully). Thirdly, even though the settlement probably did relatively little to improve relations between the British and the Baganda, it did prevent them from getting worse; and in an era when the Mau Mau conflict was wracking Kenya, and Federation was being imposed on Central Africa, that was an achievement in itself. Fourthly, there can be little doubt that the Namirembe agreements provided the kingdom of Buganda with a major opportunity to ensure its continued existence in a world in which there has been less and less sympathy for traditional institutions (and more particularly traditional rulership and all its works), and in which the logic of Cohen's insistence upon a unitary constitution for Uganda was extremely strong. The carefully contrived opportunity was, however, never seized, and a decade later nemesis followed. In May 1966 troops under the orders of President Obote of Uganda stormed the palace of the Kabakas of Buganda. The Kabaka escaped to Britain with his life, but the Kingdom of Buganda as such was left in ruins behind him[92].

NOTES

1. Earl of Durham, *Report on the Affairs of British North America*, edited by C. P. Lucas, 3 vols., Oxford 1912.
2. S. D. Waley, *Edwin Montagu*, London, 1964, p. 136.
3. *The Cambridge History of the British Empire*, Vol. VIII, chs. 17, 24.
4. G. Bennett, *Kenya, a Political History*, London 1963; L. H. Gann, *A History of Northern Rhodesia*, London, 1964, *passim*.
5. Statement about Colonial Territories in East Africa, 13 December 1950, *Hansard*, 1950–51, vol. 482, cols. 1167–9.
6. In Tanganyika in 1953 there were 14 unofficial members of the Legislative Council (4 Africans, 3 Asians, 7 Europeans); the Kenya ratios were 6 Africans, 6 Asians, 2 Arabs, 14 Europeans.
7. Claire Palley, *The Constitutional History and Law of Southern Rhodesia 1888–1965 with special reference to imperial control*, Oxford, 1969, pp. 366–8, 384–400.
8. J. S. Nye, *Pan-Africanism and East African Integration*, Cambridge, Mass., 1966.
9. See, for example, Colin Leys and Cranford Pratt, *A New Deal in Central Africa*, London, 1960, *passim*.
10. J. H. Oldham, *New Hope in Africa*, London, 1955.
11. 'Uganda's Uncertain Future', *The Times*, 21 Nov. 1953. The most substantial account is by R. C. Pratt in Low and Pratt, *Buganda and British Overrule 1900–1955*, London, 1960, Appendix I, 'The Crisis of 1953–1955'.
12. Until they learnt better – about 1906 – the British followed the Zanzibaris in calling Buganda, Uganda. 'Uganda' subsequently came to refer to the larger Protectorate which stretched well beyond the kingdom of Buganda at its centre.
13. D. A. Low, Religion and Society in Buganda 1875-1900, *East African Studies No. 8*, Kampala, 1956; Low and Pratt, *op. cit.*
14. A. I. Richards, *Economic Development and Tribal Change*, Cambridge, n.d., p. 77 (something like a third of these were migrants from surrounding areas).
15. *East African Royal Commission 1953–1955 Report*, Cmd. 9475, p. 457.
16. C. C. Wrigley, 'Crops and Wealth in Uganda', *East African Studies No. 12*, Kampala, 1959.

17. The Kabaka of Buganda, *The Desecration of My Kingdom*, London 1967, chs. 5 and 6.
18. *Report of the Commission of Inquiry into the Disturbances which Occurred in Uganda During 1945*, Entebbe, 1945. *Report of the Commission of Inquiry into the Disturbances in Uganda during April 1949*, Entebbe, 1950.
19. For a general statement of his viewpoint see Sir Andrew Cohen, *British Policy in Changing Africa*, London, 1959.
20. C. A. G. Wallis, *Report of an Inquiry into African Local Government in the Protectorate of Uganda*, Entebbe, 1953.
21. *Government Memorandum on the Report by Mr C. A. G. Wallis of an Inquiry into African Local Government in the Uganda Protectorate*, Entebbe, 1953, p.3.
22. See Chapter 6.
23. *Memorandum on Constitutional Development and Reform in Buganda*, Entebbe, 1953.
24. *Correspondence relating to the Composition of the Legislative Council in Uganda*, Entebbe, 1953.
25. See Chapter 5.
26. *East African Standard*, 3 July 1953.
27. Low and Pratt, *op. cit.*, pp. 254–8, 285–8.
28. *The Times*, 12 Aug. 1953. (It should perhaps be explained that throughout the crisis the author was Kampala correspondent of *The Times* and wrote the items bearing that bye-line.)
29. *Withdrawal of Recognition from Kabaka Mutesa 11 of Buganda*, Cmd. 9028, London, 1953.
30. D. A. Low, *The Mind of Buganda* (forthcoming) seeks to illustrate this, and some related matters.
31. As the Kabaka put it: 'The multi-racial complexion of Legco was not seen as the beginnings of self-government, but as a possible plan to change Uganda from an African to a multi-racial society in the style of Kenya or Rhodesia', *op. cit.*, p. 117.
32. J. M. Gray, 'Mutesa of Buganda', *Uganda Journal*, vol. I, pp. 22–49.
33. Kabaka Daudi Chwa, *Educational, Civilisation and Foreignisation*, Kampala [1935].
34. The Kabaka's own account is in *op. cit.*, ch. 7. The formal record is to be found in the originally secret minutes of meetings at Government House, Entebbe, on 15 August, 29 October, 3, 6, 27, 30 November 1953. These were produced in evidence in the Uganda Civil Case No. 50 of 1954, S. K. Mukwaba, J. Tomusange, and A. Kasule v. D. M. Mukubira, M. K. Wamala, A. Nyanzi, Y. Y. Kyaze, and the Attorney-General. A copy was made available to the author by the Attorney-General of Uganda in the courtroom. The minutes of the first meeting on 15 August 1954 contain the following passage: 'The Kabaka then raised the question of altering the agreement and separating Buganda from the rest of the Protectorate. He and his Ministers could no longer feel happy about Buganda's position under the agreement; apart from the danger of federation they considered that the policy of developing a unified system of government on parliamentary lines must inevitably result in Buganda becoming less important in the future. They were

worried about Buganda's future and felt that they must now take
steps to secure it. Acceptance of their wishes about separation was one
of the few things that would satisfy them. Buganda did not wish to be
associated with development on parliamentary lines and could not
accept the idea of non-African participation as of right in the Government of a Uganda Protectorate which included Buganda.' The contrast with the Government's statement quoted on p. 105 is stark.

35. 'After the Buganda crisis: looking back on the Kabaka's methods and
motives', *The Times*, 16 Feb. 1954.
36. See *Uganda Express* for November 1953.
37. Cmd. 9028.
38. *Ibid.* For the text of Article 6 see p. 355 above.
39. *The Times*, 1, 2, 3, 5, 7, 9 Dec. 1953.
40. *The Times*, 2, 3 Dec. 1953.
41. Kabaka, *op. cit.*, p. 121; *The Times*, 1 April 1950.
42. *The Times*, 14 Dec. 1953.
43. *The Times*, 3 Dec. 1953.
44. Colin Legum, *Must we lose Africa?* London, 1954 (Part one of which is
entitled 'Crisis in Uganda') gives a good insight into the thinking of
what might be called *The Observer*-reading public in Britain, not least
on points like this. *The Observer* played an important part in events
at the London end. Mr Legum was its Colonial Correspondent.
45. *Hansard*, 16 Dec. 1953.
46. 'If it hadn't been Andrew, there'd a' been a bloody row,' Mr James
Griffiths said to the author when visiting Government House, Entebbe
in August 1954. Personal notes.
47. For his personal account of the crisis see *The Memoirs of Lord Chandos*,
London, 1962, pp. 417–24.
48. *Hansard*, 2 Dec. 1953.
49. The story goes that Cohen used this phrase in a radio-telephone
conversation with Lyttelton an hour or so before the debate; that
Lyttelton used it without consulting the Colonial Office; and that the
Office was both dismayed and unforgiving towards Cohen. It will be
interesting to see what light the eventual opening of the Colonial Office
records cast on this story.
50. *The Times*, 7, 13 Feb. 1954.
51. J. M. Gray, 'The Year of the Three Kings of Buganda', *Uganda
Journal*, XIV, pp. 15–32.
52. *The Times*, 17 June 1954.
53. *The Times*, 10 Feb. 1954.
54. Cohen's speech to the Lukiko, 3 March 1954, is reported in *The Times*,
4 March 1954.
55. Specifically Professor K. C. Wheare in Central Africa, and Professor
W. J. M. Mackenzie in Tanganyika.
56. Author's personal notes.
57. *The Times*, 4, 7, 11, 23, 26 March 1954.
58. *The Times*, 8 April 1954.
59. *The Times*, 23 April 1954.

60. *The Times*, 6 May 1954.
61. *The Times*, 28 May 1954.
62. *The Times*, 1 April, 31 May, 1 June 1954.
63. Author's personal collection.
64. *The Times*, 23 June 1954.
65. Minutes of the Buganda Constitutional Committee, 24 June – 31 August 1954, and of 'the Namirembe Conference', 30 July – 17 Sept. 1954. At its final meeting the Conference agreed that the period during which its minutes and papers should remain confidential might be shorter than is normally the case. In accordance with the conditions laid down by the Conference I have availed myself of this provision, and I am extremely grateful to one of the two Secretaries of the Conference, now Professor S. A. de Smith, for making his personal copies available to me. It should be emphasised that not all of the documentation which is extant is at present open to inspection and that this chapter is based solely on material available from non-official sources.
66. *The Times*, 24 June 1954.
67. Although see *The Times*, 28 June 1954.
68. See the photograph facing p. 180.
69. *The Times*, 15 July 1955.
70. The narrative which follows in this section is based on the minutes of the first twenty-one meetings of the Buganda Constitutional Committee. There were twenty-two in all.
71. It should perhaps be made crystal-clear that, while the Baganda were strongly *opposed* to Uganda's (and therefore Buganda's) incorporation in a Federation of the three East African territories (Kenya and Tanganyika being the other two) since they feared that this would be dominated by the local Europeans of Kenya, they were very much in *favour* of a federal structure *within* Uganda. When 'federal' ideas were discussed this distinction was crucial.
72. *The Times*, 27 July 1954, contains hints of this.
73. Except where otherwise stated the whole of this section is based on the Minutes of the twenty-eight meetings of the Namirembe Conference proper. The dates in the text provide a guide to the minutes of particular meetings at which particular points were made. All quotations are from the minutes. They were always carefully agreed to, if necessary after amendment.
74. He had succeeded Oliver Lyttelton, who had recently retired.
75. *The Times*, 16 Aug. 1954.
76. Entebbe 1954.
77. Uganda Protectorate, *Report of the Constitutional Committee 1959*, Entebbe, 1959.
78. There is a useful reprint of Macmillan's speech of 3 Feb. 1960 to the two houses of the South African Parliament in *Documents and Speeches on Commonwealth Affairs 1952–1962*, edited by Nicholas Mansergh, London, 1963, pp. 347–51.
79. *Cf.* the numbered paragraphs on pp. 107–8 above.
80. *The Statement by the Governor* declared that if ever the question arose in

future, not only would local public opinion not be disregarded, but the Buganda Government would be fully consulted about how its views should be ascertained.

81. Articles 8–23.
82. *The Times*, 17 Sept. 1954.
83. Uganda Civil Case No. 50 of 1954. See *The Times*, 28 Sept. – 8 Oct., and 5 Nov. 1954. For the text of Article 6 see p. 103 above.
84. *The Times*, 17 Nov. 1954; *Uganda Protectorate, Buganda,* Cmd. 9320, London 1954.
85. *The Report of the Sub-Committee of the Lukiko which was set up to examine the Recommendations made by the Hancock Committee,* Entebbe, 1955.
86. *The Times*, 10 May 1955.
87. *The Times*, 1 Aug., 6, 15 Sept. 1955.
88. *The Times*, 18, 19 Oct. 1955.
89. It should be appreciated that they have only been treated here in a most summary fashion.
90. *The Times*, 26 Nov., 18 Dec. 1957 *et seq.*
91. See Chapter 7.
92. The Kabaka's account is in *op cit.*, chs. 1 and 11.

5

The Advent of Populism in Buganda

I

It has not always been quite certain that analysts of political forces in Africa have been looking in all the right corners. The day was after all when African nationalism crept up unawares on one generation of experts; and if, to take a wider example, one looks at studies of Indian politics before about 1950 it is remarkable how little analysis there is of the role of caste.

In 1961 Professor Apter drew attention to what he called 'populism' in Buganda.[1] This was a political ingredient which had not often made its presence felt in discussions of constitutional change or political party leadership in Africa (except in the vaguest possible way), yet in Buganda at least it was obviously a phenomenon of first importance and there were signs, that, to go no further afield, it was not without counterparts elsewhere in Uganda as well.[2] Certainly anyone who lived in Uganda during the decade of the 1950s (however much he may have confined himself to privileged circles) was aware that there were people politically active in the country, whom it was tempting to dismiss as 'rowdies',[3] but who periodically had a substantial political impact. One had the uncomfortable feeling too that they might make their presence felt to a far greater degree in the future. This disquiet was born of ignorance; and this chapter is an attempt to distinguish these very important forces for what they were, by way of an attempt to adumbrate their fortunes in Buganda over the previous three-quarters of a century.

II

We may begin then, by noting that it is reasonably clear that there have been two basic patterns permeating Buganda's society.[4]

The first may be called the Bataka pattern – the Bataka being the heads of the exogamous totemic clans which tradition suggests were originally localised and originally institutions enjoying much independent political authority. These clans, however, became subject to the Kabaka, the ruler of Buganda (in his capacity as Sabataka, or head of the clans), and then became largely dispersed. The Bataka pattern has thus been based on the principles and values of unilineal descent, and has been represented pre-eminently in the clans. For ease of reference we call the second pattern the Bakungu pattern. This is a pattern of dyadic relationships of subordination and super-ordination between each individual and his lord, culminating in the authority of the Kabaka over all his chiefs. The Bakungu were the most important of his directly appointed territorial administrative chiefs; and the Bakungu pattern has thus been based upon the principles and values of appointment to office and place, and was represented pre-eminently in the hierarchy of appointed chiefs. By reinforcing each other, these two patterns have given the Baganda a remarkable degree of tribal-wide cohesion. For every Muganda has been at once a member of a clan and the subject of a chief; and in both capacities was under the ultimate dominion of the Kabaka.

The evidence is, however, that by the nineteenth century the political power of the Bakungu pattern had come to predominate over the Bataka pattern,[5] and that by the end of the nineteenth century the various agreements which regularised the political relations between the newly arrived British Protectorate authorities and the Buganda kingdom were not far from the mark when they characterised the Baganda as divided, in political terms, within what is here called the Bakungu pattern, into the three categories of 'Kabaka, Chiefs and People'. Chiefs and people may appear to be somewhat arbitrary categories, but they are understood by the Baganda when they distinguish between *bwami* (people who rule; here chiefs) and *bakopi* (peasants; here people).[6] The essence of the distinction between them, as Dr Lucy Mair has put it, was 'between persons with the right to allocate land and persons who depend on them for land to cultivate'.[7]

In the nineteenth century, pre-British version of this triad the Kabaka had come to enjoy a very considerable measure of autocratic authority over his chiefs.[8] Chiefs were promoted or demoted, honoured or murdered, at the Kabaka's own behest. They were frequently moved from one office to another on his orders alone; and he controlled the appointment not only of the most senior chiefs but of the merest subordinates as well. There were, moreover, in broad terms by the 1880s, three separate sets of hierarchies of royally appointed chiefs – the *Bakungu*, strictly so-called, and their subordinates, who had territorial administrative jurisdictions; the *Batongole*, the Kabaka's own personal agents or personal stewards; and the *Mujasi* and *Gabunga* (the General and the Admiral), the military and naval specialists, who had their own subordinates as well. These three sets of chiefs were spread throughout the country; in each instance their authority flowed directly from the Kabaka; and they each acted on his behalf as a check upon the others. Few African rulers had as powerful a grip over their subordinate staffs as nineteenth century Kabakas of Buganda.

The relations between these chiefs and the people of Buganda stood for the most part upon a clientage basis.[9] The ordinary peasant attached himself as a client-follower to a chief whom he undertook to supply freely and serve faithfully, so long as the association between them lasted. The chief for his part was expected to provide for his client by political advancement (if that was desired), by the allotment of land, and by the provision of largesse – both from what was captured in war, and from the superabundance which a chief's position allowed him to collect. Although the jurisdiction of chiefs could be very authoritative, the relation between chiefs and people does not seem to have been as autocratic as that between the Kabaka and his chiefs. For while chiefs were frequently on the move from one position to another, and while they were as liable to rapid disgrace as to rapid promotion, the people were free to attach themselves to a popular and successful chief, and equally free to desert (or intrigue against) an unpopular and unsuccessful one. This was in a situation where there was an abundance of land, and a relative scarcity of labour. All this is not to suggest that there was here a wholly idyllic period for the ordinary peasant. But it is to suggest that since the chiefs were never at this period an irremovable deadweight; that since people participated through their linkages with their Chiefs in the great benefits which nineteenth-century Buganda's success as a predatory state brought to it; and that since people enjoyed a clear position of psychological dependence[10] upon their chiefs, they were on the whole well satisfied.

Plainly, however, the chiefs were not. The major point of tension in later nineteenth century kiganda society, as viewed in terms of its dominant triad of Kabaka, Chiefs and People, lay not between the chiefs and people, but between the chiefs and the Kabaka. Plainly, moreover, the 'dependence' of the chiefs upon the Kabaka was by no means secure. This is nowhere better illustrated than in the very elaborateness of the counter-balancing network of chiefly hierarchies which was in operation in nineteenth century Buganda, and in the excessive precautions taken by successive Kabakas, by this means and others, to prevent any appointed chief from establishing sole effective control over any one portion of the kingdom in particular.

III

It was displayed too in the spectacular upheavals which occurred in Buganda in the last two decades of the nineteenth century. There can be little doubt, for instance, that one of the main ingredients which went to the making of the so-called Christian revolution[11] in Buganda between 1888 and 1897 was the determination of some of the younger chiefs at the Kabaka's court to curtail his autocratic authority and establish a new order. For once they had gained power in Buganda (around 1888–90)[12] they took to themselves much of the authority which the Kabaka had formerly possessed, and in particular took into their own hands the responsibility for appointments to chieftaincies. As one missionary observer wrote late in 1888 after the first set of upheavals: 'The poor king was but a child in the hands of his Officers and Ministers. His time was chiefly occupied in giving his consent and approval to the distribution and division of the various chieftainships.'[13]

A year later he was writing again that the Kabaka was 'much displeased with the arrangement and division of the country [and] complains that he is helpless and King only in name';[14]

apparently he was 'hankering after the position of absolute monarch, that he once had'.[15] As one other missionary put it, 'all past history may have been leading up to this. The people[16] have learnt their strength, and the king for all time to come, has been taught his weakness. . . . The chiefs intend to have a voice, and that a loud one in the affairs of the kingdom.'[17] Furthermore, when Kabaka Mwanga revolted in 1897 against the settlement which these Christian chiefs made during the early 1890s with the newly arrived British administration, very few chiefs – only those, in fact, who had themselves come into conflict with the new regime – joined him in his revolt; the great majority of them stood by the British against him. Patently one major factor in their decision was a determination to defend the oligarchical revolution which they had by this time effected. And with Mwanga's defeat and deportation two years later (and despite the appointment of his infant son Daudi Chwa as his successor) a substantial change in the distribution of power between Kabaka, chiefs and people in Buganda in favour of the chiefs, was confirmed for the future. It constituted a major shift in the locus of political authority in the Buganda Kingdom. Political power within Buganda now resided with the oligarchy of administrative chiefs.[18] This was brought about through the coupling of an open breach in the relations between the Kabaka and a group of younger chiefs (who were both converts to Christianity and, as it happened, the leaders of the Kabaka's best-armed 'regiments') with the advent of British imperial authority which showed itself ready to support these chiefs in their ambitions.

For the moment, however, the pre-existing relationships between chiefs and people in Buganda remained intact. When the powerful oligarchy of Christian chiefs parcelled out[19] the land which was made available under the terms of the Uganda Agreement of 1900 which the Christian chiefs made with the British, there was for a year or so a tremendous amount of movement in Buganda as peasant followers of chiefs moved from their old estates to their new ones.[20] This extensive criss-cross migration in the years 1900–01 is clear evidence that the people were still closely attached as clients to and dependents upon their chiefs, and that the former nexus between them still obtained.[21]

It is the key argument of this chapter that as between the hierarchy of senior chiefs and the people of Buganda – to pursue the language of the dominating pattern of the Bakungu triad – these relationships were during the first half of the twentieth century gradually breaking down. This was not because the chiefs sank into impotence. On the contrary it was in part at least in reaction to the shift in the balance of authority in favour of the chiefs which occurred at the turn of the century.

IV

There can be no doubt that during the first quarter of the twentieth century the hierarchy of senior administrative chiefs – particularly the ministers in the Kabaka's Government, the county and the sub-county chiefs – enjoyed very considerable authority.[22] As the arch exponents of the currently dominant ideology of cultural advancement in co-operation with European missionaries and European administrators, they displayed a zest and confidence which no one else could display. As highly efficient and effective chiefs they were warmly supported by the British Administration. While, moreover, enjoying much of the previous power and position of Baganda chiefs, they had not only successfully usurped many of the Kabaka's functions, but they were no longer subject to the previous curbs upon their authority. They were far less liable to frequent movement from one post to another.[23] The rival hierarchies of appointed chiefs had virtually been amalgamated into a single Bakungu hierarchy; and one way and another they now had a far greater security of tenure. What was more, with the redistribution of land under the terms of the Uganda Agreement of 1900 the chiefs in power at that time no longer relied for their control over land – and in consequence over peasant-clients – upon their retention of political office, since they now held their land under the terms of the Agreement, in quasi-freehold tenure.[24] Many of the ingredients of this greatly increased power continued to obtain until the 1950s. Throughout the chiefs controlled a good deal of the machinery of government in the kingdom. They also presided over its courts, and practically monopolised its native council, the Lukiko.

But already by the 1920s the pre-existing relationship between chiefs and people was suffering strain, and a rift between them was appearing. This was in part at least in reaction to the greatly increased power and permanence of the chiefs in office; for the peasantry now found itself saddled with an apparently irremovable hierarchy of chiefs whose authority could not easily be circumvented. Because, moreover, of the marked linkage between these chiefs and the whole disconcerting gamut of change which the European advent was bringing the loyalty of the members of the hierarchy towards many of the values which the peasantry held dear was suspect. Relations between chiefs and people thus began to deteriorate. And they worsened too as a result of the substantial increase in the economic exploitation of the peasantry which many chiefs and land-holders took to in the second decade of the twentieth century.[25] Chiefs were not looking after their peasants as they had in the past. 'Clearly', one contemporary observer remarked, 'the lot of the peasant was not an easy one, and clearly here were all the makings of agrarian unrest.'[26] Simultaneously the old relations between chiefs and people were being adversely affected because the chiefs in office were becoming more and more of an administrative bureaucracy[27] whose fortunes depended, not as in the past upon their ability to marshal large numbers of peasants in the service of the kingdom, but upon their ability to fulfil the tax-collecting, jural and bureau-cratic decrees of the British Protectorate authorities and of the Buganda Government under its guidance. A chief's position, therefore, became less dependent upon his retention of the goodwill of his peasants, and there was accordingly less pressure upon him to take the personal interest in them which he and his predecessors had generally shown previously. This particular change was underscored by the consequences of the land settlement under the terms of the 1900 Agreement. For land was now held by an individual personally and without political obligation. This meant that whatever might be the political fortunes of the landowner he could still continue to hold his land when he ceased to hold office.[28] For this reason too he was less concerned to retain the personal support of the peasants who were settled upon it under him. By undermining the nexus between chiefs and people such conditions[29] served to strain the psychological dependence of the people upon their chiefs and to exacerbate the discontent which the very greatly increased power of the chiefs was generating concurrently.

The whole position was considerably aggravated because at the same time the people in one way and another were themselves becoming less and less personally beholden to their chiefs. If they had relations with a landlord as most of them continued to have, the chances were that because of the break which the land settlement of 1900 had instituted between land-holding and chieftainship,[30] the landlord would no longer always be a chief. A peasant might now have no tenancy relations with a chief – that is with a member of the chiefly hier-archy – as he had usually had in the past. (The position is a little complicated in that all landowners continued to be thought of as having chiefly status, and all chiefs in the adminis-trative hierarchy were expected to hold land. But increasingly the likelihood was that even if a peasant enjoyed a close relation-ship with his landowner, this was less and less likely to carry with it any personal connection with a chief of the administra-tive hierarchy). Since, moreover, under the terms of the 1900 Agreement (as confirmed by the Buganda Land Law of 1908) land could be freely bought, sold and bequeathed amongst Africans in Buganda, there developed a wholly new stratum of Buganda's society, which consisted of independent, individual landholders, owing no political allegiance for their holding of land to anyone. This introduced a distinction, and a division, between the hierarchy of administrative chiefs, and many non-chiefly landowners; and although in relation to the peasantry the latter might count themselves, and be counted, as chiefs, in relation to the chiefs of the administrative heirarchy – and in particular to its upper reaches – they were likely to act as people.

Simultaneously the ordinary peasant was wrenching himself free from his former reliance upon the largesse of his chief[31] for the procurement of wants above the subsistence level – for he was now growing his own crops, first cotton and then coffee; and it was not long before he was becoming his own independent provider of luxuries and other wanted goods. It has been very clearly demonstrated, moreover, that by the 1920s a critical change had occurred in the organisation of native agriculture in Buganda. Formerly peasants had grown cotton communally under the control of (and probably largely for the benefit of) their chiefs and landowners. Now 'production was passing into the hands of peasant cultivators' and (ominous note) 'the land-owner-chiefs were steadily being transformed into a rentier class, living off tribute and tithe and playing no longer even a supervisory role in the process of production'. This transformation occurred all over Uganda, but it 'appears to have been swiftest and most far-reaching in Buganda'. And the result was that

during the inter-war period there took shape a new pattern of agrarian society. At the bottom was an undifferentiated mass of free peasant cultivators, the *de facto* proprietors of small holdings which yielded both food and a modest money income. Above them was an administrative hierarchy of salaried chiefs, who, apart from the residual *busulu* and *nvujjo* in Buganda, no longer derived any direct profit from the land or its profits.[32]

After 1927, moreover, under the Busulu and Nvujjo Law of that year (passed by the Buganda, Lukiko, the Buganda Council, under pressure from the British administration) peasants were guaranteed occupation of their small-holdings on the payment of what became a modest rent. This relieved the immediate agrarian tension; and in the long run it meant that the ordinary peasant was no longer beholden to his chief or his landlord for his continuing occupation of the land he culti-vated.[33] Thus, one way and another, the rift between peasants and chiefly-landlords, and *a fortiori* between peasants[34] and the administrative hierarchy of chiefs – between, that is, the twentieth century version of chiefs and people – was growing.[35]

This afforded little comfort to the people. Since the dispersal of Buganda's exogamous totemic clans, corporate face-to-face relationships in the Buganda countryside were in any event not very strong. Now with the atrophy of the personal nexus between chiefs and people they became more brittle still. For a time the church-school complex introduced in the rural areas at the turn of the century by Christian missionaries served an ameliorating purpose. Local pride came to attach to these institutions scattered across the countryside, and they provided one of the few, badly needed, foci of local cohesion in the changing rural scene. The strength, however, of the local church community declined wherever pastoral care was not sustained, and when in the mid-1930s the Anglican Church went into partnership with the Protectorate Government for the improvement of education, and concentrated upon the more efficient primary schools, many of the simple bush schools were left to wither away. Such schools may have been educationally very imperfect, but at least they served as a nodal point for local co-operative endeavour. It seems plain that their atrophy increased the distance between the rural peasantry and the chiefly (and ecclesiastical) hierarchy. The fact that the Roman Catholics in Buganda have retained a greater corporateness than the Anglicans may be traced in part at least to the greater attention which their larger numbers of clergy – European and African – allowed them for pastoral work at the local level. It is not altogether surprising, moreover, that the Anglican revival movement of the *Balokole* (the Saved Ones) should have got under way in Buganda in the 1930s, for it was in many respects a typical response to the atrophy of the face-to-face relationships which by that time was becoming such a marked feature of the Bakungu pattern there. Nor it is surprising that the Balokole should so instinctively have turned for their organisational model to that other basic Buganda pattern, the Bataka pattern, which in several notable respects they reproduced,[36] for this was quite regularly resorted to upon such occasions.

V

Thus from a variety of angles it looks as if by the 1940s the bonds between chiefs and people in Buganda, which had once been so strong, were becoming seriously weakened, and that in consequence a growing number of Baganda peasants were feeling both aggrieved[37] and footloose. Initially this alienation, as one might expect, affected only a minority. But by the 1940s a significant number of people were displaying an increasing antagonism towards the chiefs in power. This was aggravated by a phase of acute rivalry within the chiefly hierarchy itself, by the discontent of a number of western-educated Baganda at their failure to establish themselves in satisfactory careers, and by economic discontents caused partly by the impact of

Kabaka Daudi Chwa and company at Namirembe Cathedral on the
day of the British King Edward VII's Coronation, 1902.

Martin Luther Nsibirwa, Katikiro of Buganda (1928–41, 1945), and
Serwano Kulubya, Omuwanika of Buganda (1928–45).

the second world war, partly by the stringent economic policy of the British Protectorate Government,[38] and partly by the close grip of non-African entrepreneurs over the processing and marketing of the African peasant-grown cotton and coffee crops. There can be no doubt that the British authorities were much less sympathetic towards this ferment than they had been towards the agrarian discontents of the 1920s. But what is especially significant for our present purpose is that there occurred at this time the rise of demands for a great increase in the election of members to the Buganda Lukiko, or Council (which had previously consisted entirely of chiefs) and even for the election of chiefs themselves. Such were the origins of populism.

So serious did the cumulative discontents become that there were riots in Buganda first in 1945 and again in 1949. In 1945 the major objective of the rioters was the removal from office of Serwano Kulubya, the long-standing, and by any reasonably objective standards, especially notable *Omuwanika* (Treasurer) of Buganda.[39] This determination was no doubt largely inspired by his rivals within the chiefly hierarchy itself; but it is of first importance to notice how successfully it could be exploited as the focal point of the people's discontent for as a symbol of the now deepening purpose of the most aroused sections amongst them, it possessed a quite unusual appositeness.[40] At the height of the rioting Kulubya resigned. Shortly afterwards, however, under pressure from the British, the position of the old chiefly hierarchy was for the time being restored (more particularly in the person of Kawalya Kagwa – the son of Sir Apolo Kagwa, the former long-standing Katikiro of Buganda[41] – who himself now became Katikiro in September 1945), and for the best part of another decade, with periodic support from the British administration, it remained in the saddle.

It is one of the many paradoxes in the story that this chiefly hierarchy despite its linkages with the British, had, on the whole, been remarkably successful in maintaining a real measure of autonomy for their kingdom; and since on this issue the people were in support of their chiefs, the important consequence followed that the people as a result seem to have confined their arena of political activities to the four walls of the kingdom. They saw the solution, that is, to Buganda's ills within Buganda itself. The irony of this outcome to so many of the successful achievements of the chiefly hierarchy had been illustrated already in 1945, when the rioters had directed their hostility mainly against an overmighty chief, rather than against, for instance, the British Protectorate authorities. It was illustrated again in 1949 when, in conjunction with acute economic discontents, there were further riots in Buganda, during which the chiefs, on a wider scale than before, became the main butt of the rioters' maraudings – numbers of chiefs had their houses and offices burnt down – and in which the major demonstration took place at the entrance, not of the British Residency, but of the Kabaka's palace.

The petition which the rioters' delegates thereupon presented to the Kabaka contained five requests:

I. Your Highness should open the rule of democracy to start giving people power to choose their own chiefs.

II. We want the number of sixty unofficial representatives [in the Lukiko] to be completed.

III. We demand the abolition of the present [Buganda] Government.

IV. We want to gin our cotton.

V. We want to sell our produce in outside countries, that is free trade.[42]

The first three requests were directed against the existing chiefly hierarchy; the last two against the existing structure of cash crop processing and marketing in Uganda, including, among other things, the strong position held in both enterprises by the Asians in the country. Mr John Stonehouse, the British Labour MP who for several years during the 1950s lived closer to some of the popular leaders of the Baganda than any other European in the country (except his American and Italian colleagues) has not inappropriately called these events 'the Peasants' Rebellion'.[43] It was soon suppressed.[44] But the ferment behind it persisted. Mr Fenner Brockway, another British Labour MP who visited Uganda in 1950, described how he was met at Entebbe airport by a crowd of about 3,000 people and was then taken by his Baganda hosts to hold meetings at twenty different places they had prepared in the Buganda countryside, at which there were anything from 500 to 5,000 persons present.[45]

These meetings were organised, it seems, by the Federation of Uganda African Farmers which had been heavily involved in the riots. It is of great significance, however, that the dis- content of the peasants in the 1940s was directed as well by an organisation which called itself the Butaka Union. For by this invoking that other pattern in Buganda's society – the Bataka pattern – it brought into action against the much disliked hierarchy of administrative chiefs, who now represented so pre-eminently the Bakungu pattern, that other pattern in Bu- ganda's society which already had such a long history of conflict with it. It had been the same in the 1920s. One vehicle of peasant discontent at that time had been the so-called Feder- ation of the Bataka.[46] During both these periods there were Bataka (clan and lineage heads), strictly so-called, who were active in the movement, because they were anxious to recover the position which they believed Bataka had held in Buganda in the past. But in the ordinary way such men found it difficult to procure much popular support.[47] Whenever, however, there was a strong, popular, anti-chief movement their symbolic value was immense.

VI

During the early 1950s the economic grievances of the Baganda people began to be met.[48] Nevertheless there were still demands for an elected Lukiko and elected chiefs, and on at least one occasion in 1952 the Ministers in the Kabaka's Government (at the apex of the chiefly hierarchy) became very seriously worried about the pressure which was building up against them on the latter point.[49] This pressure was somewhat relieved in March 1953 when the Kabaka and the Protectorate Govern- ment jointly announced that in future the Lukiko would have a majority of elected members and that the Kabaka would appoint his Ministers after consultation with a committee of the Lukiko;[50] but the pressure by no means disappeared.

Eight months later in November 1953, in circumstances which have already been discussed,[51] the Kabaka of Buganda was deported by the British from his country after a head-on collision with them over future policy. The details of this clash were little understood by the people of Buganda: since the dispute had something to do with the advance of Uganda towards self-government they assumed that the Kabaka was right and the British wrong. There were many aspects to the crisis; but the point which is of first importance to note here is that it suddenly provided the people of Buganda with a golden opportunity to rectify the imbalance in the relations between chiefs and people against which the more active amongst them had for some years kicked so strongly but without so far very much noticeable success: for the British were obviously one of the strongest supports of the overgrown authority of the chiefly bureaucracy; it was fairly plain that the position of the Kabaka like that of the people had suffered substantially from the increase in the authority of the chiefs. (Perhaps because it was instinctively recognised that for this very reason the Kabaka ought to be on the side of the people, the practice had already grown up for the people to look to the Kabaka for a settlement of their grievances.)[52] If he, therefore, as now seemed apparent, had the makings of an effective political protagonist,[53] then there was more than half a chance that if the people supported him against the British they might come within striking distance of, among other things, reducing the overgrown dominance of the chiefs. Or, in other words (to use the terms of the basic Bakungu-type triad of Kabaka, chiefs and people) the people now looked to the Kabaka to bring the chiefs back to heel.[54] Anyone who attended the garden party which the Kabaka gave on his return to Buganda in 1955; or saw the public march past at that time at which he took the salute; or recalls the attacks, sometimes accompanied by violence, which were made upon a number of chiefs, in the two months that followed, would be aware that such political readjustments were occurring.[55]

It has frequently been asserted that the Baganda supported their Kabaka during his period of exile from 1953 to 1955 because they were profoundly and devoutly attached to their monarchical institution. If the truth of this need not be denied, it does not explain why the Baganda supported their Kabaka when he was exiled by the British in 1953, but had not supported their Kabaka when he was exiled by some of his own courtiers in 1888, or when he revolted against the British in 1897.[56] On the latter occasion indeed most of the people of Buganda followed their own chiefs in supporting the British against their own Kabaka. The suggestion here would be that they acted differently in 1953–5, partly, no doubt, because political relations between the British and the Buganda kingdom had altered in the meanwhile,[57] but also because political relations within Buganda itself had altered in the interval as well. With the eventual triumph of the Christian oligarchy in the 1890s the aggressive feelings which had hitherto been directed against the Kabaka had been reduced. Aggressive feelings were now mainly directed against the chiefs; and the nexus between them and their people had been considerably weakened. Consequently those chiefs who for various reasons were luke-warm in 1953–5 in their attitude towards the Kabaka were never in a position to mobilise support amongst the people for the British against him, as their predecessors had managed to do in 1897; and by the time the Kabaka returned from exile in 1955 an alliance between Kabaka and people had been forged which ensured that those chiefs who had not been un-equivocally loyal to him during his exile lost their offices.[58] To him and his closest associates they were traitors; to the people they were the hateful symbols of a chieftainship which was out of step with general Baganda requirements. An important consideration here was that with the twilight of the colonial period upon them the British refrained from intervening on the chiefs' behalf. The props of overgrown chiefly authority were therefore patently buckling, and all the chiefs of Buganda had had a clear warning that the distribution of political power in the kingdom was now no longer what it had been for the past half century.

After 1955 it was made clear indeed not only that the hier-archy of chiefs in Buganda had lost its former largely independ-ent powers, but that the people in Buganda were a much more powerful political force than they had ever been before. The magnitude of the support which the Kabaka enjoyed was just one expression of this. For the people the Kabaka was the person who had broken the serious impasse which the most seriously disturbed of them had felt they had reached with their chiefs.

VII

But this was not the only contemporary manifestation of Buganda's populism. One of the curiosities of Buganda's political history during the 1950s was the relatively small support which nationalist-minded political parties procured.[59] It may be suggested that one reason for this was the suspicion amongst the people in Buganda that the young western-educated political leaders who were always forming these parties would probably be, in several important respects, only one more generation of dominating chiefs. It was not merely that these leaders were frequently scions of chiefly families. It was also that since chiefs in Buganda have most usually been drawn from successive generations of the best educated people in Buganda, who have congregated about the focal points of power and authority in the Kingdom, these younger educated men seemed in so many respects (and for all their protestations to the contrary) of much the same timber as the chiefs. In Buganda there had on previous occasions been periods of substantial constitutional changes; yet it had always been this same type of elite group which (on every occasion during the previous hundred years at all events) had scrambled to the top.[60] The new young elite may have wished to see a major change in the system – from power being exercised by chiefs to power being exercised by political leaders; but for the people this had all the marks of a distinction without a difference.[61] This being so, one can readily understand why from their point of view increased authority in the hands of the Kabaka promised, not irresponsible monarchical authority (as many of the political party leaders saw it) but the safeguarding of effective popular control against the independent ambitions of yet another elite generation.

It is certainly significant that in the absence of strong anti-imperialist nationalism in Uganda,[62] no political party in Buganda in the 1940s and 1950s was able to gain extensive support until it had managed to link its fortunes with an issue which was of first importance to the people. The Bataka Union in the 1940s owed it strength not to its leadership of various groups of the elite *manqué*,[63] but to its (often crude) articulation of the economic and political grievances of the peasantry. A party like the Uganda National Congress, which was founded in 1952, enjoyed from time to time considerable support, partly, of course, because it was periodically especially vehement in its attacks upon both the British Government and the Asian minority in the country, but partly too because it seemed readier than any other party to make room for leaders who were truly 'of the people', and partly as well because it seemed more genuinely opposed to the established order in the country than any other party. But a party like the Progressive Party (founded 1955), or the United Congress Party (founded 1957), or the Uganda National Party (founded 1959), all of which patently represented little more than the interests of the new western-educated elite, never won popular support.[64]

On the other hand popular support was forthcoming for those who supported the Kabaka. Whenever, for instance, in the period after 1955, the Kabaka's Government of the Buganda Lukiko made a move to uphold the Kabaka's status, either against local party leaders, or against the British Protectorate authorities, or against the non-Baganda in the rest of Uganda, they were assured of considerable popular approval. This was not just because the people felt obliged to the Kabaka. It may be suggested as well that it was because the people felt that by supporting the Kabaka they would ensure that no counter-attack by either an old or a new ambitions elite would be successful. A new system of political relations in Buganda had been made possible by the outcome of the events surrounding the Kabaka's exile and return; but it had not yet achieved a definite form, and the most active minds amongst the people seem to have determined not to let the new opportunity slip from their grasp through their own inactivity.

Against this background the equivocal position in which the Kabaka's Government stood in the years following the Kabaka's return from exile in 1955 throws a good deal of light upon the strength of populism. The Kabaka's Government, it must be remembered, was still largely drawn from the chiefly stratum of Buganda's society, so that to the most aroused elements of the people it was still periodically suspect. Its leadership of popular forces in Buganda was in consequence never wholly secure, and in fact only operated fully in the intervals between the activities of other prominent pace-setters, who were either drawn more directly from the people, or who had in one way or another successfully established more direct linkages with them. The difficulties in the position of the Kabaka's Government were especially discernible whenever popular forces – for one reason or another – took the law into their own hands. The Kabaka's Government, and for that matter the Kakaba himself, were almost certainly not the fomenters of popular upheaval on these occasions. They were in no position, however, to oppose it firmly. Even the Kabaka himself had to walk warily, since he was by no means the master of the situation at these times which both his most vehement detractors and his most vehement supporters claimed him to be.[65]

VIII

The classic example of these truths was afforded by the popular boycott of Asian traders in Buganda in 1959–60. The political changes of 1955–6 had altered the role of the chiefs in the rural areas of Buganda, but it had done nothing to that other aspect of rural life which had been so disliked by the people of Buganda (and about which little has so far been said here) – namely the penetration into its midst of Asian entrepreneurs both as owners of factories processing African peasant-grown primary products, and as the dominating influence in rural retail trade. The most frequent explanation of the exacerbation which this had caused has been the belief that Africans had very frequently received short measure at Asian hands. If the truth of this need not be denied, its importance does not stand alone. For Baganda exacerbation with Asian traders also had an ideological foundation – the belief that in a very profound sense these Asians did not *belong* to the Buganda countryside:[66] and in a rural society where localised corporate linkages were in any event tenuous enough any who as sharply as the Asians stood outside of them were naturally the butt of much ill-will.[67] For those, moreover, who were already feeling a sense of alienation within their own society this state of affairs was especially serious.

The beginnings during the 1950s of Government aid to African co-operatives in the taking over of processing factories from Asians,[68] and the beginnings of aid for the advancement of Africans (rather than Asians) in trade[69] were for the people a step or two in the right direction, but there were patently many leagues to be travelled yet; and such ameliorating influences as these reforms may have had, tended to be offset by the Protectorate Government's simultaneous support, or apparent support, for the establishment of 'multi-racial' government in Uganda[70] – a concept which at that time was anathema not only to the Baganda chiefs and party politicians, but to the people in Buganda as well; for they saw here a means by which, if they did not take care, the existing economic and social position of the Asians in Buganda might be entrenched for all time. While the efforts of the Kabaka's Government, of the party politicians, and of others, seemed likely in the period after 1955 to be succeeding in making the British remove themselves from the life of Buganda, despite a number of press campaigns in the local Luganda newspapers, there was no sign of any progress in the movement to remove the Asians from the life of Buganda. On the contrary further constitutional reform seemed to promise, if the British Colonial Office had its way, to entrench the position of the Asians, not only by including them upon a common electoral roll but by instituting at the same time constitutional 'safeguards for minorities'.[71]

Existing as it did under the eye of the Protectorate Government (who in the event showed its strength by cutting its financial grants to the Buganda Government) the Kabaka's Government in Buganda was in no position to do more than protest. The most aroused elements amongst the people, however, determined to take action on their own, and soon set about ridding the countryside of the Asian trader by a campaign of boycott, arson, crop-slashing and violent attack, directed as much against those who had dealings with Asians, as against Asians themselves. At the outset this campaign was linked with the establishment of a new political party in Buganda, the Uganda National Movement, which significantly enough became in its short life by far the most powerful which the country had so far seen. It is equally significant for our present purposes that its proscription, and the rustication of its leaders, did very little to stop the popular campaign, which proved to be no more dependent upon the leadership of party politicians than it was upon that of the Kabaka's Government. Boycott instructions were given – by leaflet – in the name of one 'Muzinge' (who does not seem to have been any single, identifiable person). Such other organisation as there appears to have been, seems to have been based, significantly enough, not upon any Bakungu-type pattern, but on a Bataka-type pattern.[72] And in the event the boycott was for the most part singularly successful in ejecting Asian traders from the Buganda countryside.[73]

By 1960–2 popular feeling in Buganda was chiefly exercised with the problem of Buganda's participation in the larger and prospectively self-governing Uganda.[74] The Buganda Government having by 1961 agreed to participate in this on terms,[75] the need arose for a political organisation to defend Buganda's interests within the agreed framework. It called itself, significantly enough, *Kabaka Yekka* (the Kabaka alone). It represented – very effectively it seems – the popular forces at work in Buganda. Well over half the candidates it chose for the crucial elections to the Buganda Lukiko in 1962 – which it won by sixty-three seats to three – were farmers or traders.

We may note, however, that at the same time a crucial role in the electoral organisation of Kabaka Yekka was played by the Kabaka himself in close conjunction with the hierarchy of administrative chiefs, now, it seems, in a somewhat chastened mood; and that six of the seven Ministers in the new Buganda Government, which was formed shortly afterwards, belonged to the younger political elite. What seemed to be emerging here were the elements of a new political order. As controllers of the one functioning political bureaucracy in the kingdom the chiefs had no rivals as organisers – certainly not in the ranks of the Bataka or those who aped them; they had their uses, therefore, as a political machine: while the new Government promised to be as effectively dynamic as anything which Buganda could otherwise have produced.[76] At the same time it is quite clear that both chiefs and ministers (and, to a lesser degree, the Kabaka) were only able to assume the roles they did, because they had learnt (through some bitter experience) that they must be acutely responsive to the militant populism of the Baganda people – a populism which had been fermenting for years and which had broken forth in the years between 1955 and 1960 into political prominence.

All in all it looks as if in the mid 1950s there was a substantial switch in the *locus* of political power in Buganda, away from the chiefs as such, to the people and those in whom they chose to repose their confidence. And lest these should in any way betray that confidence, the people had already shown their ability, on more than one occasion, to reach for alternative ways of securing their ends.

IX

Over a period of three quarters of a century there were therefore two shifts in the *locus* of political power within Buganda: between 1888 and 1897 away from the Kabaka to the chiefs; in the mid 1950s away from the chiefs to the people.

It is important, however, to note that the structure of the Bakungu-type triad of Kabaka, chiefs and people in Buganda remained intact. The Christian chiefs of the 1890s never thought to abolish the Kabakaship; the popular forces of the 1940s and 1950s never thought to abolish the chieftainship. Throughout, the existence of these institutions was accepted. That is why a good many Baganda were able to feel, and to act, as if nothing had changed. In fact, of course, there had been substantial changes – two quite radical changes, indeed, in the distribution of political power within the triad. In both cases the changes had been more than rebellions though less than full revolutions. They had been changes not of the structure itself but of the distribution of political power within it.

We may note, moreover, that they were effected, not by determined mass movements (either of the chiefs on the first occasion,[77] or of the people on the second) but by aroused minorities – the Christian chiefs in the 1880s and 1890s; the 'political malcontents' (as Professor Pratt has called them[78]) in the 1950s. In many respects these minorities may not have been typical of their order: but in a Burkean sense they were nevertheless representative of it. And it may be suggested that it is just because they were so successful in securing successive redistributions of political power, as tension built up, that on the one hand there was no necessity for determined mass movements, and on the other the basic structure never came under any major attack.

We may note too that the changes which these minorities

effected owed a great deal to their fortuitous conjunction in time with major changes in the balance of external authority impinging upon the country. The shift in the 1880s and 1890s was intimately linked with the advent of European rule; that of the 1950s and 1960s with the removal of European rule. They were linked too with the emergence of new political formations: on the first occasion the Christian parties; on the second with various attempts to create popular political organisations. Primarily the Christian parties displayed the characteristics of the Bakungu pattern, though they had important correspondences with the Bataka pattern as well.[79] But populism, as we have seen, mainly displayed characteristics of the Bataka pattern. Since this has a natural tendency to thrust against the hierarchical elements in the Bakungu pattern it provided an admirable frame of reference for populist activity. And because it represented an alternative legitimate expression of Buganda values to that expressed by the Bakungu pattern, it gave impetus and legitimacy to the opposition to the overgrown status of the chiefly hierarchy which populism was concerned to express. Populism, in short, has its roots in the relative egalitarianism of the Bataka pattern. For all that, in a manner that is characteristic of the other, Bakungu pattern, populism showed that it could be led – in the 1950s and early 1960s the Buganda Lukiko, the Kabaka, 'Muzinge', and the leaders of the Butaka Union, the Uganda National Movement, and Kabaka Yekka discovered that. It would not however be led by the nose.

In appearance populism in Buganda concerned itself mainly with two objectives: the reduction of economic disabilities, and the smooth articulation of the kingdom's corporate solidarity. But at the same time, it was dependent upon a growing sensitivity both to economic interests and to political possibilities, and above all it came to be propelled by the determination of the people to control the terms of their own society, whether political, social, economic, or psychological. It became a force which no one concerned with Uganda's politics could afford to ignore.

This chapter has been an attempt, in the first place, to draw attention to all of this; secondly to sketch out an introduction to its analysis (a full analysis has still to be made); and thirdly, by offering in one instance a few signposts, to suggest the importance of giving attention to subliminal factors in African politics.

NOTES

1. David E. Apter, *The Political Kingdom in Uganda: A Study in Bureaucratic Nationalism*, Princeton, 1961, p. 195 ff.
2. *Report of the Commission of Inquiry into the Disturbances in Certain Areas of the Bukedi and Bugisu Districts of the Eastern Province during the month of January, 1960, Uganda Protectorate*, Sessional Paper No. 3 of 1960.
3. Professor Pratt called them, specifically, 'political malcontents', R. C. Pratt, 'Nationalism in Buganda', *Political Studies*, IX (1961), p. 162.
4. I owe the use of the word 'pattern' to the Reverend F. B. Welbourn.
5. It is admirably surveyed in Martin Southwold, 'Bureaucracy and Chiefship in Buganda', *East African Studies, No. 14*, Kampala, 1961. I have to thank Dr Southwold for his most helpful comments upon my original draft. He must not be held responsible, however, for such errors as remain.
6. Professor Fallers has a valuable discussion of this in his chapter on 'Social Stratification in Traditional Buganda' in L. A. Fallers, ed., *The King's Men*, London, 1964.
7. Lucy P. Mair, 'Clientship in East Africa', *Cahiers d'études Africaines*, II (1961), p. 318.
8. Apolo Kagwa, *Basekabaka be Buganda*, 2nd ed. Kampala 1927, Chs. 12–16, gives perhaps the most comprehensive account of nineteenth century Buganda. See also J. Roscoe, *The Baganda*, London, 1911, esp. Chs. 5–10.
9. Mair, 'Clientship in East Africa', pp. 318–9, 322–4. I am aware that chiefs were also in some sense clients of the Kabaka, but I suggest that it might be misleading to emphasise this. For whereas there were many chiefs from whom a peasant could choose his lord, and whereas these chiefs had only a limited security of tenure, the chiefs had only one Kabaka to look to, and by the nineteenth century his security of tenure had become considerable. The relation between chiefs and people had, I suggest, in Buganda at this time a greater element of choice in it for the subordinate party than the relation between chiefs and the Kabaka. In focusing my account on these relationships I have tried to bear these differences in mind throughout.
10. For this whole notion see O. Mannoni, *Prospero and Caliban*, English translation, London, 1956.
11. Between 1888 and 1889 a Muslim oligarchy was in supreme power in Buganda. Analytically its role was identical with that of the Christian oligarchy that succeeded it, which is the centre of interest in this chapter. After 1893 a rump of the Muslim oligarchy attached itself to the Christian oligarchy. See Chapter 1 above.
12. J. M. Gray, 'The Year of the Three Kings of Buganda', *Uganda*

Journal, XIV (1949), pp. 15–52; C. C. Wrigley, 'The Christian Revolution in Buganda', *Comparative Studies in Society and History*, II (October 1959), pp. 33–48; D. A. Low, 'Religion and Society in Buganda 1875–1900', *East African Studies*, *No. 8*, Kampala, 1957; Southwold, pp. 15–77.

13. Gordon to Lang, 7 November 1888, G3 A5/O5, Church Missionary Society Archives, Salisbury Square, London.
14. Gordon to Mackay 3–21 October 1889, G3 A5/O5, CMS Archives.
15. Walker to I.W., 1 Nov. 1889, Walker Papers, CMS Archives.
16. In the original the context makes it plain that this is *not* meant to refer to 'the people' in the sense employed in this chapter.
17. Walker to W. C. Walker, 2 December 1889, Walker Papers. See also Walker to B. W. Walker, 10 October 1889, *ibid.*; and Gordon to Lang, 7 November 1888; Walker to Lang, 19 October and 19 December 1889; Gordon to Mackay, 3 October 1889; Mackay to Lang, 28 December 1889; Mackay to Ashe, 3 January 1890, G3 A5/o5, CMS Archives.
18. The most important of them, Apolo Kagwa, was Katikiro (Chief Minister) of Buganda for thirty-seven years (1889–1926).
19. Amongst themselves, their followers and all those who would accept their dominance. Low and Pratt, *Buganda and British Overrule*, Ch. 5.
20. E.g. A. R. Tucker, *Eighteen Years in Uganda and East Africa*, London, 1911, new edn., pp. 287, 290.
21. There is plenty of other evidence for this, e.g. 'the chiefs have to be very gentle in making the people work for them for fear of their leaving and going to some other chief'; and (about the payment of rents in cash) 'The chiefs are afraid to press the point lest the people leave them', Memorandum by Walker for Hayes Sadler, 20 July 1902, Entebbe Secretariat Archives A22/1.
22. Perhaps the two most striking manifestations of their power were first their supervision in 1907 of the removal of the whole of the population living within two miles of Lake Victoria's shore as one of the measures taken to combat the Sleeping Sickness epidemic which was rampant at that time, and, second, their enforcement of the stringent Cotton Rules of 1908 (which saved the reputation of Uganda Cotton on the British Market at a critical moment). Both were effected without open conflict. Half a century later this would have been inconceivable. Sir Hesketh Bell, *Glimpses of a Governor's Life*, London, 1946, pp. 163–4, 176–7.
23. I have detailed some of this in my chapter on 'Uganda: the establishment of the Protectorate 1894–1919' in the Oxford *History of East Africa*, Vol. II, Oxford 1966, pp. 91 ff.
24. Low and Pratt, pp. 141–5.
25. This included steady increases (with British support) of the rents which tenants had to pay; e.g. P. G. Powesland, 'Economic Policy and Labour,' *East African Studies*, *No. 10*, Kampala, 1957, pp. 6, 22.
26. H. B. Thomas, 'An Experiment in African Native Land Settlement', *Journal of the African Society*, XXVII (April, 1928), p. 244.

27. Oxford *History of East Africa, loc. cit.*
28. Low and Pratt, pp. 142–3; A. B. Mukwaya, 'Land Tenure in Buganda, Present Day Tendencies', *East African Studies, No. 1*, Kampala, 1953, p. 16.
29. L. P. Mair, *An African People in the Twentieth Century*, London, 1934, pp. 166 ff., 183, 275–7.
30. Low and Pratt, pp. 142 ff.
31. Or, for that matter, his landowner.
32. C. C. Wrigley, 'Crops and Wealth in Uganda', *East African Studies, No. 12*, Kampala, 1959, pp. 48–9, 55. *Busulu* was a tribute (or rent), *nvujjo* a tithe.
33. I think the critical point in the difference between the Buganda situation and that amongst the Mambwe and Tonga, described by Watson and van Velsen, probably lies here. Cf. William Watson, *Tribal Cohesion in a Money Economy*, Manchester, 1958 (the crucial point is summarised in Professor Gluckman's Introduction on p. x); J. van Velsen, 'Labour Migration as a Positive Factor in the Continuity of Tonga Tribal Society', in Aidan Southall (ed.) *Social Change in Modern Africa*, London, 1961, pp. 230–41.
34. And in certain respects landowners who were not administrative chiefs.
35. This is not the place to set out a further account of the political events of the 1920s. A campaign to dismantle the land settlement under the 1900 Agreement, so as to restore their traditional lands to the Bataka, was mounted. This attracted support from various groups which were then opposed to the existing chiefs. It was eventually decided that it would be impossibly complicated to untangle the land settlement; instead there were changes in the personnel of the chiefs; and the Busulu and Nvujjo Law checked the former exploitation of the peasants. It is significant that these last two changes removed the immediate force of the agitation, although the most overt objective had been in no way attained. There are important studies of Buganda in the mid-1920s in R. L. Buell, *The Native Problem in Africa*, New York, 1928, Vol. I, Section VI; and Thomas, *loc cit.*; and of the 1920s and 1930s in Apter, Ch. 6 ff.; Low and Pratt, Ch. 9; P. G. Powesland, Chs. 2–3; C. C. Wrigley, Ch. 4; and Mair, *An African People, loc. cit.*
36. On the story of the Anglican Church at this time see J. V. Taylor, *The Growth of the Church in Buganda*, London, 1958, Ch. 4. See also F. B. Welbourn, *East African Rebels*, London, 1961, esp. p. 190.
37. Professor Apter (*Political Kingdom*, p. 90) makes an important point when he asserts that by the 19th century the Baganda – or at all events, their upper echelons – had switched from 'consummatory' to 'instrumental' values. See also D. E. Apter, 'The Role of Traditionalism in the Political Modernisation of Ghana and Uganda', *World Politics*, XIII (1960), pp. 45–68. But so much of the history of Buganda since then (e.g. as outlined in this paper) looks remarkably like a revulsion from that switch.
38. Mr Wrigley remarks of this period: '. . . since . . . the peasant producers were receiving very much less than the export value of their crops, there

can be no doubt that the rural population was markedly less well off than it had been before the war – a fact which goes far to explain both the unrest and general malaise which characterised Uganda in these years . . .', 'Crops and Wealth', p. 69.

39. He had held this office since 1928. He had made a considerable mark in London by the dignity and forthrightness of his evidence to the Joint Select Committee on Closer Union in East Africa in 1931.

40. *Report of the Commission of Inquiry into the Disturbances which occurred in Uganda during January 1945*, Entebbe, 1945. (With this, as with the Report on the 1949 riots, it is frequently more important to read between than to read on the lines.)

41. He was the foremost member of the first Christian oligarchy.

42. *Report of the Commission of Inquiry into the Disturbances in Uganda during April, 1949*, Entebbe, 1950, p. 21.

43. John Stonehouse, *Prohibited Immigrant*, London, 1960, Ch. 3 ff. See also G. W. Shepherd [Stonehouse's American colleague], *They Wait in Darkness*, New York, 1955.

44. Apter, Chs. 11–12; Low and Pratt, Ch. 11.

45. Fenner Brockway, *African Journeys*, London, 1955, Chs. 4–6.

46. Thomas, pp. 245 ff.; Buell, pp. 594–9.

47. E.g. although there were complaints at the loss of their lands under the terms of the Land Settlement of the 1900 Agreement as early as 1902 (Low and Pratt, pp. 109, 144) these never enjoyed much popular backing until the 1920s.

48. E.g. in 1953 the Uganda Government abandoned its former policy and agreed to the payment of cotton and coffee prices to producers on the basis of the best estimate possible of the world price, Despatch from the Governor of Uganda to the Secretary of State for the Colonies on subject of the East African Royal Commission, 1933–1955, Uganda Protectorate, Sessional Paper No. 4 1956/57, pp. 14–15; see also Wrigley, 'Crops and Wealth', p. 78.

49. This was at the time when the de Bunsen education committee was collecting evidence. Personal recollection.

50. Memorandum on Constitutional Development and Reform in Buganda, Entebbe, 1953.

51. Low and Pratt, Appendix I, contains the fullest available account. See Chapter 4 of this book.

52. This had occurred in the 1920s (e.g. Low and Pratt, pp. 234–5), and, as we have just seen, in the 1940s.

53. He had previously given a very different appearance, e.g. during the 1949 riots.

54. Cf. Bendix's summary of Weber; 'Patrimonialism appeals to the masses against the privileged status groups: not the warrior-hero but the "good king", the "father of his people", are its prevailing ideal. That the patrimonial ruler sees to the welfare of his subjects is the basis on which he legitimizes his rule in his own and their eyes', Reinhard Bendix, *Max Weber: An Intellectual Portrait*, London, 1960, p. 364.

55. For the events of this time see *The Times*, 24 October, 1, 9, 14, 17, 22, 24, 28 November, 6, 22, 24, 28, 29, 30 December 1955.
56. See chapter 1.
57. See Chapter 3.
58. See references to *The Times* above.
59. I discuss this at greater length in the next chapter.
60. See Chapter 3.
61. Professor Fallers in *The King's Men*, p. 189, shows that although 'today there are somewhat more places in the hierarchy at levels above the lowest than there were formerly', there is still a broad, undifferentiated base making up some six-sevenths of the population; a middle group of approximately one-seventh, consisting of the relatively few men engaged in the more specialized forms of production and exchange; and a tiny elite of the wealthy, educated and powerful.'
62. Pratt, *Nationalism in Uganda*, pp. 157–78. See Chapter 6
63. For some of these see, for example, Stonehouse, Ch. 7.
64. Pratt, *loc. cit.*
65. All this was exemplified both at the end of 1955 when there were violent attacks upon 'traitors' in Buganda, and in 1959 during the boycott of Asian traders: see the Luganda newspapers for these periods, *passim*.
66. Cf. the way in which Africans who are *not* Baganda are assimilated in Buganda when they immigrate there, even if this process is not without its difficulties, A. I. Richards, *Economic Development and Tribal Change*, Cambridge, 1954, esp. Ch. 7 and Plate I.
67. Two groups – the African rural shopkeepers (who were in direct competition with Asian shopowners – and very frequently belonged to the small Muslim community) and the African taxi drivers (who were in sharp rivalry with Asian bus owners) – had an important influence on, and played a key role in, the boycott; but neither could have built up the boycott to the scale it eventually reached had there been no wider-ranging dissatisfactions to draw upon: see e.g. Stonehouse, pp. 90–1, 94.
68. The decision about this reform was taken by Mr James Griffiths when British Colonial Secretary in 1951. He visited Uganda at the time.
69. *The Advancement of Africans in Trade*, Uganda Protectorate 1955.
70. E.g. the terms of reference of the Constitutional Committee set up in 1959, *Report of the Constitutional Committee 1959*, Entebbe, 1959, p. 1.
71. *Ibid.*; and *Elections to Legislative Council*, Sessional Paper No. 4 of 1957/58, p. 4.
72. E.g. Welbourn, *Rebels*, p. 240 (n. 22).
73. It is impossible to give detailed references for the boycott. I have used *Uganda News* published almost daily by the Department of Information, Kampala, and its regular *Summary of the Local Press*. I have also to acknowledge my debt to valuable typescripts, dealing with the boycott by Miss Lalage Brown, and Rev. F. B. Welbourn. See also Pratt, 'Nationalism in Uganda', pp. 167–70.
74. E.g. Leader on 'A Fight for Democracy', *The Times*, 28 October 1958.
75. *Uganda: Report of the Uganda Constitutional Conference, 1961, and Text of the*

Agreed Draft of a New Buganda Agreement initialled in London on 9th October 1961 (Cmnd. 1523).

76. For further details, see the next chapter.
77. Most of the older chiefs abstained from the upheavals of 1888.
78. See footnote 3 of this chapter.
79. See Chapter 1.

6

Political Parties in Uganda 1949–62

I

On 27 April 1949 the Bataka Party in Buganda was proscribed. On 23 May 1959 the Uganda National Movement, which was also largely confined to Buganda, was proclaimed an unlawful society. During the intervening decade no political party in Uganda was outlawed, but no powerful countrywide political party emerged. There was nothing in Uganda to be compared in vitality with the Convention Peoples Party in Ghana, the National Council for Nigeria and the Cameroons, the Tanganyika African National Union or the Malawi National Congress in Nyasaland. Noting this failure, the Report of the Uganda Constitutional Committee of 1959 declared 'that persons who are genuinely seeking to establish and lead political parties on a national basis in Uganda' were 'performing a vital function in the development of the country's political institutions', and it went on to try and analyse the difficulties which in its view dogged them. Political parties in Uganda, it declared, had been inhibited by the paucity of elections; by the fact that a high proportion of educated people were employed in civil service positions, which prevented them from participating in, and contributing to, party politics; by the operation of British policy which (particularly through its development of District Councils) had maintained the tribal units into which Uganda had been divided; and by the absence of a *lingua franca*. This lack of a *lingua franca*, it concluded, and this division of the country into tribal units, presented a political party 'seeking to operate on a national basis with formidable problems'.[1] Yet all these obstacles to party development could have been found elsewhere in British colonial Africa, but it was only in Uganda that a powerful, extensive, nationalist political party failed to develop during the 1950s. What is more, with one exception (whose significance will be considered in its place), all the factors which the Constitutional Committee noted persisted, yet in the years immediately after 1959, when the Report of the Constitutional Committee was published, two political parties and a further political movement thrust to the fore in Uganda, and showed themselves to be the equals in vitality and effectiveness of such contemporaries as the NCNC and the Action Group in Nigeria, or KANU and KADU² in neighbouring Kenya. The complaint that Uganda had no effective political parties was as a result no longer heard. The roots of these later developments went back to the period before the 1959 Report, and their appearance was not so sudden as a reference to the statements of the Report might lead one to suppose. However, the general statement remains true that whereas during most of the 1950s political parties in Uganda failed to become really effective, in the early 1960s political parties of some considerable strength in the end made their appearance. This chapter attempts to answer the question why all this was so.³

II

In the 1950s Uganda had a European population of about 11,00, hardly any of whom were settlers; a resident Asian population of about 73,000, most of whom were engaged in commerce; and an African population of close on six millions, of whom up to two millions lived in Buganda.⁴

Apart from political changes the European impact upon Uganda had two major facets to it, both of which were fundamental to any general consideration of the country's affairs. First, Christian missionaries had had an extensive influence.⁵ They had at the same time been sharply (and almost exclusively) divided into Anglicans (generally here called Protestants) and Roman Catholics; the division between the two creeds ran deep through most parts of the country, and frequently dominated its local politics. Secondly, Uganda's economy was based for the most part upon expert-directed peasant farming designed to produce exportable primary products which would bring a lucrative return.⁶ For almost half a century cotton was the most valuable export, but by the end of the 1950s, cotton had been overtaken (though by no means displaced) by coffee. A good proportion of the resulting profit found its way into African hands; and even though the Protectorate Government appropriated much of the remainder, it eventually channelled a substantial proportion of it into an African Development Fund which in the 1950s made extensive social development possible, especially in education. In Uganda there was little of the grinding poverty that ran through Asia, and even through parts of neighbouring Kenya. There was apparently more literacy than in Ghana. Uganda was for long noted, by contrast with its East African neighbours, Kenya and Tanganyika, for its steady and relatively rapid advance from a 'traditional tribal' to a 'modern African' society. Yet it was not until 1951 that a political party was founded in Uganda which was at all comparable to the Kenya African Union which was founded in Kenya in 1944 and was itself the heir to several earlier African political organisations there. There was never anything in Uganda comparable to the countrywide Tanganyika African National Union,[7] and in the event Tanganyika, in many other respects by far the most 'backward' of the East African countries, preceded Uganda into independence. In the realm of modern political progress Uganda's earlier promise was plainly, therefore, in the 1950s not fulfilled.

III

Before offering any detailed explanation of this failure it will be convenient to begin by noting the five phases, extending over a considerable period of time, into which the political history of the key central kingdom of Buganda may usefully be divided. The first phase is hidden in the perhaps legendary past,[8] perhaps up to 500 years ago when 'the people lived on the estates and under the rule of their respective clan heads'. At this time, it would seem that political authority rested in the hands of the heads of localised clans and lineages. Subsequently there was a switch to a second phase, when Buganda took to itself a ruler, the Kabaka, who became Sabataka, the supreme head of the clans and clan heads; and then a third phase in which the Kabaka after a protracted struggle, which did not culminate until the nineteenth century, reached the point where, despite the continued existence of the clan heads, he 'administered [the kingdom] through officers whose appointments were highly dependent upon his favour', an achievement which gave the Kabaka very considerable autocratic power.[9] This was the position which Buganda had reached when the first Europeans visited the kingdom in the 1860s and 1870s. To a considerable degree as a result of Buganda's increasing contact with Europeans thereafter, which culminated in the declaration of a British protectorate over the kingdom in 1894, its politics had by 1900 entered a fourth phase – one which persisted in most of its essentials, as we shall see, into the 1950s. During this fourth phase ultimate political power rested in the hands of the British protectorate authorities. They chose, however, to retain Buganda as a monarchical native state with its own structure of government under the umbrella of British colonial jurisdiction. But for reasons which were intertwined with the whole story of the establishment of British authority over Buganda the configuration of political relationships within Buganda itself was now no longer what it had been at the end of the third phase. For simultaneously with the advent of British supremacy an oligarchical revolution had occurred in Buganda and political power within the kingdom now rested, not in the hands of an autocratic Kabaka, but with an oligarchy of senior chiefs. This oligarchy, as it happened, was itself divided into three religio-political parties – two large (a Protestant party and a Catholic party) and one small (a Muslim party) – which arose in part out of the conversions in Buganda to Islam from 1860 onwards and to Christianity from 1880 onwards, and also out of the so-called Christian revolution in Buganda in the 1880s and 1890s.[10] Between them these three religio-political parties monopolised both the important positions in the chiefly bureaucracy and the membership of the native council or Lukiko. Since these parties held such undisputed control over offices of state, and since their leadership was *ouvert aux talents*, they were joined by large numbers of Baganda, the only requirement for *de facto* membership (there was never any *de jure* membership) being adhesion to the relevant religious community. They never established a formal political organisation; they never had presidents or secretaries, committees or branches. They were not concerned to advance any separate programmes for the general good of society. Nor did they represent any pre-existing social, economic or political groupings. Their purpose was to promote and defend the interests of their members, and more especially of those amongst them who had, or aspired to have, place and prestige. After the first generation when adherence to one or other party was largely a by-product of adherence to one or other mission station, recruitment was mainly an accident of birth. If born of Protestant parents, and therefore baptised in a Protestant church, an aspirant was educated at a Protestant school and thereafter automatically found himself a member of the Protestant party. I have shown elsewhere that the dominance of these parties over the main offices of state and over the membership of the Buganda Lukiko remained virtually unchanged between 1900 and 1956, as did the balance of power between them.[11]

During that same period the institutions of this fourth phase of Buganda's political history were exported to almost all the smaller kingdoms and districts which surrounded Buganda and which then went to make up with it the modern state of Uganda.[12] So that by the 1950s wherever one went in Uganda one tended to find in each of its kingdoms and districts, as in Buganda, a distinctly African native government headed by three senior appointed chiefs, who topped a three (sometimes four) tiered hierarchy of territorial administrative chiefs; a native council which, as in Buganda (but not as in neighbouring Kenya), was a purely African council with no British officer presiding; and more often than not a division amongst the people, if not between Muslims, Catholics and Protestants, then between Catholics and Protestants, that was reflected, as in Buganda, both in the allotment of positions in the chiefly bureaucracy and in the membership of the local council or assembly. So long as British colonial authority predominated, these fourth phase institutions – as, for convenience, we may call them for the whole of Uganda[13] – reigned supreme and political conflicts within its kingdoms and districts were confined to the arena which they circumscribed.

But by the end of the Second World War a new phase was looming up; for it now began to seem probable that Uganda would eventually emerge as a self-governing nation-state on an equal footing with others in the modern world. To the most

'advanced' Africans in Uganda,[14] it seemed that membership
of this modern world would demand the formation of new
political and constitutional structures, and from their knowledge of the experience of other self-governing nation-states
they drew the conclusion that one essential requirement would
be some new political parties, which in their particular circumstances as a colonial people would be in the first instance
nationalist and anti-imperialist, and would then, when the
British colonial authorities had been forced to withdraw,
become contenders for the right to control the government of
the future independent Uganda nation-state. All this involved,
as they saw it, a transition to a further (or fifth) phase of
politics, and this time – in the aftermath of the fourth phase
not just for Buganda alone, but for Uganda as a whole. In
considering the formation of political parties which would be
appropriate to such a fifth phase – 'new-style' political parties
as they will be called here[15] – these 'advanced' Africans took
their cue not from the formulas which had governed the religio-
political parties of the fourth phase, but from the rough
impression they had procured of some features of the organisation and structure of the Conservative, Liberal and Labour
parties in Britain, the Republican and Democratic parties in
the United States, the Socialist and Christian Democratic
parties in Western Europe, the Indian National Congress, and
the Convention Peoples Party in Ghana. These notions were
the common parlance of 'advanced' Africans in many other
African territories; but as has already been intimated they were
not put into practice in Uganda either as early or initially as
effectively as elsewhere. The first point for consideration, then,
is an explanation for the tardy emergence of political parties
of – in Uganda terms – this fifth phase kind.

IV

The explanation falls under several heads. In the first place, by
contrast with India or West Africa, hardly any Africans from
Uganda had before the 1950s been educated in, or had visited,
Britain or America. The tiny minority which had been abroad
for further education had been in the main either to Trinity
College, Kandy, in Ceylon, to Fort Hare in South Africa, or

in one or two instances to Achimota College in the Gold Coast; several of these were prominent in later life. Ignatius Musazi, the founder of the Uganda National Congress, was educated in part at Trent College, Nottingham, England. It is difficult, however, to think of any other significant Uganda figure of the 1950s who had an English schooling. Two well-known personalities went to American universities – B. J. Mukasa and Dr E. B. Kalibala – but only the former returned permanently to Uganda; for many years he flourished as a prominent public figure, but he never at this time aspired to be a new style political leader.[16] The considerable influence wielded by this small handful of men suggests how important a larger contingent of people who had 'been-to' might have been for Uganda's affairs. As it was they were a tiny minority, and hardly any of them, let alone any others, had gained even a layman's knowledge of western politics.

At the same time by contrast with Kenya, Tanzania, Malawi, Zambia, Rhodesia and South Africa, where non-African political organisations provided an invaluable stimulus to modern African political movements, there were in Uganda no such organisations for Africans to emulate. Asian political organisations were not unknown in Uganda, but they were never as important as the Indian Congress in Kenya, or even the small Indian Nationalist Association in tiny Zanzibar. (During the 1950s there existed in Uganda a Central Council of Indian Associations, with, for a period, a full-time European Secretary; and a Central Council of Muslim Associations, dominated by the Aga Khan's Ismailis. But the object of both was to preserve Asian interests, not so much by overt political action, but rather by preventing issues affecting the Asian communities from becoming the sport of politics.) As for the Europeans, there was never any specifically European political organisation in Uganda. If the Governor of Uganda wished to address himself specifically to the European community, almost the only opportunity available to him was the annual, dinner of the Caledonian Society. Other expatriate groups in Uganda, more especially African migrants from neighbouring Kenya and Ruanda-Urundi also had their tribal societies, but none of these organisations, European, African, or indeed the various Asian communal organisations either,

173

were ever in any significant sense political. They certainly never provided anything for African politicians to copy.

A further reason for the slow emergence of African political parties in Uganda, by contrast with all its East and Central African neighbours, was to be found in the lack of any country-wide political issues, and the absence of any long-lived conflicts between Europeans and Africans, which might have stirred African feelings deeply. After a short-term heyday for European planters in the second decade of the twentieth century, there was never any suggestion of European non-official domination in Uganda; nor was there ever any prolonged and substantial discrimination in favour of Europeans against which (as everywhere else in East, Central and South Africa) there might have been strong African opposition. There were, moreover, few economic discontents;[17] and there was generally ample space for the educated African minority in the chiefly, ecclesiastical and educational hierarchies of the country. When these two last considerations ceased to be true – in Buganda in the 1940s – there was considerable political discontent, which, significantly enough, eventually provided the basis for the first new-style political party in Uganda in 1952. The only issue prior to this which had ever provoked any widespread African hostility had been the proposal to create an East African Federation. In the 1920s the establishment of an East African Federation was seriously debated, and since this would almost certainly have meant non-official European domination from Nairobi in Kenya, African representatives from Uganda went to London in 1931 to give evidence of their profound opposition to the whole idea before the Joint Select Committee on Closer Union in East Africa.[18] But the proposal was then dropped. Its revival in the modified form which led to the establishment of the East African High Commission in 1948,[19] and Lord Chandos'[20] hint of 'still larger measures' in June 1953, caused on both occasions a political stir, the latter indeed provided the spark which touched off the major crisis that eventually resulted in the deportation of the Kabaka of Buganda in November 1953.[21] But East African Federation was only a potential, never an actual danger, and it never inspired the establishment of an extensive new-style political party.

Another important reason for the slow emergence of new-style political parties was the very liveliness of fourth phase politics in Uganda, which occupied, absorbed and satisfied a great many Africans with political interests. There is still all too little detailed information about the course of African politics in Buganda and the surrounding kingdoms and districts down the years. But there can be no doubt of their vitality. The fact that the various kingdom and district councils were wholly African bodies made them free to discuss a very wide range of questions with as much vehemence as they chose. From 1937 onwards some of these councils began to include Africans who did not belong to the chiefly hierarchy, and by the middle 'fifties 'non-officials' everywhere occupied an overwhelming majority of their seats. Since discussion was in the vernacular, and since the councils were obtaining more and more authority,[22] many Africans who would have had little chance of cutting a figure in national politics found in them a highly rewarding outlet for their energies. The chiefly hierarchy, and particularly the three senior positions at its apex, offered powerful, lucrative and coveted positions, *ouverts aux talents* and constituting a distinctly 'native' government, not merely under, but over against, the British Administration. These positions presented a pinnacle of unusual power, influence, accessibility and autonomy, and the activities of those who held them were as a result always the subject of intense scrutiny by those with political interests. Yet despite their complexity, their extensive and effective African participation, the long prevalent notions of indirect rule which buttressed them, and the *point d'appui* they provided in the struggle for place and prestige, one of the most notable features of these fourth phase governmental and administrative structures in Uganda was the paucity of their functions. Their duties were for the most part limited to tax collection, the upkeep of roads, the maintenance of law and order, and the settlement of customs and conflicts within society. For a long time they had little or no responsibility for education, health or agriculture, and compared with the governments of the larger Northern Nigerian Emirates, for instance, their duties were severely limited. In such circumstances the struggle for power and position, rather than the intricacies of a developing administration, provided the focal point of African public life, and from time to time this struggle could be fierce.

There is no space to elaborate this. Suffice it to recall that local political pressure in Buganda succeeded in forcing the resignation of a Katikiro (Chief Minister) of Buganda in 1941, and then of an Omuwanika (Treasurer) of Buganda in 1945, both of whom were at once long-established and powerful figures, enjoying the warm approbation of the British Administration; or again, that when there were economic and other grievances in Buganda in the 1940s – there were riots in Buganda in 1945 and 1949 – popular political hostility was 'directed against the Buganda Ministers rather than the British Protectorate Government. Much politics could thus operate within the fourth phase framework, and there were men who knew how to manipulate its forces to dramatic effect.

Outside Buganda, as various occurrences during the 1950s were to show, fourth phase politics could also be exceedingly lively. Practically everywhere there was a Catholic party and a Protestant party, and sometimes other political factions representing the different elements which went to make up a single administrative district. Such groupings were frequently very active politically.

The only political organisation of the 1940s which might be thought *prima facie* to have displayed features characteristic of fifth rather than fourth phase politics was the radical Bataka Party in Buganda, or as it more usually called itself the Butaka Union. It would be a mistake, however, to see here a fifth phase political party. It certainly aped some of the attributes of a new-style party; but in the main it drew its inspiration from the traditions of the first phase of Buganda's politics – the Bataka proper are clan and lineage heads – from those of the second phase – in which the Bataka under the Kabaka formed the aristocracy of Buganda – from those of the third phase – in which the Bataka were one of the chief obstacles to the rise of the Kabaka's directly appointed hierarchies of chiefs – in order to express the economic and other grievances of the discontented masses in Buganda with conditions in the fourth phase, and not least the greatly inflated power of the chiefly hierarchy which was such a distinctive feature of the fourth phase régime.

In this connection a further factor militating against the formation of fifth phase political parties may be discerned. For in Buganda by the 1940s there was very considerable popular hostility against the chiefly hierarchy, and one of the major facets of the riots which occurred in Buganda both in 1945 and in 1949 was the very great antagonism and even violence displayed against numbers of the chiefs in power.[23] Now these chiefs were drawn, as in each generation for well over a century past they had been drawn, from the most 'advanced' members of Buganda's society.[24] As late as 1956 the chiefs in the Buganda Lukiko were the best-educated group, in the western sense, in its total membership.[25] Popular opposition to the chiefly hierarchy tended, therefore, to become popular opposition to the 'advanced' elite. The new younger generation of educated men who were looking forward to a fifth phase régime might perhaps proclaim that their purpose was to replace the previous authority of the chiefs by that of new-style political party leaders, but to the great majority of people who had little chance of reaching the pinnacles of power this seemed a distinction without a difference. It was not merely that many of the new 'advanced' generation were patently scions of chiefly families. It was rather that the mass of the people in Buganda had several times before seen such elite groups attain to power over them, and were now highly suspicious of any who seemed to offer little more (except a new uniform) than the old dominance of such small elite groups. This obstacle to fifth phase politics at the very core of the country was a major stumbling block to the formation of new-style political parties.[26]

V

There were a number of reasons, therefore, why the climate for the creation of new-style political parties in Uganda was initially unpropitious. Nevertheless during the 1950s attempts were made to form political parties appropriate to what was thought by 'advanced' Africans to be the demands of fifth phase politics. Uganda was not immune from the anti-colonial fever. The example of the South Asian and West African Commonwealth in their advance towards self-government began to be felt. The establishment of the Federation of Rhodesia and Nyasaland,

Mau Mau in Kenya, self-government in Uganda's northern neighbour the Sudan, and the deportation of the Kabaka of Buganda, served, each in a somewhat distinct manner, to stir political interest out of its fourth phase mould – though, as we shall see, nothing impinged in a sufficiently extensive and decisive manner to galvanise the whole country into a single political movement, as the whole tenor of British policy in Kenya,[27] Lord Twining's last few years as Governor of Tanganyika, and the inclusion of Nyasaland (Malawi) in the Rhodesian Federation, propelled the Africans of those other East African countries into monolithic new-style political movements in each instance. In Uganda – or rather more precisely, in this context, in Buganda – new-style political parties were only formed when leading groups of factions from within the fourth phase order decided that the time had come for them to express themselves in a substantially new form.

The first new-style political party to emerge, in 1952, was the Uganda National Congress; and since it purported to be the embodiment of Uganda nationalism we must consider its fortunes at some length. It took its name, of course, from the Indian National Congress, its purpose being to register a pre-emptive claim, like that of the Indian Congress itself, to be the one true nationalist party (though immediate inspiration probably came from the Indian and African Congresses in South Africa[28]). The UNC sought at the outset to include all races. But this did not last, and from time to time it showed itself both anti-European and, more especially, anti-Asian in outlook. Its main strength came initially from Buganda – from those who had been economically and politically discontented there during the 1940s. From the outset its President-General was Ignatius Musazi, who as President of the Federation of Uganda African Farmers had played such an active part in the political upheavals in Buganda which culminated in the Buganda riots of 1949. Those riots were not particularly successful. The Federation did not provide a sufficiently strong platform upon which its leaders could operate. Congress was formed to serve their radical political purposes more effectively.

Outside Buganda, Congress was at first dependent upon the existence of similar radical elements within fourth phase régimes

178

elsewhere. The first cause which it championed concerned the creation of the Queen Elizabeth National Park in western Uganda; it supported the elements in Toro who were opposed to the reservation of land for this purpose;[29] but as soon as this issue died away, Congress lost its original momentum there. Its following in Bugisu in eastern Uganda came from the members of the Bugisu Coffee Union, who for several years pursued a battle with the Protectorate authorities over the management of the Union. In Busoga, immediately east of the Nile, Congress was dependent upon those in the district who were angry at the Protectorate Government's refusal to grant recognition to all of its small hereditary chieftainships, and to the claims of its chiefs to own land. Its dependence upon local impulses was well illustrated by the protest of its Busoga branch in 1958 against the transference of the headquarters of Uganda's Eastern Province from Jinja in Busoga to Mbale, the capital of Bugisu District, a move which was warmly welcomed by its Bugisu branch. Where there was no local issue within the fourth phase régime to arouse radical feelings, it was difficult for Congress leaders from Buganda to secure much of a welcome. Congress, in consequence, enjoyed a very chequered support. It was fundamentally radical in outlook. It made the typical nationalist demands. It never, however, issued more than the briefest manifesto. It preferred to rely almost entirely upon the unsurpassable slogan 'Self-Government Now'.

In time its radical, and only very partially western-educated, elements were joined by a small group of people, most of whom were Baganda, who had had some form of higher education. But during its first two years (because of its so far ineffectual programme) it failed to win to its membership any significant number of 'advanced' people. This failure was of considerable importance, for these two years proved to be those which immediately preceded the Kabaka of Buganda's deportation, and during the crisis which followed one such group of western-educated men successfully snatched the initiative from Congress, went their own way, and made respectable the creation of further new-style political parties which were unattached to Congress. This constituted a serious breach in the leadership of the embryonic nationalist movement.

Nevertheless during the Kabaka's exile Congress was loud in

its denunciations of the British Government's action, and as early as December 1953 organised a deputation to London to protest. Its leadership, however, was soon in disarray. The President-General remained away in Britain. The original Secretary went off to King's College, Cambridge, as an undergraduate, and the first acting President-General was rusticated in March 1954 on a sedition charge. In May 1954 under a second acting President-General Congress organised a trade boycott in protest against the Protectorate Government's Deportation Ordinance. A year later it made a clamorous demand for immediate self-government; and in April 1956 it vociferously denounced the Governor's *Statement on Elections*.[30] But, since these moves were largely ineffectual, they actually lost Congress support, and on each occasion it found it necessary before very long to retract. At the first election in 1955 for a Katikiro of Buganda it failed, moreover, to procure the nomination, much less the election, of any of its members in the Lukiko. It did, however, in the same year, obtain four of the five seats at the first, indirect, elections for Legislative Councillors[31] for Buganda, and in 1956 and again in 1957 fairly successful 'Congress Weeks' were also organised, in the course of which Congress leaders toured the whole country making speeches and enlisting new members.

The organisation of these 'Weeks' owed much to the small clique of 'advanced' western-educated men who during 1955 decided after all to join Congress rather than any of its rivals in the hope that they might be able to stir its supposedly latent energies into life. Yet it was their presence within Congress which generated its subsequent splits. These all revolved around the personality of Musazi, the President-General, who by this time had returned to the country. If he lacked the ability of an Nkrumah, Awolowo, Azikiwe, Mboya or Nyerere, he had been active in Buganda politics since 1938, which was some fifteen years longer than any of his detractors. During that time, moreover, for all the moderation he had sometimes shown, he had never betrayed the radical elements. He was by far the most widely recognised political leader in the country. So he was none too easily evicted. But to the fury of the 'advanced' members of his party, moderate as well as radical, he never showed any inclination for any positive programme. An

The Namirembe Conference, 1954: Photograph taken on the lawn of
Bishop's House, Namirembe. *Back Row* (left to right): Father J. K.
Masagazi; J. P. Musoke, Kyambalango; A. K. Kironde; E. M. K.
Mulira; E. Z. Kibuka, Secretary; Y. K. Lule; J. G. Sengendo Zake;
T. A. K. Makumbi; S. A. de Smith, Secretary; Dr E. B. Kalibala; and
Father J. Kasule. *Front Row* (left to right): Y. Kyaze; S. W. Kalubya,
Member, Uganda Executive Council; M. Mugwanya, Omulamuzi;
Professor Sir Keith Hancock, Chairman; Sir Andrew Cohen, Governor
of Uganda; Bishop J. Kiwanuka; and J. P. Birch, Resident of Buganda.

'Populism' in Buganda: waiting outside the Lukiko hall, Mengo, 1954.

initial breach between him and the better-educated was healed in 1956, by the return of the 'advanced' group which had broken away, on condition that J. W. Kiwanuka – at that time an intermediate figure – should be installed as Chairman of the Congress Executive. But in July 1957 a second breakaway led to the formation, by a majority of the 'advanced' leaders, of the United Congress Party. On this occasion Kiwanuka and a few of the more important figures stayed with Musazi, chiefly because they knew that he still retained his unrivalled hold over the radical-minded peasantry. The original Congress was soon afterwards gravely embarrassed, however, when towards the end of 1957 two of its former Legislative Councillors – one for Buganda, the other for neighbouring Busoga – who had transferred their allegiance to the new party, the UCP, sought to create a constitutional crisis in Uganda by resigning from the Legislative Council in protest against the Government's refusal to agree at that stage to direct elections to the Legislative Council throughout the whole country. But as it happened their resignations played straight into the hands of those people in Buganda who wished, for reasons to which we must return, to be rid of Baganda participation in the Legislative Council altogether. When these successfully prevented the holding of any further Baganda elections to the Council, the new United Congress Party was quite nonplussed, and before very long disappeared into obscurity. The remnant of the original Congress managed, however, to survive, and before long was even gathering into its ranks a growing number of politicians and their followers from outside Buganda, who were anxious to find a home in an avowedly nationalist party.

VI

Meanwhile two other new-style political parties had been formed in Buganda. Within two days of the Kabaka's deportation in 1953, the political initiative was seized not by Congress (Musazi quickly escaped across the Sudan border), but by a tiny group of 'advanced' western-educated men who had just been elected to the Buganda Lukiko. The most prominent of these was Eridadi Mulira. During the following months it was he and his companions who steered the Lukiko through the prolonged crisis which ensued; and it was this same group which dominated the Buganda Constitutional Committee in 1954, and laid the foundations for the subsequent resolution of the immediate issues in dispute.[32] For over a year Mulira and his group functioned entirely within terms that belonged to the fourth phase régime. Early in 1955, however, they formed themselves into the Progressive Party. This was a genuine attempt to form a fifth phase political party. It represented in the main a largely Protestant group of schoolmasters, prosperous farmers and African entrepreneurs, who had not found a niche for themselves within the Buganda Government hierarchy, but who (as Mulira's own election to the Lukiko in 1953 as one of the three members for the most central country of Buganda indicates) had latterly begun to play an important part in the fourth phase order. Many of them were old boys of the leading Protestant School, King's College, Budo, which had earlier replaced the Kabaka's own household as the main seminary for the country's elite. In outlook the Progressives tended, however, despite their name, to be somewhat conservative, and were certainly less radical than Congress. But they distinguished themselves by publishing a manifesto, in which upon issues other than self-government (which, of course, they advocated too) they made a long list of promises which they hoped would attract support.[33] However as they privately admitted, their task was exceedingly difficult. They could not invent a more urgent slogan than the 'Self-Government Now' of Congress, and upon social and economic questions they found it difficult to step ahead of the vigorous policy of the then reforming Governor, Sir Andrew Cohen. They never enjoyed much support outside Buganda (they rather rashly adopted Luganda mottoes). Mulira's leadership was not particularly imaginative. No member of the party ever looked like winning a seat in the Legislative Council, or, on the party ticket, in a District Council or Lukiko either. By 1958 the Progressive Party was almost as moribund as the UCP.

VII

The third element in Buganda to spill over from a fourth to a fifth phase form called itself the Democratic Party. Perhaps its title would be better explained if one were to say that it was a *Christian* Democratic party. It was almost exclusively Roman Catholic in origin, inspiration and membership, and at first sight would appear to have been the natural opposition to the largely Protestant Progressive Party. It is true that before the party was formed the Roman Catholic Bishops approached the Anglican Bishop of Uganda, and asked if he would join them in sponsoring a joint Christian party. He, however, declined. In so far as the Protestants had a specifically political purpose it was in any event being well served by the existence of the Progressive Party with a leading Anglican layman, Eridadi Mulira, at its head. The Roman Catholic Bishops therefore went ahead upon their own. Coming, as most of Uganda's Roman Catholic Fathers did, from Quebec, France, Germany, Holland and Italy – each with its tradition (unlike Britain, from which the Anglican Bishop came) of close ecclesiastical interest in politics – this was to be expected. From the outset their Catholic Action movement worked in harmony with the new party. Roman Catholic priests assisted its organisers' activities, and some European Roman Catholic laymen proffered their services in support.

The main political target for the Roman Catholic hierarchy was undoubtedly at this time Congress, which they believed was prone to Communist fellow-travelling.[34] Some support for such beliefs was furnished by the 'Foreign Mission' that Congress maintained at this time in Cairo, sponsored originally by Egyptian agencies, and plainly linked with the Communist-inspired anti-imperialist front which operated from there. Moreover, by 1958, of Congress' top leadership, one member had been to Moscow, another to Peking. None of this, however, constituted the dominant issue for the Democratic Party's following in the country. Their chief concern was with the furtherance of the interests of the Catholic elements in the country, and popular support for the Democratic Party was primarily dependent upon the deep hostility amongst Catholics all over Uganda at the preference which *de facto* had been accorded to Protestants in procuring positions within fourth phase régimes. There were certainly grounds for this feeling. In Buganda, for instance, there had never been any but Protestant Katikiros since before the British occupation; there had always

been ten Protestant county chiefs, compared with eight
Catholics; and in the Kabaka's Government which was formed
in 1955 four of the Ministers were Protestants, one a Muslim
and only one a Catholic; yet there were assuredly more
Catholics in Buganda than Protestants, and certainly many
more Catholics than Muslims.

Within the fourth phase order, as we have seen, the Catholics
had long been a party; they were, indeed, together with the
Protestants, one of the two main parties which, with the British,
had helped to create the fourth phase régime there in the first
place. Here and elsewhere the Catholics usually looked to the
chiefs whom they had thrown up for their leaders. In this
instance the transition from a fourth to a fifth phase form can be
especially vividly illustrated. When the Democratic Party was
formed in 1956, it chose as its first President Matayo Mugwanya,
who had been Omulamuzi (Chief Justice) of Buganda – the
highest position to which a Catholic could aspire. He had also
been the unsuccessful Catholic candidate at the first elections
for the office of Katikiro, held after the conclusion of the new
Buganda Agreement of 1955. In 1958, however, his place as
President of the Democratic Party was taken by the leading
African Roman Catholic lawyer, Benedicto Kiwanuka.[35] This
personal change exemplified the transformation of the party
from fourth phase Catholic to fifth phase Democratic.

A number of lesser parties were also formed; for example, the
Uganda Taxpayers Party, the Uganda Labour Party, the
Uganda Nationalist Party, the Uganda Reform Party. None
of these was important; most were one-man affairs, and they
need not detain us.

VIII

There was, however, by 1955 one other grouping of first
importance in the political life of the country, namely Buganda's
neo-traditionalists. They need to be distinguished from all
pre-existing groupings, although like the new-style political
parties they arose out of them. But they cut across, indeed over-
laid, the fourth phase religio-political parties in Buganda. They
included Protestants, Catholics, Mohammedans, as well as
chiefs, radical followers of the Bataka Union, and a number of

younger educated men. Members of all these groups had been deeply scandalised by the Kabaka's deportation in 1953, not only as an insult to their intense tribal pride, but as a portent of the possible destruction of the hard-won privileges and autonomy of their hitherto pre-eminent native state. The more uncompromising of them began to work together as an informal grouping of 'King's Friends', and as the most vociferous supporters of the Kabaka during his exile in Britain they gained control of the Buganda Government on his return to Buganda in 1955. There they soon operated a Cabinet system, together with a number of other instruments of an embryonic nation-state. Their leaders were almost all as well educated as the rest of the country's contemporary elite; they made the most of palatial modern offices, and large German cars. Yet they were at the same time much more atavistic than most of their contemporaries; they remained intensely jealous of the position of the Kabaka and of the status of Buganda; for the most part they abhorred new-style political parties as a threat to traditional values; and the very idea of an overriding central Government for a united self-governing Uganda was anathema to them. Their figurehead was the Kabaka. Their most articulate spokesman was James Lutaya, the county chief of Singo. Their ablest mind was Amos Sempa, Minister of Health and Works in the Kabaka's Government. By 1957 they had established a firm grip over the Buganda Lukiko which had been elected in 1953. They managed to secure the expulsion of about five per cent of its members who would not toe their line. They successfully prevented the holding of direct or any other kind of elections in Buganda to the Uganda Legislative Council in 1958. Having killed the prospect of direct elections to the Lukiko, they won the subsequent indirect election in 1959. They then procured the re-election of their candidate, the outgoing Protestant Katikiro, Mikaeri Kintu, with a considerably increased majority (he was no longer, as in 1955, opposed by a Catholic candidate, but by Y. K. Lule, a Minister in the Protectorate Government, who, though a Protestant and not a political party member, represented the 'advanced' and Catholic forces in Buganda); and having already purged the chiefly hierarchy of all whom they believed to be its weaker elements, they very adroitly ruled Buganda, leaving the Protectorate

Government, for the most part, politically powerless to intervene.

During 1957 and 1958 the question was whether the neo-traditionalists, would, after all, turn themselves into a new-style political party, akin, say, to Ghana's National Liberation Movement. The Ministers in the Kabaka's Government flirted with the existing parties (all of them at once, some averred). Then with something of a flourish, one of the smaller parties which had mushroomed during the Kabaka's exile, and which was headed by the former chairman of the unofficial members of the Lukiko, which had called itself the All-Uganda Party (another overspill from fourth to fifth phase forms) suddenly changed its name to the All-Buganda Party. Its purpose was plain. It hoped to provide a channel for those who wished to preserve and enhance – they themselves said 'restore' – the autonomy of the Buganda Kingdom. This bid failed. The leaders of the All-Buganda Party were not particularly adroit in their public pronouncements, and the real leaders of the neo-traditionalists declined to be wooed.

For the moment the neo-traditionalists decided, it seems, that if they formed themselves into a new-style political party they might be forced to fight their battles upon their opponents' terms. They sought at one stage to refurbish the political role of the clan leaders, which was to hark to the first and second phases of Buganda's political history; but since the Kabaka is, as Sabataka, head of the clans, this was a not unnatural expedient to try. A Council of clan heads was, therefore, formed. It was granted use of the old Lukiko hall within the Kabaka's royal enclosure,[36] and it was held in readiness as a weapon with which to trounce the opponents of the neo-traditionalists. Every Muganda is a member of one clan or another, so that the strengthening of the clan organisation affected every one of them, more especially because the clan heads have unusually extensive powers over inheritance and succession.

Only the outcome of the general elections to the Uganda Legislative Council which in 1958 took place in most districts outside Buganda forced the neo-traditionalists in Buganda itself to think again.

IX

The Uganda Legislative Council was constituted in 1921. Its first African members (three in number) were appointed in 1945. By 1958 it had altogether sixty-three members, over half of whom were Africans, although the Protectorate Government retained a bare majority. This was achieved by the appointment of Africans both as Ministers in the Protectorate Government itself, and also to the Government's own backbench of nominated unofficials.[37] Upon the opposite side of the Council (known as the Representative side), there were six Asian and six European members, and places for eighteen Africans – five from Buganda, two each from Ankole and Busoga, and one each from every other district except Karamoja.[38] The European and Asian seats were filled on the Governor's nomination after he had consulted with 'leaders' of the various non-African communities.

At the time of the negotiation of the Buganda Agreement of 1955[39] the Protectorate Government was pressed by the Baganda negotiators, headed by the later Katikiro of Buganda, Mikaeri Kintu, to agree to the holding of direct elections for Buganda to the Uganda Legislative Council at the next elections. The Protectorate Government reluctantly agreed. There then came pressure from the members of the outgoing Legislative Council for the holding of direct elections throughout Uganda. This was fully supported by the non-African members, who felt that it was undesirable that Buganda should enjoy a special position in this respect, or that there should be two grades of African Representative members, one directly and the other indirectly elected. The new Governor, Sir Frederick Crawford, eventually agreed in 1957 that direct elections for the eighteen African Representative seats should be held throughout Uganda in 1958, if the District Councils in each instance so desired. As a result of Catholic-Protestant rivalries in Ankole, the Protestant group there managed to prevent the *Eishengyero* (District Council) agreeing to the holding of direct elections, so in 1958 Ankole's two seats were filled by two Protestants, according to the pre-existing system under which the Eishengyero sat as an electoral college.

There was at the time a widespread demand in Uganda (which was supported by most non-Africans) for an increase in the African Representative members.[40] Bugisu District Council accordingly informed the Governor that they would not agree to direct elections unless the number of African seats was increased. The Governor, however, refused to accept their condition, and proceeded as if they had declined the direct elections offer; in the event he had to nominate a member for Bugisu. Meanwhile the neo-traditionalists had effectively consolidated their position in Buganda, and (for reasons to which we must return) had managed to prevent the Lukiko reaching agreement with the Protectorate Government on the essential details of the holding of direct elections to the Legislative Council: so direct elections were not held in Buganda either.

The seats to be filled by direct election were thus reduced to ten, and elections for them were held in October 1958. There were forty-five candidates. Although the franchise was restricted, the qualifications for electors were set fairly low, and 626,000 electors were registered (which may be compared with only 127,000 for the 1957 African elections in Kenya, and a mere 29,000 for the five constituencies that in 1958 returned members in the first round of Common Roll elections in Tanganyika). In six constituencies there was a poll of over eighty per cent, and in two more one of over ninety per cent. In Toro there was a poll of only fifty-one per cent, but this reflected a recent quarrel within the fourth phase régime. It was from the organisers' point of view, therefore, a highly successful election.[41]

The results had several interesting features. Although two former Legislative Councillors were among the twenty candidates who lost their deposits, six of the ten seats were won by members of the previous Council. One of these had been a Parliamentary Secretary in the Protectorate Government; the others were former Representative members re-elected in their old constituencies. While special considerations accounted for these results in one or two instances, in several Districts the post of Legislative Councillor seems to have come to be regarded as analogous to that of a senior office holder in the fourth phase régime, a position which in practice a man was deemed to hold much as he might hold the local Treasurership.

The two members with the highest number of votes, Obwangor (Teso) with 76,510, and Obote (Lango) with 40,081, were both the elected Chairmen of their District Councils. Obwangor stood as an Independent; Obote for Congress. In two places only was there a close fight. In Acholi the Congress candidate beat the Democratic candidate by 320 in a 33,000 poll. In Kigezi the Protestant beat the Democratic candidate by just over 5,000 in a 78,000 poll. In the latter, and to a considerable extent in the former, the essence of the struggle was Protestant versus Catholic. The state of the parties at the conclusion of the election was Uganda National Congress five, Democratic Party one, Independents[42] four. The indirectly elected members from Ankole and the nominated representative member from Bugisu were also Independents, making an Independents grand total of seven.

In a vitally important, indeed seminal, development this position was quickly upset. One of the Congress members, Nadiope (N. Busoga), after first being claimed by the Progressive Party, was very soon involved in the foundation of a new party altogether, the Uganda Peoples Union. The UPU was largely inspired by another nominal Congress member, Magezi[43] (Bunyoro), and from the outset the new party also included the two indirectly elected members from Ankole; it was joined by the nominated member from Bugisu, and by two of the directly elected Independents. The state of the parties amongst the African members of the Legislative Council (none of whom were, of course, from Buganda) was therefore very shortly UPU seven, UNC three, DP one, Independents one, vacant one. A party that did not exist at the time of the elections had thus within two months of their completion become the largest in the legislature. The explanation of this *bouleversement* takes us straight into the heart of Uganda's politics in the years after 1956.

X

There had long been widespread jealousy and dislike of Buganda in the remaining parts of the country. Sometimes there were specific reasons for this. Bunyoro, for instance, had for over 50 years been trying to recover the counties which at the turn of the century it 'lost' to Buganda at the instance of the British. But there were some more general complaints too. Buganda had always had more and better schools. It enjoyed a system of individual land tenure which prominent people elsewhere would have liked to secure for themselves, but had long been prevented from attaining by the Protectorate Government. Buganda obviously benefited considerably both from its very much larger size, and from the presence in its midst of the Protectorate's commercial and administrative capitals. Under the British the Baganda had in the past exercised jurisdiction, moreover, in many other parts of the country, and many Baganda obviously still looked upon their neighbours with considerable disdain. During 1957 and 1958 there were various rumours that the old and widespread hostility against them which had thus been generated would become channelled into a new-style political party. In 1957 C. J. Obwangor, the Legislative Councillor for Teso in eastern Uganda, actually announced the formation of the Uganda Peoples National Liberation Movement; but it never flowered, and at the 1958 elections Obwangor stood as an Independent. The UPU, however, was obviously a more extensive affair than this. It was, indeed, an attempt to organise along new-style lines the non-Baganda parts of the country; and its formation represented not just a new outlook in the less advanced parts of the country, but a direct reaction to the establishment in a strong position within Buganda of the Baganda neo-traditionalists.

That establishment had already had an important impact upon the political parties based upon Buganda itself. For during the years 1956–8 the neo-traditionalists had taken steps to strike down the leaders of the new-style Buganda-based political parties lest they betray or undermine the neo-tradition alist régime there. Mulira (President of the Progressive Party) was prevented from attending the Lukiko while a tendentious charge of insulting the Kabaka wound its way through the courts; Mugwanya (the Democratic President) was prevented – actually by the Kabaka himself – from taking the seat in the Lukiko which he had won at a by-election; and Kiwanuka (Chairman of Congress) was arraigned on a trumped-up charge of plotting to kill the Kabaka. The neo-traditionalists then tried to outlaw the political parties altogether; they arranged for the clan heads to issue a statement condemning any Muganda who joined one; and they protested to the Governor against his talks with the party leaders, who, they implied, were seeking to usurp the Lukiko as Buganda's one true voice. These events led the Buganda-based parties in 1958 to form for a time a united front against the Kabaka's Government and the Lukiko.

A parallel story affected Buganda's neighbours. At a meeting of the Lukiko in 1957 the Omuwanika (Treasurer) let slip the remark that Uganda ought to become a 'Federal state under the Kabaka'. In 1958 a committee of the Lukiko announced that they had asked the Protectorate Government to see that the Kabaka became 'King' of the self-governing Uganda. These statements provoked a crescendo of hostility in the rest of the country. The Katikiros of the Western Province kingdoms talked of forming a Western Provincial Council: whereas the Buganda Lukiko had always hoped to unite the District Councils throughout the country against the Legislative Council, the non-Baganda Legislative Councillors now organised the non-Baganda District Councils to pass angry resolutions against the pretensions of the Buganda Lukiko; and after the 1958 elections, when newly returned members from all over Uganda met in the new Legislative Council (by which time the impotence of the Buganda-based parties in Buganda itself had become very plain), the UPU was formed. One of its joint Presidents came from Ankole, the largest district in the Western Province, the other, Nadiope, from Busoga, the largest in the Eastern Province. Over the previous two years the Buganda-based political parties had themselves become increasingly conscious of the need to woo and accommodate the non-Baganda parts of the country; the breakaway UCP, for instance, always had a non-Baganda President, and Congress itself made strenuous, and at first not altogether unsuccessful, efforts to give direction to political activity in areas outside Buganda. But the UPU was, in essence, different from any one of them. It did not represent any one particular element from within the fourth phase order. It was the first party to be formed by non-Baganda. Its leaders all belonged to the Legislative Council; and potentially it represented three-fifths of the whole country, not upon any particularly anti-colonial platform, but primarily in opposition to Buganda and to its neo-traditionalism in particular.

As if to underline the ineffectiveness of the Buganda-based parties, the Congress chose this very moment – early 1959 – for its third major split. This time many who had stood by Musazi in the past broke away. The precipitating cause was a contre-temps over the status of the Congress Foreign Mission in Cairo; but the breach was fundamentally a revolt by the party's 'advanced' members against Musazi's undistinguished leadership. Out of it emerged a rival Congress[44] which elected as President A. M. Obote, the Legislative Councillor for Lango, who, after a political apprenticeship in Nairobi in Kenya, had established himself as the most articulate of the Protectorate Government's critics in the Legislative Council. This break-up left Musazi with a feeble rump. It also undermined the united front which Congress had momentarily established before the elections with the remnants of the other Buganda-based parties. Most of their leaders now wandered frustratedly in the political wilderness.

XI

It is not surprising therefore that they should now have been ready to seize any opportunity to rehabilitate themselves. Their chance came much more quickly than they can have hoped with one other occurrence which followed the 1958 elections. For in accordance with the programme laid down in 1956 by the then Governor, Sir Andrew Cohen, the Protectorate Government now proceeded to establish a Constitutional Committee, largely composed of Legislative Councillors, to draw up plans for elections to the Legislative Council in 1961 upon a Common Roll, together with 'adequate safeguards . . . for non-Africans'. This had long been a contentious issue since hardly any Africans wished to see any prescribed representation for Asians and Europeans maintained in the Legislative Council once self-government came into prospect. The leaders of the UPU and Obote's Congress nevertheless accepted seats on this committee in the well-justified belief that they would have little difficulty in circumventing its terms of reference.[45]

But their acceptance precipitated a further stage in the political story, for those new-style Baganda politicians who had lately seen their parties wither away immediately determined to seize the initiative in denouncing any further toying with special rights for non-Africans, and swung into active opposition against the Constitutional Committee and its members. They were quickly able to draw on the alarm of the Baganda neo-traditionalists at the formation of the UPU (as a barely veiled line-up of the non-Baganda against them), and out of this conjunction of view-points, managed to form a new political party, the Uganda National Movement, in which Musazi of the UNC, Mulira of the Progressive Party, and several former members of the UCP joined with a number of new, and less 'advanced' leaders of the Baganda populace to give themselves a new platform upon which to operate. With the full support of the neo-traditionalists' following in Buganda the UNM quickly became the most powerful political party which either Buganda or Uganda had ever seen. In protest against the Protectorate Government's apparent support for special representation for non-Africans in the Legislative Council (as expressed in the terms of reference it handed down to the Constitutional Committee) the UNM called for a boycott of non-African trade. This was so patently designed to embarrass the leaders of the UPU and Obote's Congress that the non-Baganda soon decided to have nothing to do with it; in consequence both the UNM and the boycott were practically confined to Buganda. Before long the latter had led in a number of places in Buganda to violent and destructive attacks upon trade, people and property. The Protectorate Government eventually decided to intervene, and on 23 May 1959 declared the UNM an unlawful society. Its leaders riposted by changing its name, and in reply to further Government proscriptions, changed it again, but within a week six of them, headed by Musazi and Mulira, had been deported by the Protectorate Government to northern Uganda,[46] and the death knell of the movement, though not, as we shall see, of the boycott, was sounded. In March 1960 the leaders of the UPU and Obote's Congress, in reaction to these events in Buganda, eventually joined forces in a new party called the Uganda Peoples Congress. This, as it happened, was for the moment similarly destructive of new-style party politics, for the leaders of the UPC now held such an overwhelming majority of the African representative seats in the Uganda Legislative Council that they proceeded to function in the main, not through any party organisation but through the Representative Members Organisations of the Uganda Legislative Council. As a result it was not modern party delegations which during 1960 went from Uganda to London to wrestle with the Colonial Secretary over the major issue of how power should be distributed in a self-governing Uganda, but a delegation from the Legislative Council on the one hand and from the Kabaka and his Government on the other. The attempt in Uganda to create fifth phase political parties once more seemed largely abortive.

XII

In reality new-style political parties in Uganda during the 1950s never seized control of the political life of the country for very long. It is time to try and summarise the reasons. In the first place most of the factors which had originally retarded the establishment of new-style political parties continued to operate. Even in the mid-1950s there were still very few Africans from Uganda who had returned from a sojourn in Britain or America. There were still no non-African organisations to copy. Nor was there any major political issue to stir the whole country. The deportation of the Kabaka of Buganda in 1953 was much disliked in the rest of the country, and the rulers of the three western kingdoms were profoundly disturbed at its implications for their own positions. But the issue never aroused Buganda's neighbours to strenuous political agitation in protest, and even in Buganda itself it was never an issue to stir into life a fifth phase political organisation. The handling of the crisis on the Baganda side was conducted not so much by new-style party politicians as by the Lukiko, which in the process – by making protests, sending deputations, etc. – brought its techniques up to date. The whole crisis in fact moved essentially within the framework of Buganda's fourth phase régime, rather than along any fifth phase lines.[47]

Such continuing vitality in fourth phase politics militated severely against the strong development of new-style politics. The Buganda-based political parties, for instance, never fully incorporated the fourth phase groupings out of which they arose. Because, moreover, the major crisis of the decade concerned the Kabaka their potential following was all too easily filched from them by the neo-traditionalists who were most vociferous in his support and came to power upon his return in 1955. Nor was the continuing strength of fourth phase politics confined to Buganda. To take some of the most dramatic examples: in Busoga in 1955 there was rioting because a chief of one religion was appointed county chief of an administrative county which was felt to be the preserve of another religion.[48] Throughout the 1950s there was acute rivalry between different groups in Ankole.[49] In Bugisu there was continuing agitation surrounding its powerful Coffee Growers Cooperative Union.[50] There was acute conflict in Teso between its two major halves – the Iseera and the Ngoratok.[51] And in January 1960 there was rioting in both Bukedi and Bugisu Districts *inter alia* against local chiefs.[52] The continuing importance of fourth phase politics was plainly exhibited too in the elections to the Uganda Legislative Council in 1958. For it was necessary, it seems, even when candidates stood upon new-style party tickets,[53] for any successful candidate to the Legislative Council from outside Buganda to have established himself in the local fourth phase régime, either by being the nominee of a Catholic or Protestant party; or by securing election to the chairmanship of the District Council; or by having, as the sitting member for the constituency, grafted himself onto the local government hierarchy; or by being heir to a locally important but officially excluded royal line; or by a combination of two or more of these processes.[54] Fifth phase politics were still essentially exotic.

There were further difficulties as well. There were no large towns in Uganda. In consequence very few Uganda Africans were town dwellers. The mile-long main road that ran through Katwe, the suburb of Kampala which was the main centre for the country's politics, had no parallels elsewhere in Uganda, and was tiny when compared with the political beehives of Accra, of the Copperbelt in Northern Rhodesia, or of Nairobi in neighbouring Kenya. Allied to this was the lack of trade unions or other organisations (tribal, cultural, etc.) that might have provided the urban base which so many other African political leaders all over the continent enjoyed. Almost all such organisations in Uganda, and more especially the trade unions, were primarily composed of non-Uganda Africans. It is difficult to think of any such organisations which were dominated by Uganda citizens. The lack of large towns meant too that politicians encountered great difficulties in calling together large crowds for political meetings, and that there were grave problems in circulating newspapers. As the 1959 Report explained, there is, moreover, no *lingua franca*. Literacy rates were relatively high, but it was mainly literacy in the vernacular. This made it difficult for politicians to make themselves understood throughout the whole country or for newspapers to circulate at all widely.

The newspaper position casts a specially important light upon political activity in Uganda. Throughout the decade there was an active African press, with a regular production of four or five different newspapers. It was largely confined, however, to Buganda and to its language Luganda, which outside Buganda was only used freely in Busoga. At the outset these newspapers were all weeklies; but by 1959 there were three dailies, at least one of which was selling over 10,000 copies an issue. None of them, however, boasted a foreign news service, and they were all very thin upon country news too. For most of the period they were in essence not newspapers but 'views papers'. Each had its own political bias, but none of them was tied for very long to one party in particular. Their concentration in Buganda meant that Buganda's politics were stirred much more easily and much more frequently than the politics of the rest of the country, and their lack of hard news meant that if any political party, however insignificant, issued a statement it was always sure of procuring a considerable publicity; it was given, that is, a prominence which the real extent of its following never deserved. But the success of the most successful of the Luganda newspapers emphasises that there was no lack of ability in Uganda, not least in matters political (upon which the newspapers largely concentrated). This never produced, however, at this time a powerful nationalist party.

XIII

'We are all Johns waiting for a Messiah', a Uganda politician once remarked, and there can be no doubt that the situation might well have been transformed had a really dynamic political leader appeared. As it was, no leader of any political party, except Musazi, ever captured the public imagination, and he failed most lamentably in the task of leading his own immediate colleagues. In consequence the effective leadership of the various political parties in Uganda fell into the hands of small cliques of 'advanced' men, who belonged, for the most part, to the upper echelons of Baganda society. Their numbers were always small, yet there were rather too many of them to allow any single one of them to assume on his own a prominent position with the lesser-educated populace. For all of them membership of a party's central committee was a *sine que non* of their support for a political party. Messrs. Mulira, Makumbi and Basudde long dominated the Progressive Party, Messrs. Musazi, J. W. Kiwanuka, Paulo Muwanda, S. M. Sekabanja, Apolo Kironde, and Dr B. N. Kununka were variously influential in the Congress. Luyimbazi Zake tried his hand at running the All-Uganda Party, but in 1957 joined the 'advanced' members of Congress, led by Erisa Kironde and Senteza Kajubi, to form the UCP in which David Lubogo, Dr E. M. K. Muwazi and Godfrey Binaisa were prominent too. Benedicto Kiwanuka eventually took charge of the Democratic Party. The fortunes of the various parties followed closely the political inclinations of the small co-operative cliques which these relatively few men formed. But with the possible exception of the first three UNC names, and later Benedicto Kiwanuka, none of them was ever a full-time politician. They were all primarily active professionally as lawyers, doctors, editors, schoolmasters, accountants, etc. They were never more than 'week-end' politicians.

Such organisation, however, as the parties displayed was almost invariably the work of these few men – most usually upon their free week-ends. Parties had executive committees in which they sat with a certain number of others. Very occasionally – once, perhaps, in three or four years – a party convention would be held. Subscriptions were sometime paid, but it was said that when the UCP leaders broke finally with Musazi in 1957 there was considerably less than £10 in the Congress treasury. Party branches were nominally established in many parts of the country, and from time to time political excitement might be sufficient to stir local rural leaders into activity. But more frequently, party organisation lay moribund. It was only in the Congress outside Buganda that branches ever displayed any considerable activity on their own, and even the course of these upcountry branches was sometimes chequered. In Uganda, in the 1950s, one saw nothing at all comparable with the signboards marked 'TANU Headquarters' which, by 1956, were appearing in many townships and trading centres throughout Tanganyika. It was only very slowly that the parties opened headquarters in Katwe, the political centre on the edge of Kampala. These never comprised more than a one-roomed office, a clerk (perhaps), a typewriter and a signboard outside. Even Congress never worked its widespread radical following into a strong party organisation. Such failures were aggravated, not so much, as the 1959 Report suggested, by the paucity of elections – they were just as infrequent in Kenya and Tanganyika – as by the relatively large electorate (626,000) which was able to register for the 1958 elections in the areas outside Buganda. This was a far larger number than any of the new-style political parties in Uganda with their restricted organisations could ever have hoped at this time to have reached. Small wonder that politics still subsisted very largely in fourth phase terms.

XIV

There can be no doubt too that there were serious obstacles to the formation of new-style politics in Uganda because of the cross-currents which were affecting Buganda at this time. Some of these have been touched on already, and will be referred to again. But one development in the 1950s seems, in conjunction with the other events of the decade, to have taken on a special importance.[55] We have noted already that by the 1940s the chiefly hierarchy in Buganda was intensely disliked by large numbers of the ordinary populace in the kingdom. In 1949 at the height of the riots in that year the rioters presented a petition to the Kabaka containing five requests, the first three of which were:

I.   Your Highness should open the rule of democracy to start giving people power to choose their own chiefs.
II.   We want the number of sixty unofficial representatives [in the Lukiko] to be completed.
III. We demand the abolition of the present [Buganda] Government.[56]

But these riots availed little; they were soon quelled; and the chiefly hierarchy remained for the time being firmly in the saddle. In March 1953 the Kabaka and the Governor of Uganda made a joint announcement which promised that for the first time there would now be a majority of elected members in the Lukiko, and that the Kabaka would choose his Ministers after consultation with a committee of the Lukiko;[57] but these reforms had only been partially executed when on 30 November 1953 the Kabaka was deported.[58]

The crisis which followed presented the populace of Buganda with a quite unusual opportunity for striking a crippling blow at the over-mighty authority which the chiefly hierarchy in Buganda had enjoyed since the turn of the century. The Kabaka was in conflict with the British; and the British were now the major support of the greatly extended authority of the chiefs. The Kabaka's authority, moreover, had suffered decline throughout the fourth phase of Buganda's political history (by comparison with its autocratic position at the culmination of the third phase), so that if the Kabaka were to prove himself a resolute political protagonist – as at last he now seemed – a popular movement in his support, which gave him a very much greater measure of authority than he had had for well over half a century, had as good a chance as anything else of reducing the inflated authority of the chiefs. One of the major developments which underlay the so-called 'Kabaka crisis', therefore, was the formation of a formidable alliance between the Baganda populace and the Kabaka, which, at the conclusion of the immediate crisis in 1955, brought the chiefs in Buganda, after their long years of being responsible to no-one but their fellows and the British Administration, firmly back into the position where they were once more under decided obligations both to the Kabaka and to the ordinary people of Buganda. For two or three months after the Kabaka's return from exile in 1955 there were serious attacks, often accompanied by violence, against those chiefs who were thought to have been disloyal to the Kabaka (and in consequence to popular feeling) whilst he was in exile. These attacks belonged essentially (to a degree which appears to have escaped notice) to the same sequence of events as the attacks upon chiefs in Buganda in 1945 and 1949. Certainly it was only now, in 1955–6, that the old, and formerly largely abortive, popular campaign against the overgrown authority of the chiefly hierarchy achieved its most resounding success. It was only in 1955 that the chiefs lost their former very considerable measure of independence, and it was only in the years after 1955 that they found themselves subjected to every wind of popular feeling. A popular desire for this very considerable change in the political structure of the Buganda kingdom had been fermenting for at least a generation past. In consequence its attainment had a special importance for great numbers of Baganda, and this helps to explain why they should now have showered so much loyalty upon the Kabaka; for they were delighted at the part he had played during the crisis over his deportation, which, among other things, had enabled them to break the chiefs' previous hold; and in the aftermath of this achievement a re-establishment of his former autocratic authority looked like being the most likely guarantee against the rise of any new oligarchy.

All this was of first importance to the fate of new-style political parties. For as has already been noted, their leaders were to many of the populace only one more version of the old, ambitious, overmighty elite. Furthermore, although the educated political leaders and the populace both felt the need to break out from the fourth phase régime in Buganda, the former thought that it should be replaced by a régime in which political parties (in which they, of course, would predominate) should rule, whilst the latter were chiefly concerned to ensure that the very concept of a privileged power elite should be done away with altogether. It is notable that those parties – in particular the Progressive Party, the breakaway United Congress Party, and the later Uganda National Party – which patently represented very little more than the interests of the new elite never won popular support; that Congress itself was prominent only when it championed causes with a wide popular appeal – as on its formation, and periodically during the Kabaka's exile; and that the most powerful movements in Buganda in the years that followed were those which were of special concern to the ordinary populace.

Following the long-awaited victory over the chiefs at the time of the Kabaka's return in 1955 the populace in Buganda became a formidable political force. Because their interests and those of the 'King's Friends' (amongst the Buganda chiefs, in the Buganda Lukiko and in the Kabaka's Government) coincided – the elevation of the Kabaka to an autocratic position admirably suited the purposes of all of them – their co-operation in the neo-traditionalist movement in Buganda was readily effected, and gave it great power. But the full force of the newly dynamic energies of the Baganda populace was not demonstrated until the boycott of Asian and other non-African trade in Buganda in 1959–60. The Uganda National Movement, which was responsible for launching this, became very powerful precisely because its educated leaders, having reached a dead-end with their new-style political parties, went into partnership in a much more co-operative manner than they had ever done hitherto with the populace and with the less educated and less 'advanced' men,[59] who were giving the populace leadership. For the educated leaders, and even for the Kabaka's Government, the boycott mainly represented, as we have seen, an attack upon the Constitutional Committee of the Legislative Council and particularly its non-Baganda (not to say anti-Baganda) members. For the Baganda populace, however, the boycott was directed primarily against the grip which Asian entrepreneurs in particular had established over the economic life of the rural areas. This grip provoked anger elsewhere, but outside Buganda such sentiments were held in check, partly no doubt because the populace elsewhere was not so politically aroused, but chiefly because most non-Baganda were now primarily concerned to do nothing to support those in Buganda who were opposed to the Constitutional Committee and its non-Baganda members. The really significant fact, however, about the boycott in Buganda for present purposes was that it continued to flourish long after the educated leaders of the UNM (and its reincarnations) had been deported to northern Uganda, and even after the Kabaka's Government had turned its face against it. All too little is known, to outsiders, about how the boycott was sustained. But its continuance into 1960 is plain evidence that there were popular forces at work in Buganda which were capable of acting quite independently both of new style political leaders and of the Kabaka's Government – both of whom, as embryonic élite groups, tended in popular terms to be highly suspect.

At the very hub of Uganda, therefore, in the one place where there were any number of 'advanced' people to give shape to new-style politics, there existed a popular political ferment, whose dimensions new-style political party leaders never properly discerned. The objectives of those involved in this ferment were in critical respects diametrically opposed to those of the political leaders, and their full co-operation was only available on their own highly particularist terms. The one prominent party politician who, for all his lack of success in other directions, had long-standing links with these popular forces was Ignatius Musazi, the long-continuing President-General of Congress. Here was the basis of his political strength, which was otherwise quite incomprehensible.

XV

Yet even this consideration – added to all the others which have been adduced – does not provide the final explanation of the chequered story of Uganda's political parties during the 1950s. For variations on most of these themes existed elsewhere, yet elsewhere they were generally submerged, as they never were in Uganda. For the Uganda story there yet remains to be noted the most important consideration of all. This is simply that the emergence of fifth phase politics in Uganda was inhibited above all because there was no deep-rooted sense of urgency behind the nationalist demands which at this time the new-style political parties made their especial *raison d'être*. This was emphatically not because Africans in Uganda did not want to become self-governing. On the contrary it was primarily because they knew they were going to become self-governing.

It is this consideration which at bottom set Uganda apart from many other colonial territories. It was not until almost the eve of Indian independence in 1947 that most Indians, after many long years of vociferous nationalist pressure, began to feel that the British really might transfer political power into Indian hands. Similarly in West Africa it was by no means certain until the beginning of the 1950s that the British would grant independence to African countries without Africans having to display the political pressure which the Indians had had to bring to bear. On the other hand, by 1953, when Lord Chandos, the British Colonial Secretary, declared that Uganda would one day have self-government as a 'primarily African state', and certainly by 1955, when the immediate crisis over the Kabaka's deportation had been resolved, it was becoming fairly certain that a major political struggle was not going to be required in British Africa before self-government was attained – at all events in those territories, such as Uganda, where there were not settled non-African minorities sitting in positions of power. By 1957, when Ghana attained its independence, all serious doubts were removed. Although there was much concern in Uganda over the constitutional position of non-Africans in the country, they were never at this time, and never really looked like being, the political problem for African nationalists in Uganda that they most decidedly were for Africans in Kenya and central Africa, and even in Tanganyika. The only obstacle, it seemed, to self-government for Uganda was the British Government, and on their record in South Asia and West Africa, it looked fairly certain that they would be true to their commitment to transfer power to African hands in Uganda as well. For these reasons the urgency was removed from nationalist politics in Uganda, before nationalist parties, such as the Congress, had secured a widespread hold upon the country, and anti-colonial sentiments were never sufficiently aroused to thrust the obstacles to new-style politics, which we have noted, into second place. Two preliminary but important results followed. Very few men of ability were ready to devote themselves to the peculiarly fortuitous life of a full-time politician in Uganda, and there was no compulsion resting upon those with nationalist sentiments to pull together whatever the cost. Modern political parties basing themselves upon nationalist demands were as a result left peculiarly rudderless.

But even this was not the whole story; for there was a further consequence of the utmost importance as well. During the mid-1950s no-one troubled for a time to probe the full implications of the assurances and probabilities about self-government very deeply. But at the beginning of 1957 the crucial point was seized upon by Buganda's neotraditionalists; and in consequence they became the pivot upon which the newly dynamic polarities in Uganda's politics swung. They were the first to have their eyes opened to the political realities underlying the changing scene because they suddenly became frightened by the much-publicised actions which in 1957 the CPP took against the traditionalists in Ghana, whom the Baganda neotraditionalists saw as their own counterparts there. At the time of Mr Edusei's fulminations against chiefs and the National Liberation Movement shortly after Ghana attained its independence, friends of the Kabaka in Buganda, and supporters of the neo-traditionalists there, began to inquire very anxiously how democracy could be *prevented* from setting foot in Uganda. They also began to ask how any Muganda could ever hope to become Prime Minister of Uganda. They grasped, that is, the vital fact about Uganda's politics by this time: the real issue was not the attainment of self-government – that was assured – but the question of the *locus* of power upon its attainment.

Their agitated inquiries gave a new urgency to two related issues, which were by no means new, but which now began to dominate the political life of the whole country: first, the question of the security of the neo-traditionalist régime within Buganda itself, and secondly the possibility that in a self-governing Uganda, Buganda might be at the mercy of a hostile combination of its neighbours. These were, of course, related issues, and in due course became conjoined in a widely felt determination to defend the autonomy of Buganda.

The crucial change in the political life of the country is best illustrated by the *volte face* of Mikaeri Kintu, Buganda's Katikiro. In 1955 he had led the demand for direct elections to the Uganda Legislative Council, because he believed that they would constitute an important advance towards self-government. But by 1957 he had come to have second thoughts, and soon set about preventing direct elections in 1958 in Buganda for the Uganda Legislative Council (or for the Buganda Lukiko) because he feared that they might throw the gates open to domination within Buganda itself by those – the new-style political parties – who in the long run might well make very little effort to preserve its neo-traditional régime; and because he feared that if heads alone were counted in Uganda, Buganda, which only contained two-fifths of the population of the whole country, would soon be dominated by those – the non-Baganda – who constituted its majority.

From all this the political developments of the later 1950s followed. It was because the Buganda neo-traditionalists grasped so firmly the truth about the political issues which *really* had to be resolved in Uganda that they outgeneralled so adroitly most of the Buganda-based parties, killed the opportunity for them to participate in direct elections, and took every step to attack them as so many snakes in the grass. So soon as the non-Baganda began to grasp equally firmly the issue which the Baganda neo-traditionalists had thrust to the fore they formed the UPU. To this step the alliance in the UNM between the neo-traditionalists and those party politicians in Buganda who found themselves without a following (and shared the neo-traditionalists' concern at the appearance of anti-Baganda solidarity amongst the surrounding peoples) was the answer; and the amalgamation between Obote's dissident Congress and the UPU to form the UPC constituted the further reply from the non-Baganda. This realignment of political forces into new political parties did not for the moment, however, offer any immediate prospect of a healthier existence for new-style political parties, for the UNM expired shortly after it was proscribed; and against the pretensions of the Baganda the non-Baganda preferred for a time to operate through the Representative Members Organisation of the Uganda Legislative Council rather than through the UPC. The nadir in the fortunes of new-style party development in Uganda had been reached.

XVI

Nevertheless a strenuous political struggle in Uganda had now been joined. Most Baganda were now determined that immediate steps should be taken to ensure that upon the attainment of self-government the autonomy of their kingdom should be assured, and many of them felt that the only effective safeguard would be the establishment of Buganda's separated independence entirely on its own. This view found expression in a series of documents which the Katikiro of Buganda published in January 1960 under the title *Buganda's Position*.[60] Most non-Baganda, however, were now determined that no such future should be granted to the Baganda, and for their part were anxious that a unitary constitution, or at all events a strong central government for the whole of Uganda, should be established without more ado. This was not only because they wished to curb the pretensions of the Baganda, and press forward with the opportunity which now presented itself to them for the first time to lord it over the Baganda; it was also because the excision of Buganda (incorporating as it did the hub of Uganda) could only have a very seriously disruptive effect on the whole of the rest of the country. The charter of the non-Baganda by this time was the Report of the 1959 Constitutional Committee which had recommended direct elections to the Legislative Council on a Common Roll throughout the country, and the establishment thereafter of a mainly African central Government headed by an African Chief Minister – proposals which in their existing form were anathema to the Baganda.

The Baganda completely failed, however, to get the Protectorate Government to agree to the separated independence of their country. But (for fear of too sharp a reaction from them) they did cause the Protectorate Government to hesitate, and in February 1960 when the Government announced that it accepted most of the recommendations of the 1959 Committee, it also announced, not only that a Commission would be established to consider the future relationship between Buganda and the rest of the country, but that it could not accept the recommendations of the Constitutional Committee for the early establishment of a largely African central Government headed by an African Chief Minister. This last decision outraged the non-Baganda (and those few in Buganda who were opposed to the neo-traditionalist régime there). It led many Baganda, however, to give their attention once again, as they had occasionally in the past, to the less drastic solution than the one they had recently championed, of trying to safeguard the interests of their kingdom by creating a federal constitution for Uganda.

It had long been the hope of the neo-traditionalists in Buganda that one of the ways by which they might direct events along the lines they desired would be to enlist the local governments and councils spread throughout Uganda in support of an attack upon the central Uganda Legislative Council, in an effort to ensure that it never became all-powerful over them. This idea enjoyed considerable appeal so long as it looked as if the Legislative Council was little more than the rubber stamp of the British Protectorate Government, and for a long time the Protectorate Government not unnaturally opposed all attempts to call a meeting of representatives along these lines. But after the new constitution of 1958 and the successful elections outside Buganda to the central Legislative Council in that year, and after the formation of the UPU and all the events which had led up to it, there was no longer very much danger of an effective line-up between the non-Baganda councils and the Buganda Government and Lukiko against the Legislative Council and all that it represented as the foundation for a strong central government for the whole country. Rather the danger now was that the Baganda and the non-Baganda would refuse to co-operate with one another altogether. In consequence the Protectorate Government now warmed to the idea of conferences between the non-Baganda governments and councils and the Buganda Government and Lukiko as a first step towards bringing the two sides together. Discussion at these conferences quickly centred upon the issue of whether Uganda's future should be as a federal or as a unitary state. At the end of the second conference, at Makerere in June 1960, the Katikiro of Buganda found himself in a minority of one in favour of a federal constitution for the whole of Uganda. For the Baganda it was a moment of truth. Their long-standing hope that the non-Buganda local governments could be enlisted in a campaign against a strong central government for Uganda was shattered. Now fully aroused, the non-Baganda for their part shortly afterwards sent a delegation of their Legislative Councillors to London to press the British Colonial Secretary to proceed with the implementation in full of the recommendations of the 1959 Constitutional Committee. They were quickly followed, however, by the Kabaka of Buganda who went to impress upon the Colonial Secretary the adamant opposition of the great majority of his people to the whole proceeding. A corresponding moment of truth occurred for the non-Baganda immediately afterwards; for upon his return to his kingdom the Kabaka received a vociferous welcome back from his people.

Many were bewildered by these events; it did not look as if the delegations had made any impression upon the mind of the British Government. But the two moments of truth were amongst the most encouraging events for years; for they brought both sides up against sharp political realities. It was now plain not only that, short of force, the Baganda could not make the non-Baganda toe their line, but also that the non-Baganda could not coerce the Baganda either. One urgent question, however, remained: were the elections to the Legislative Council, which were now due, to be held before or after the Relationships Commission had reported? The British Government decided that the elections should come first. This decision was criticised in some quarters because it was clear that large numbers of Baganda would not participate in the elections lest this should in any way prejudice the future of their kingdom. But the Relationships Committee was only now being established, and postponement of the elections until it had reported would have infuriated the non-Baganda. What was more it would have allowed the Baganda to feel that they could dictate further concessions, and it would have removed the opportunity for gauging the exact strength of the forces which were opposed to Buganda and to its neo-traditionalists. Many Baganda, however, were so infuriated by the decision that on 1 January 1961 the Lukiko declared Buganda independent. Yet this availed little, and in March 1961 elections to the Legislative Council were held nevertheless. Strenuous efforts were made by the Protectorate Government to register voters in Buganda; in the event, however, only 35,000 names out of an estimated 1,000,000 who were eligible were enrolled. But by contrast with 1958 all the necessary election formalities were completed in Buganda in 1961 and 20 Baganda members were returned to the Legislative Council (albeit on a minuscule vote). Outside Buganda the elections were an even greater success than in 1958; the total number of votes cast was 983,718 – over half as much again as in 1958.

XVII

The 1961 elections undoubtedly marked a distinct step forward into fifth phase politics. In the months preceding them yet another party had mushroomed in Buganda, the Uganda National Party; it failed, however, to win any seats. The final rump of the original Uganda National Congress, moreover, was trounced; it secured only a single seat. For the rest two new-style political parties practically swept the board between them.[61]

With the advent of an election the leaders of the non-Baganda could no longer operate through the Representative Members Organisation of the Legislative Council, and so fell back upon the parties to which they belonged. The chief of these was the UPC whose prime function – opposition to the pretensions of the Baganda – fitted precisely the widespread anti-Baganda feeling in the rest of the country which was now running high, and in the event the UPC won thirty-five seats in the Legislative Council. Its President, A. M. Obote, however, only became Leader of the Opposition, for the majority of seats in the Council was won not by the UPC but by the Democratic Party (even though the UPC beat the Democratic Party in sheer voting strength at the polls by 488,334 votes to 407,416).

This outcome must be explained. The Democratic Party still primarily represented the Catholic forces in the country. Its leader, Benedicto Kiwanuka, however, was a Muganda and it was still based in Buganda. But the DP was the only one of Buganda's new-style political parties which had not sunk its fortunes in the Uganda National Movement in 1959. For the leadership of the UNM was predominantly Protestant, and the Buganda Government, with which the UNM was at first in partnership, was predominantly Protestant also; and if these forces were to be successful in gaining control over the future destinies of Buganda, there was little chance that the balance of political advantage in Buganda would be readjusted in favour of the Catholics (as the census figures clearly warranted). Like the populace in Buganda, and like 'advanced' Protestants, many Catholics were anxious to break out of the mould in which Buganda's political history had been cast for the past half century. But whereas the populace wanted to reduce the power of all élites, and whereas 'advanced' Protestants wanted to see political power pass to new-style political parties (but were very well satisfied with the Protestants' *de facto* predominance), the primary objective of many Catholics was to ensure that in any advance to a fifth phase in the political history of the country they had a share of élite positions which should be much more commensurate with their numbers than in the past. At the same time because the Democratic Party withheld its support from the UNM and other manifestations of neo-traditionalism, it came to represent – for there was little else to represent – those (admittedly very small but not altogether insignificant) elements in Buganda who were opposed to the entrenchment there of the existing neo-traditionalist régime. Both of these strands, the Catholic and the anti-neo-traditionalist, were represented in the Democratic Party's President, Benedicto Kiwanuka, and in some of his leading colleagues, and the existence of the anti-neo-traditionalist strand even attracted some Protestants to the Party.

Upon the establishment of Protectorate Government machinery to run the 1961 Legislative Council elections in Buganda, the Democratic Party proved to be the only party in Buganda which had the following to contest them in the teeth of neo-traditionalist opposition. In consequence, on a remarkably low poll, they won nineteen seats in Buganda. Elsewhere they picked up a further twenty-four seats. These were won wherever there were considerable numbers of Catholics, who were now fearful of the *de facto* dominance of Protestants in the UPC.[62] It was from this medley of political configurations, therefore, that the Democratic Party won a majority of seats in the Legislative Council. So that for all the advance to fifth phase politics fourth phase politics plainly still obtruded. When, however, the new Legislative Council met, a Democratic Party Government, led by its President Benedicto Kiwanuka (who became Minister without Portfolio and Leader of the House), faced a solid UPC Opposition, and throughout the life of this Legislative Council a clear, and firmly based, 'two-party system' operated. This result gave these new-style political parties a confidence which none of them had ever enjoyed before.

XVIII

With the conclusion of the elections, however, nothing else or great significance could eventuate until the Relationships Committee appointed to advise on the future relationship between Buganda, the rest of the country and the central African Government of Uganda, had reported. This is perhaps an appropriate moment, therefore, to consider Buganda's position at this time with the somewhat greater attention which its crucial importance at this juncture deserves.

Buganda, it has to be remembered, has a history stretching back for anything up to five hundred years. Growing up under the shadow of what was once the very much larger neighbouring kingdom of Bunyoro-Kitara, its struggle for survival was not without setbacks, but by the nineteenth century its independence from Bunyoro was assured, and it was fast becoming the most formidable kingdom in its area. Under the impact of this success its people had come to contemplate their future with great confidence. From the middle of the nineteenth century, however, they have been engaged in defending the autonomy of their kingdom against a whole series of formidable threats to it. In the 1850s they defended its autonomy against some Zanzibari traders; in the 1870s against the threat of an Egyptian advance from the northward; in the 1880s and early 1890s against European conquest; between 1897 and 1926 against the administrative ambitions of the British Protectorate Government; in the 1920s and 30s against the embryonic Uganda Legislative Council; during the same period against the threat of an East African Federation dominated by the Kenya settlers; between 1926 and 1955 against the administrative encroachments of the

Protectorate Government; in the later 1940s against the possible results of the establishment of the East African High Commission; after that time against a greatly strengthened Uganda Legislative Council; in 1953 against the suggestion once again of East African Federation; in 1953–5 against the conceivably dangerous implications of the deportation of the Kabaka; during most of the 1950s against both the threat of 'multi-racial' government, and the Protectorate Government's plans for a unitary state in Uganda. With limited exceptions, however, every threat was sooner or later warded off. Since the 1890s Buganda had lost its ultimate independence to the British Protectorate Government, but even this had never destroyed its autonomy; it had so far only circumscribed it. Yet as the one persistent curb upon Buganda's freedom of action it is no doubt understandable that by 1 January 1961 the Buganda Lukiko should have reached the point where they were anxious to cast it off altogether, more especially since by this time they were faced by a very grave problem which made the decision especially urgent; for it now looked as if Buganda was facing the greatest crisis in its whole history. For if the Protectorate Government, and more particularly the non-Baganda, were to have their way, the autonomy of Buganda would now be submerged in a unitary Uganda nation-state, with the consequence that after all these long centuries of strenuous and hitherto almost invariable success, it was in very grave danger of being lost beyond recall.

For a great many Baganda this was an issue of profound importance. And it did not stand alone. During the previous hundred years Buganda had never ceased to undergo regular political and constitutional reform. It would be tedious to compile a further list. Suffice it to say that it is difficult to think of a single decade during the previous hundred years during which there had been no political or constitutional reforms in Buganda. The result, by 1960, was that there existed at Mengo, Buganda's capital, many of the institutions of a modern nation-state: a parliament (with a 'Speaker'), a cabinet, a civil service, a treasury. What is more, on successive occasions many of the most 'advanced' elements in Buganda had found their way into the inner circles of power in the kingdom. This had been true for the 'Christians' in the 1890s – witness the career of Sir

Apolo Kagwa, Katikiro of Buganda from 1889 to 1926; it had been true for the youthful generation of the 1920s – witness the career of Serwano Kulubya, Omuwanika (Treasurer) from 1928 to 1945; while perhaps the most striking example in the 1950s was the accession to the Ministry of Education in the Kabaka's Government in 1958 of Abu Mayanja, formerly the first Secretary-General of the Uganda National Congress.[63] The truth is that many of the most 'advanced' Baganda had seen in their kingdom's autonomous government something which deserved their ungrudging allegiance, since at no time had it been allowed to become fossilised.

In this connection it is a serious mistake, to imagine that neo-traditionalism in Buganda was just a plot of the 'King's Friends'. It becomes important to distinguish five themes in its course following the Kabaka's return from exile in 1955. At first the 'King's Friends' were concerned to be rid of those who had not been 'loyal' to the Kabaka whilst he was away. Then those 'King's Friends' who had gained office were anxious to consolidate their hold upon place and power in Buganda; and we have already noticed that, for reasons of their own, the Baganda populace were keen supporters of neo-traditionalism as well. To these earlier concerns there had been added by 1959–60 the fears of numbers of other Baganda not only for the now threatened autonomy of their kingdom but for their own fate in a unitary Uganda dominated by the non-Baganda. It became common, for example, to hear suggestions that the overseas scholarships and other educational grants which Baganda had been enjoying hitherto would be cut. There were in fact a great many Baganda who, without supporting the more extravagant postures of the neo-traditionalists, were now genuinely worried about how the non-Baganda, who in a unitary state would be on top of them for the first time, might decide to treat them.

Behind all this lay one more issue whose features if hazy it is essential to visualise. The African world as we are frequently yet correctly informed is undergoing a massive transformation which to an uncomfortable extent has been dependent upon the organisational and technological discoveries of the West. In this torrent of change it is hardly surprising that people should be profoundly concerned about the bases of their personal and collective identity, and that there should be a search for, and a clinging to, those guide lines which are indubitably autochthonous. Now this search was peculiarly difficult in Africa. An Indian could turn to the patent richness of his own historical, cultural, religious and philosophical heritage, and like Jawaharlal Nehru could find in his 'Discovery of India' the life-line which he needed. But Africa (and it would be a mistake to suggest otherwise) has for the most part no such abundant riches readily to hand. It became imperative, therefore, that the best use should be made of what riches were available; that the search should be on for the values of 'Negritude' and 'the African Personality' (the kind of search which would be superfluous to a Nehru); and that the spirit of Pan-Africanism should be fostered so vigorously.[64] It was hardly surprising, too, that the Gold Coast, for example, should become Ghana, and the Southern Rhodesian African National Congress the Zimbabwe African Peoples Union, even if both were a little contrived.

For many, very many, Baganda, however, this problem hardly arose; their identity lay with their age-old but constantly reinvigorated kingdom – until its whole future was challenged, as it undoubtedly was, by any demand that it should submerge itself in a unitary state in which it would be seriously outnumbered by its potentially iconoclastic neighbours. These neighbours, of course, had their own problems too. For too long (many of them felt) they had been satellites of Buganda. However strong, moreover, might be the appeal of neo-traditionalism to the Baganda, it had for them far too many archaic and autocratic overtones to be at all acceptable; their conflict with the Baganda by 1960–1 was, therefore, at bottom, a conflict about the values and cultural identity of the wider country to which they now belonged. To many Baganda it seemed nothing less than sacrilege to lay hands upon an identity which was already in full flower; but to the non-Baganda the scent was abhorrent. Here, then, was no petty conflict of rapacious interests alone; but a drama with a high purpose. It was made especially acute, moreover, because of the existence of a sub-plot.

XIX

Much of the drama of Buganda's internal politics over the last hundred years had, it must be noted, lain in the never-ending succession of groups who had felt that whatever the undeniable advantages safeguarded by the preservation of Buganda's autonomy, the genius of the country forbade it to curl up into its shell. Although it had always been careful to defend its autonomy, it had been equally careful to avoid becoming moribund. This may be illustrated by the actions of three key figures. Kabaka Mutesa 1 (1856–84) established a valuable nexus with Zanzibari traders and Christian missionaries, which made Buganda the strongest and most forward-looking kingdom of the area. Apolo Kagwa (Katikiro 1889–1926) led the Christians in Buganda in an alliance with the early British Administration which assisted Buganda to adapt to the advent of British authority to a more fruitful extent than perhaps any other traditional state in Africa. Serwano Kulubya (Omuwanika 1928–45), in association with a second generation of British administrators, won for Buganda the invaluable reputation of being one of the most outstanding 'native states' of its day.

In 1960 Benedicto Kiwanuka, by his refusal to join in the campaign to break Buganda's relations with the new forces which in the shape of the rest of Uganda were impinging upon it, epitomised this other Baganda tradition. There were many in Buganda who considered his actions as little short of treachery: it had been the same for his forebears in the tradition. But successive exponents of this tradition had always felt that they alone were being true to Buganda's real interests; and there was a great deal in the point which, by implication, they had always made that Buganda had only been great when it had kept its communications with the outside world open. When its neighbour Bunyoro closed its doors against outside influences, first in the 1870s and again in the 1890s, it had set on foot the sharp decline in its fortunes which in the twentieth century had such a demoralising effect upon its people. Moreover, those who had opposed the exponents of this tradition had only succeeded in storing up trouble for themselves in Buganda itself. When Kabaka Mwanga had persecuted the Christian and Mohammedan minority in Buganda in the late 1880s they revolted and turned him off his throne. When Sir Apolo Kagwa clung to office in his old age in the 1920s, an association of junior chiefs was formed to oppose him, amongst whom a leading figure was Serwano Kulubya. Buganda's genius over the last hundred years had thus been to accommodate itself, in due course, to the new forces springing up around it and in its midst. Many of its most perceptive figures had, therefore, been fully seized of the great disservice it would have been to allow it to withdraw completely into its shell; and by the time of the Constitutional Conference in London in 1961 it was plain that while on the one hand there were excellent reasons why the claims of the Baganda for the maintenance of their kingdom's autonomy should be treated with great respect – by the non-Baganda as well as by the British – there were also signs that the suggestion that it should seek independence on its own under a neo-traditionalist régime, which was anxious to become permanent, were being resisted even in Buganda itself. Not all Baganda, it now appeared, wished to be saddled with an all-powerful, long-persisting, neo-traditionalist régime, without very much chance of external appeal. Benedicto Kiwanuka had shown that, contrary to many people's expectations, a Muganda who played his cards skilfully could become head of an all-Uganda Government; and before long there were plenty of expressions in the Luganda newspapers of the strength of the tradition that refused to shut Buganda's doors with the outside world which he and his DP colleagues in 1959–60 had represented. To a growing number of people in Buganda some working compromise between Buganda and the rest of the country began to hold out some promise of serving the best long-term interests even of Buganda itself. The Baganda delegates who went to the Constitutional Conference in London in 1961 were therefore not in a mind to be completely inflexible.

XX

The crucial conference on the future constitution of Uganda met in London from 18 September to 10 October 1961[65]. It had before it the report of the Uganda Relationships Committee which, although a somewhat unimaginative lawyer's document, made the very sensible, though by this time obvious, suggestion that while Uganda should for the most part be a unitary state, Buganda's relations with the central government should be upon a federal basis, and that there should be special provisions to secure the traditional monarchical institutions of the three western kingdoms of Bunyoro, Toro and Ankole as well.[66] This, with minor amendments, was accepted.[67] There was one momentary crisis when the Baganda delegates procured a provision by which, although Baganda members were to be elected to the Uganda National Assembly (as the Legislative Council was henceforth to be called) without any obstruction from the Buganda Government, the Buganda Lukiko after a further set of elections of its own was to decide whether it would elect the Buganda Assemblymen itself or allow them to be elected directly. Kiwanuka denounced this provision vociferously but in the end was obliged to accept it, since it was accepted by the UPC.[68]

No problems were finally solved by the decisions of the Constitutional Conference, for the basic problems were not of the kind to be 'solved'. They had to be lived with. Constitutionalists may find the agreed solutions of the Conference untidy; but they should consider the position in Canada. There one group at the heart of the country, the French-Canadians, have had special privileges for nearly two centuries. This has presented a continuing problem to Canadian politicians and Canadians generally; but with give and take on all sides there has never been a breakdown. If it were to be realised that the Uganda Agreement of 1900 (the agreement between the British and the Baganda which is the original charter of Buganda's claims to a special position) was as much part of the ineradicable heritage of Uganda as it has been accepted in Canada that the spirit of the Quebec Act of 1774 (which guaranteed the French-Canadians their distinctive language, civil law and religion) is an ineradicable part of the heritage of Canada, might not Canada's efforts be repeated in Uganda? Having come this far it was quite clear that the answer rested in the end with the peoples of Uganda themselves, and that the British Government could do very little to assist them further; so on his last appearance as British Secretary of State

for the Colonies, Mr Iain Macleod announced that Uganda
would become independent on 9 October 1962.

XXI

The delegates to the London Conference thereupon returned to
continue the political conflict in Uganda itself in preparation
for the elections to the National Assembly which were to take
place before independence was attained. During 1960 a
popular neo-traditionalist organisation calling itself Mwoyo gwa
Gwanga had appeared, but by 1961 it had been overtaken by a
new political movement in Buganda called Kabaka Yekka
which by November 1961 had become the main vehicle for
the political activity of the great bulk of Buganda's neo-traditionalists. If not the lineal successor, 'Kabaka Yekka', 'the Kabaka
alone' was certainly the heir to the UNM (and its reincarnations) of 1959. Its leadership included new-style politicians,
less 'advanced' popular leaders, and members of the Kabaka's
Government. Its main enemy, however, was now the DP,
whose success at the polls in 1961, and whose dominance of the
central Uganda Government thereafter, had aroused both
jealousy and dismay in other quarters in Buganda. In the
elections to the Buganda Lukiko in February 1962, which were
to be held in advance of the elections to the Uganda National
Assembly in April 1962, KY set itself to destroy the DP in
Buganda. It began by calling upon Protestant and anti-Catholic
sentiments. Its chief election cry, however, was that the DP
wished to destroy the Kabaka-ship (and, in consequence, all
that, by this time, it symbolised).

These elections were especially important to the neo-
traditionalists in Buganda because upon them turned not only
the character of the future régime in Buganda itself, but
(according to the decision of the London Conference) the
nature of Buganda's representation in the Uganda National
Assembly. In conducting them, however, KY was confronted
by novel problems of electoral organisation such as had never
confronted the UNM. But into the breach stepped the now
chastened chiefly hierarchy, who were glad to find themselves
an active political rôle once again, and enjoyed the great
advantage of being organised already as a functioning political

bureaucracy; they were soon in action – despite denials – as KY's electoral machine, a rôle they could adopt all the more easily because KY was expressly *not* a political party; it carried forward, that is, all the old aversions to new-style political parties which the neo-traditionalist movement in Buganda had long possessed. Indeed its very name – Kabaka Yekka – marked a step further along the pure neo-traditionalist road than any taken by the UNM in 1959. What was more, for all the part played in its leadership by 'advanced' politicians, and by the chiefly hierarchy, KY had very close links with the populace; well over half the candidates it chose for election to the Lukiko were farmers or traders. In the event it won a sweeping victory at the polls, taking sixty-five seats in the Buganda Lukiko to the DP's three. The accusation against the DP that they were 'against the Kabaka' proved to be a crushing one. For all that, 19·5 per cent of the electorate voted against KY or abstained, and since 22 per cent of the potential electorate did not register, the KY vote was only about 60 per cent of the possible total. Following upon the elections, however, the Lukiko with its KY majority decided (as had been expected) not to have direct elections in Buganda to the National Assembly but to choose Buganda's Assemblymen itself.

Since the London Conference the Baganda leaders (and thereafter their chosen vehicle KY) had been in alliance with the non-Baganda (not to say anti-Baganda) UPC. At first sight this looks astonishing. But a closer look makes it somewhat more understandable. For KY, after all, was, in the first place, only obeying the old nostrum which Mutesa I, Kagwa, Kulubya, and from time to time others in Buganda, had followed of 'agreeing with thine adversary quickly, whiles thou art in the way with him'. Buganda's policy for the past five years had been governed by fear; hope, however, was now returning;[69] and it was an old principle in Buganda that given the opportunity it was better to seek accommodation with an alien leviathan rather than act in complete defiance of it. This policy, indeed, had frequently yielded very handsome dividends. On this occasion an alliance with the UPC presaged a major share in the central Government of Uganda upon the attainment of self-government. This might be by far the best way to secure the special interests of the Baganda in the future. It might allow them to resume their former rôle of *primus inter pares*; while their leading politicians would have some very greatly enlarged opportunities for the exercise of political power. Several corresponding considerations moved the UPC. There were in particular two immediate points at which the interests of KY and the UPC coalesced. In their different ways they were both opposed to the DP – KY in Buganda, the UPC in the Legislative Council; and to a significant degree they both represented the old Protestant ascendancy in Uganda – KY in Buganda itself, the UPC in the rest of the country. Some at least of KY's leaders, moreover, shared much of the 'advanced' outlook of the UPC leaders; their support of neo-traditionalism arose partly from expediency – they had learnt the hard way that no politician who was not acutely sensitive to popular demands could survive in Buganda – and partly from the feeling that neo-traditionalism was for the time being the only movement which could ensure that the Baganda as a whole were not submerged by their neighbours; they were not its unyielding devotees, and the position was obviously changing.

To allow such considerations to influence political tactics was, however, to run some obvious risks – as Augustine Kamya, an important popular leader since 1955 (and former leader of both the UNM and Mwoyo gwa Gwanga), saw very clearly; so suspicious indeed did he become of the 'trimming' tendencies of KY that he formed an 'ultra' neo-traditionalist and 'ultra' popular group called 'Mabega wa Lukiko ne Nnamulondo', 'the people for the Lukiko and the throne'. But KY, for the time being at least, so successfully represented the very much wider range of variegated (and sometimes contradictory) interests held by the Baganda – it had room for 'advanced' politicians, chiefs and populace alike – that at the Lukiko elections it trounced MLN even more completely than the DP.

The subsequent elections to the National Assembly in April 1962 were at first complicated by the ardent desire of the three non-Baganda kingdoms of western Uganda and Busoga to have federal rights which would be fully comparable with those of Buganda. They were here displaying a long-standing tendency amongst the non-Baganda to safeguard their future, not as during 1958–61 by uniting against the Baganda, but by emulating the Baganda in every possible respect. Their demands, however, were eventually supported not only by the DP but by the UPC, both of whom were angling for votes in the rest of the country. The General Election outside Buganda was in fact for the second (one might even say the third[70]) time a straight fight between them. In the event DP won twenty-two seats outside Buganda; the UPC thirty-seven.[71] The National Assembly was thereupon made up of twenty-one Kabaka Yekka, thirty-seven UPC, and twenty-two DP together with the nine specially elected members. The DP Government resigned and Milton Obote, UPC's leader, formed a new UPC–KY coalition Government. A new era opened. Independence followed on 9 October 1962.

XXII

Political parties, for sure, do not exist within a political vacuum. Their fate is intimately linked with political realities. Two widespread suppositions about political realities in a colonial territory proved to be inapplicable in Uganda; the first, the suggestion that new-style politics would emerge *de novo* (how much talk there once was of 'the African political awakening'!); the second, the notion that anti-colonialism was always an overriding passion. Until the later 1950s many new-style politicians in Uganda assumed that fifth phase politics would begin with a sharp break with most that had gone before. In Uganda they were especially wrong; and they had gradually and painfully to accommodate themselves to one major, ineluctable, fact about Uganda's political history – that each phase of it has (so far) been profoundly conditioned by elements surviving from earlier phases, and especially that immediately preceding.

Politics, of course, hang about polarities – polarities of ideology, polarities of interest, polarities of expediency. It is widely assumed that in a colonial territory the major polarity was between indigenous people and colonial authority. But in Uganda this was not so; here was certainly one polarity, but in the 1950s rarely the overriding one. In consequence other polarities were especially free to operate; and as it happened a number of these were very important. Some of them may be listed thus: the polarity between 'ins' and 'outs'; between 'advanced' élites and less 'advanced' populace; between Catholics and Protestants; between Baganda and non-Baganda; between those who would defy their opponents and those who would seek accommodation with them; between those who would say in Luganda *'sitakange'*, 'what I have I hold', and those who would say *'simudda nnyuma'*, 'there is no turning back'. It is not often that these polarities firmly coincided with one another. Frequently they ran at angles to each other, so that all manner of combinations could become possible – both at one and the same time and in kaleidoscopic succession. Different combinations, moreover, could be found in people who at first sight might appear similar; they could be found too in the same person at different times.

Even so in two successive general elections coherent fifth phase political parties in Uganda had shown themselves to possess considerable electoral strength. None of them however, was in origin primarily a party of Uganda nationalism, bred in the exigencies of the struggle for independence. Rather they all had their origins in the struggle for the allocation of political power upon the attainment of independence. They were drawn forth, that is, not so much by the fear that self-government might not be attained, but by the fear that unless positive action was taken political power upon the attainment of independence would pass to other groups in the country who might pay scant regard to the interests and aspirations of those who stood outside them. Such considerations – to a far greater extent than has sometimes been acknowledged – were present in other colonial territories on their march towards independence, but they rarely proved to be so important as they were in Uganda.

NOTES

1. Uganda Protectorate *Report of the Constitutional Committee 1959*, Government Printer, Entebbe, Uganda, 1959, pp. 35–6.
2. The Kenya African National, and Democratic, Unions.
3. It is based very largely upon the information I collected as Kampala correspondent of *The Times* 1951–8. In addition to that derived from innumerable personal contacts, my major sources of information were the press handouts of the Uganda Government, and the local press;

the Luganda press in particular was an invaluable quarry. I am particularly indebted to Miss Lalage Bown, Dr Cherry Gertzal and Rev. F. B. Welbourn for letting me see their typescripts on episodes I did not myself witness. Among other studies which may very fruitfully be consulted, see especially David E. Apter, *The Political Kingdom in Uganda*, Princeton 1961; R. C. Pratt, 'Nationalism in Uganda', *Political Studies*, IX, 1961, pp. 157–78; Donald Rothchild and Michael Rogin, 'Uganda', in Gwendolen M. Carter (Ed.), *National Unity and Regionalism in Eight African States*, Ithaca, 1966; and the 'Epilogue' by A. I. Richards in L. A. Fallers (Ed.), *The King's Men*, London, 1964.

4. IBRD, *The Economic Development of Uganda*, Baltimore 1962, p. 7

5. For an important account of one side of this process, see J. V. Taylor, *The Growth of the Church in Buganda*, London, 1958.

6. C. C. Wrigley, 'Crops and Wealth in Uganda,' *East African Studies No. 12*, Kampala, 1959.

7. This was founded in 1954; its predecessor the Tanganyika African Association was founded in 1929.

8. Even if the historical distinctiveness of these phases proves doubtful, their analytical distinctiveness seems clear.

9. Cf. Martin Southwold, 'Bureaucracy and Chiefship in Buganda', *East African Studies No. 14*, Kampala, 1961; L. A. Fallers, 'Despotism, Status Culture and Social Mobility in an African Kingdom', *Comparative Studies in Society and History*, II (1959–60) p. 18 ff.

10. Cf. C. C. Wrigley, 'The Christian Revolution in Buganda', ibid., pp. 33–48; and Chapter 1 above.

11. Low and Pratt, *op. cit.*, pp. 97, 136.

12. See A. I. Richards, *East African Chiefs* London, 1960.

13. I am aware that if the enumeration of phases was based on the experiences of other parts of Uganda it would be different. But since Buganda held such a key position in Uganda it seems best to link the enumeration with its experience.

14. By 'advanced' is meant people whose values were relatively westernised and relatively modernised. This seems to have gone with a secondary school or university education so that 'advanced' is almost synonymous with having had such an education.

15. Mainly as some relief from too constant a use of 'fifth phase', with which it is largely synonymous.

16. Mr B. J. Mukasa was at one period Katikiro (chief minister) of Buganda's neighbouring kingdom, Bunyoro. He became a Minister in the (central) Uganda Government formed by the Democratic Party in April 1961.

17. During wartime and its aftermath the Protectorate Government's artificial depression of cotton prices hit the peasantry more seriously than the Government was willing to concede, while the simultaneous, and unavoidable, curtailment of developmental policies made it difficult for the gradually increasing educated minority to find jobs.

18. *Report and Evidence of the Joint Select Committee on Closer Union in East Africa* House of Commons Paper 156 of 1931, 3 vols.

19. *Inter-Territorial Organisation in East Africa*, Colonial No. 191, 1945. *Inter-Territorial Organisation In East Africa: Revised Proposals*, Colonial No. 210, 1947.
20. At that time Mr Oliver Lyttelton, Secretary of State for the Colonies.
21. Low and Pratt, *op. cit.*, appendix I. Uganda Protectorate, *Withdrawal of Recognition from Kabaka Mutesa II of Buganda, 1953–4*, Cmd. 9028. See also Chapter 4 of this book. Although the Federation issue set off the crisis it played no part in the final dispute.
22. By this I mean not just that they were obtaining greater legal responsibilities, but that as African representative assemblies they were, particularly in a country where the Buganda model had such a powerful influence, being more and more looked to as the local 'parliament', with all the moral authority that in a colonial territory subject to an imperial power having a parliament the parliamentary idea enjoyed.
23. *Report of the Commission of Inquiry into the Disturbances which occurred in Uganda during January 1945*, Entebbe, 1945; *Report of the Commission of Inquiry into the Disturbances in Uganda during April 1949*, Entebbe, 1950.
24. See Chapter 3.
25. W. P. Tamukedde, *Changes in the Great Lukiko*, mimeo, East African Institute of Social Research (no date); cf. Richards, *op. cit.*, p. 68.
26. See below, section XIV.
27. It is true, of course, that no countrywide African political *party* emerged in Kenya during this period; it was forbidden by law. Most decidedly, however, there was a countrywide political *movement*.
28. It is perhaps not insignificant that the one student political demonstration at Makerere College, the University College of East Africa, during the 1950s – and there was no ban on them – was upon Van Riebeeck's Day 1952.
29. See Fenner Brockway, *African Journeys*, London, 1955.
30. Government Printer, Uganda 1956. According to Congress' initial reaction Sir Andrew Cohen's proposals were totally inadequate.
31. These members were chosen not by the Lukiko, but by an Electoral College specially elected for the purpose.
32. See Chapter 4.
33. *Self-Government for Uganda, an African State*, Manifesto by the Progressive Party, Kampala, no date.
34. Cf. Uganda National Council for Catholic Action, *A Communist Build-up in Africa*, 1956.
35. Minister without Portfolio and Leader of the House in the first African (central) Government of Uganda, formed in April 1961; Chief Minister, July 1961; Prime Minister, March 1962.
36. The Lukiko and the Kabaka's Government having moved by 1957 to a magnificent new building upon an adjoining hill.
37. These might speak and even vote against the Government, except upon the comparatively rare occasions – which were more often than not during the Committee stage of the Budget debates – when the Government put the whip on; *Correspondence relating to the Composition of the*

Legislative Council in Uganda, Entebbe, 1953. It should be noted that at this time no more than three or four members of the Legislative Council – and only those from Buganda or Busoga – were members of new-style political parties, either UNC or UCP.

38. Karamoja was 'represented' by a nominated unofficial member on the Government's backbench.
39. See Chapter 4.
40. It was felt that constituencies of some Representative members were far too large. Teso had over 300,000 people in the District.
41. C. P. S. Allen, *A Report on the First Direct Elections to the Legislative Council of the Uganda Protectorate*, Government Printer, Entebbe, 1959.
42. Independents meaning all those who could not be enumerated in new-style, fifth phase terms.
43. Nadiope and Magezi would probably have been elected in their constituencies whichever party they had joined; Magezi in Bunyoro was the sitting member, and Nadiope was the lineal successor of the rulers of the largest kingdom which existed formerly in the area covered by his constituency.
44. During 1959–60 there were at least two Uganda National Congresses. Obote's Congress itself split into two in August 1959.
45. See Uganda Protectorate, *Report of the Constitutional Committee 1959*, Part III.
46. The UNM did not last long enough to reveal whether the unsuccessful party leaders had really captured the support of the populace, or vice versa; but a taxi-driver was overheard saying about Mulira: 'He is now our prisoner; and whoever heard of a prisoner-of-war trying to be commander-in-chief.'
47. Perhaps this is best illustrated by the contrast between the success of the Mulira group in the year before they formed the Progressive Party early in 1955, and their failure subsequently.
48. *The Times*, 22 August 1955.
49. The effects of this on the Legislative Council elections in Ankole in 1958 have been noted in section IX above.
50. *Report of the Commission of Inquiry into the Affairs of the Bugisu Co-operative Union Limited*, Uganda Protectorate, Sessional Paper No. 14 of 1958.
51. *Report of the Commission of Inquiry into the Management of the Teso District Council*, March 1958, Entebbe, 1958.
52. *Sessional Paper on the Report of the Commission of Inquiry into the Disturbances in Certain Areas of the Bukedi and Bugisu Districts of the Eastern Province during the month of January 1960*, Uganda Protectorate, Sessional Paper No. 3 of 1960.
53. More than half of those elected as Congress Members, it will be recalled, changed their allegiance to the UPU immediately afterwards.
54. See section IX above.
55. It will be appreciated in the light of earlier chapters in this book that the account which follows is highly compressed.
56. *Report (on) . . . the Disturbances . . . during April 1949*, p. 21. It must be remembered that the majority of existing members of the Lukiko

and all the Ministers in the Buganda Government at this time were members of the chiefly hierarchy.

57. *Memorandum on Constitutional Development and Reform in Buganda*, Entebbe, 1953.

58. Low and Pratt, *op. cit.*, appendix I. See also Chaper 4.

59. Some of these can be named: Augustine Kamya, Aligizanda Kisitu, Musa Bulwada.

60. Published by the Information Department of the Kabaka's Government, Kampala, 1960.

61. There were eighty-two seats for elected members in the Legislative Council by this time, based, as nearly as possible, on equal electoral districts. An additional 9 seats were 'specially elected' by the whole council, and there were three seats for official members – the Chief Secretary, the Minister of Finance, and the Minister of Legal Affairs.

62. The nexus between the UPU (which by amalgamation with Obote's wing of Congress had become the UPC) and the Protestant forces outside Buganda was already apparent at the time of the 1958 elections (see section IX above). The absence of any other party to represent the Protestants, and the activity of the Democratic Party as the *de facto* champion of the Catholics, only strengthened the UPC's links with the Protestants.

63. In March 1962 six out of the seven Ministers (Mayanja included) in the Kabaka's Government could be characterised as 'advanced'. Only the Katikiro had come up the chiefly ladder, and there were no characteristic representatives of the populace.

64. Pan-Asianism was only a very feeble counterpart.

65. The conference was attended by Ministers of the central African Government of Uganda, by elected members of the Uganda Legislative Council, by representatives of the Kingdoms and Districts of Uganda, by the Governor of Uganda and Mr Iain Macleod, the Secretary of State for the Colonies, and their advisers.

66. *Report of the Uganda Relationships Commission 1961 under the chairmanship of the Right Honourable the Earl of Munster, P.C., K.B.E.* Entebbe, 1961.

67. Colonial Office communiqué, October 1961, *Commonwealth Survey*, VII 22, pp. 1087–91.

68. See section XXI below.

69. Some of the grounds for this may be summarised: (i) the knowledge, since 1960, that Buganda could not be coerced; (ii) the 'federal' concession recommended by the Relationships Commission 1961; (iii) the élan of Baganda solidarity; (iv) the fact that a Muganda had become Chief Minister of Uganda.

70. See section IX.

71. Elections for the two seats in Toro were not held until later.

7

Buganda and Uganda:
The Parameters of a Relationship

On 24 May 1966 special forces of the Ugandan army attacked the royal enclosure of the Kabaka of Buganda. The palace was soon in flames. The royal drums were destroyed, and the Kabaka fled. It was the end – or at all events so it seemed – of the Kingdom of Buganda, at the hands of the executive President of Uganda.[1]

The confusion between Buganda and Uganda is initially a verbal one. It stems from the failure of coastal traders from Zanzibar, who were used to U-prefixes in what became Tanzania, to go over to Bu- prefixes when they reached the region between Lake Victoria and Lake Albert. When the British who followed them, established their rule here at the turn of the twentieth century, and eventually caught up with the error, they found it convenient to use the term Uganda to distinguish the wider Protectorate from the Kingdom of Buganda at its centre.[2]

There is just one reason for labouring this point. It is highly symbolic of the continually intimate, yet provocatively confusing, relationship between Buganda and Uganda. Some of its substantial features are worth recalling.

I

To begin with developments in Buganda in the late nineteenth and early twentieth century set the pattern in a number of ways for developments in the rest of Uganda. It is well known that Baganda adventurers spread Baganda rule into north-eastern Uganda around the turn of the century, and stamped their mark upon that area.[3] It is not always realised, however,

227

that Baganda chiefs were also employed by the British not just subsequently in that northeastern region, but in Bunyoro, Ankole and Kigezi at the other end of the Uganda Protectorate as well; that indigenous chiefs who had had intimate personal experience of the workings of the Buganda kingdom played a vital, creative, part early in the colonial period in both Toro and Busoga; and that a full *tour d'horizon* reveals that there were not many areas of the old Protectorate which did not feel the presence, around the turn of the century, of one or other of those two arch-exporters of the Buganda system, Semei Kakunguru – the greatest of the Baganda adventurers – and George Wilson – perhaps the most important British official in the early years of the Protectorate.[4]

The export, moreover, came to be substantial. It was not just that Baganda chiefs and their followers spread themselves over so many non-Buganda areas. In a remarkable way the shape which Buganda's political institutions came to assume following the British occupation in the 1890s came piece by piece to be replicated as the ensuing decades unfolded throughout the greater part of the rest of the Protectorate. It was essentially a haphazard process, never systematically pursued. But a seemingly inexorable one even so.[5] The characteristics of the Buganda system as it evolved can be readily itemised; a three-tiered hierarchy of appointed – not hereditary – territorial chiefs, with both administrative and judicial functions, topped by a three man group of senior chiefs – called 'Ministers' in Buganda and 'senior officials' elsewhere – one of whom was the chief executive (Katikiro or Nganzi in the kingdoms; 'secretary-general' elsewhere), the second the Chief Justice, and the third the Treasurer. Together these formed a 'government' (that really had no counterpart in either Kenya where the District Commissier was the 'government' or in Northern Nigeria where the Emir was the 'government'). Linked to this, moreover, was a real 'native council'. For several decades this was composed wholly of chiefs; but latterly following developments which first occurred in Northern Uganda it came to include elected members. One of its vital characteristics was that it was not presided over by a British colonial official (as its counterparts were in Kenya until independence). Here, that is, were institutions that in due course gave the kingdoms and districts of Uganda, African local governments that were at once African and local and governments. In Buganda; in the three western kingdoms of Bunyoro, Toro and Ankole; and in the kingdom-amalgam that was Busoga, there was a ruler at the apex. But since the prototype of the system came to maturity in Buganda when its ruler was a minor, the ruler was not essential to its effective functioning (as more than one ruler came to discover to his dismay). With the admittedly piecemeal, but nevertheless fairly complete, replication of these institutions – all of them initially fashioned in Buganda – in the rest of the country, Uganda came to comprise a congeries of little Bugandas.[6]

Two characteristics of the way in which the Buganda model operated – wherever it was exported – need to be stressed. First, because the relationship between the Buganda prototype and the British was regulated by treaty, a tradition developed under which the African local government stood over against the British administration, and was never full meshed in with it. (In Northern Nigeria, where there were no treaties, the mesh between the British administration and the native authorities was very much closer). Secondly – and flowing from this – because the British found their freedom of action curbed by the prevailing treaty relations, they preferred to work apart from the 'native administration' whenever the treaty's omissions allowed.[7] As a provincial commissioner in Buganda put it in 1917: 'In all indirect matters of administration such as agricultural progress, dealings with non-natives and government laws not in conflict with the Uganda Agreement . . . the executive lies with the British Government.'[8] As a result developmental tasks at the local level – those for example relating to education or health or agriculture – came to be not so much the responsibility of the local government as of the local officials of the central government. And this state of affairs came to prevail elsewhere wherever the Buganda model was followed.

It was not, however, just the institutional features of the Buganda model which were exported to the rest of the country. Few things were more striking than the export of the new religion, Christianity, to the rest of the country as well, very often at the instance of Baganda chiefs like Kakunguru, but also by special Baganda Christian evangelists, Catholics and

Anglicans alike.[9] It followed from this that the Christian cleavage first established in the 1880s and 1890s in Buganda came to be repeated kingdom by kingdom, district by district, in the rest of the country. This expressed itself, moreover, not just as a religious divide but as an educational and social division as well. Furthermore, as in Buganda it came to have a political expression – to such an extent indeed that in Kigezi district in the 1950s, for example, and in the Bukedi riots in 1960, there was religio-political conflict between Catholics and Protestants that came closer to paralleling the religious wars in Buganda in the 1890s than probably anything which had occurred in the interval.[10]

It was not, however, only the institutional and religious complexes which were first fashioned in Buganda that came to be replicated elsewhere. There is a good deal of evidence – from the career of Nuwa Mbaguta, the Nganzi of Ankole in in the first decades of the twentieth century, to the Teso school development programme in the 1950s[11] – that the modernising ideology of the Baganda came to be adopted elsewhere too. This revolved around a dual concern to preserve one's own cultural and political integrity while seeking to ensure that the advantages which could be gained from contact with the wider world were secured as well: a brilliantly constructed ideology, which has the chief claim to being Buganda's greatest achievement. It must be noted that the ideology was elitist in outlook, and that hand in hand with the hierarchical structures which the institutions presented – ecclesiastical let it be emphasised, as well as civil – it gave the Buganda model its most vulnerable characteristic.

What all of this led to was an extraordinary Buganda-like pattern throughout almost all the rest of the country. For a visitor in the 1950s a meeting with the senior officials of Bugisu – where the people were originally acephalous – or with a county chief in Ankole – whose lineal predecessors had been war-band leaders rather than administrative chiefs – was extraordinarily like a meeting with their counterparts in Buganda. Amongst the Baganda themselves it led to a deep sense of their own importance to Uganda, while in the rest of the country it generated a profound ambivalence towards Buganda, which in the end came to express itself more particularly in envy – that janus-like emotion which, while anxious to emulate, is resentful of any claims to superiority.[12]

II

All of this, however, is only one aspect of the importance of Buganda to Uganda. There is another whole matter to be considered as well. Its significance was probably not appreciated by the rest of the country, nor indeed by the many Africans in other parts of east and central Africa who were scarcely less affected by it as well. Elsewhere in this vast region in the opening decades of the twentieth century – from Table Mountain, indeed, to Mount Kenya – the interests of Africans became subject primarily to the interests of immigrant European settlers. The creative energies of Africans were given little release; the role allotted to them was in the main either that of an industrial or an agricultural proletariat.[13] (It was thus not for nothing that when the Reverend John Chilembwe ran his despairing revolt in Nyasaland in 1915 he should have given prominence to the decapitated head of a local estate manager – rather than a missionary's or an administrator's. It was against the régime which this represented that his whole being revolted.)[14]

But further north it was different. 'However successful colonisation may prove in Kenya', Sir Philip Mitchell, Governor of Uganda, wrote in 1939, 'it can never alter the fact that in Uganda and most of East Africa the setting and the circumstances are African and seem certain to remain African'.[15] Why was Uganda different? It is unnecessary to labour the point that the key to the difference lay in Buganda. But what was it about Buganda that made for the difference?

It is scarcely enough to argue that it was because there were so few European settlers there. During a fifteen year period – from about 1906 to 1921 – a group of European planters had an influence in Uganda that looked for a time very much like that enjoyed by their kith and kin elsewhere: if this was not sustained it was not simply that the bottom dropped out of their world market in 1921, for this was true for their countrymen elsewhere as well.[16] Nor will it do to refer to the fact that Buganda was a powerful traditional kingdom; for such were of course to be found in various places to the south as well. It may well be of some moment that there were not so many Europeans in its vicinity and that its continuous history was much more substantial. But it looks as if the chief reason for the difference which Buganda represented lay in the fact that – by contrast with the acephalous peoples of many parts of Kenya, or (on the whole) the larger kingdoms further south – it made a quite unusually positive response to the western impact when it came, which earned it a quite unusual reward.

Colonial administrators were to be found elsewhere in Bantu Africa who had no sympathy with the policy of developing the region through the proletarianisation of Africans. In a country such as Kenya, however, they had all too little to work on.[17] In Buganda, however, not only were there traditional appointed chiefs who could be expected to administer the country effectively under colonial guidance. There was a set of key figures – who became the model for many of their neighbours – who in some very remarkable ways were responding positively to, and cooperating creatively with, the British administration as they established their Protectorate over the country. The consequence of this was, as one early senior official put it in 1907, that 'Administrative Officers of experience in this Protectorate are agreed that the best method of developing the country is through the native governments, and that these governments should be upheld and established in every possible way . . .'[18] From a very early date, moreover, they were able to sustain their belief with a good deal of practical evidence of its validity. A full discussion of why there was this response to the British contact cannot be offered here. It derived in part from the basic values of the Baganda (there was a striking contrast between the disdain for and the hostility towards strangers exhibited by so many Kenyan peoples, and the eager desire to know what they had to offer which the Baganda displayed).[19] It derived as well from the conversions to Christianity which occurred in Buganda in the 1880s and 1890s; and from the mutually profitable alliance which the Baganda chiefs succeeded in making in the 1890s with the British administration.

The ready response of the Baganda did not, however, mean that they were simply *collaborateurs*. It should be emphasised indeed that their readiness to cooperate was always coupled with an unremitting determination to see that the integrity and autonomy of their kingdom was not impaired. No-one, for example, did more to uphold the admittedly reduced (but nevertheless still very largely intact) autonomy of Buganda than the otherwise arch collaborator, Sir Apolo Kagwa, Katikiro (Chief Minister) of Buganda from 1889 to 1926.[20] Similarly no-one withstood the British Parliament's Joint Select Committee on Closer Union in East Africa in 1931 more firmly than Serwano Kulubya, the Omuwanika (Treasurer) of Buganda, and in so many ways during the inter-war period the ideal African chief in the eyes of the British. Kulubya gave the Baganda position considerable precision.[21] It was superbly spelt out by none other than Daudi Chwa, Kabaka of Buganda between 1897 and 1939, in a pamphlet published in 1935 which, significantly enough, he called *Education, Civilisation and Foreignisation*.[22] He welcomed the first two; he was opposed to the third; that was the attitude of the Baganda.

Their prime achievement was to withstand the successive British proposals for an East African federation. The Baganda were aided and abetted in this by various British administrators in Uganda; by the liberal lobby in Britain; and by Sir Donald Cameron, Governor of Tanganyika. But they themselves made a major contribution to the defeat of the Federation idea.[23] They belaboured it vociferously whenever it raised its head, and were much its most substantial African opponents. After the Report of the Joint Select Committee advised against Federation in 1931, and throughout the 1940s and 1950s, they remained upon a constant *qui vive* – as their opposition to the proposals for an East African High Commission in the 1940s indicated, and as Sir Andrew Cohen found to his cost in 1953.[24]

What, we may ask, was the concern of the Baganda in all of this all about? They were, of course, fearful that if an East African federation were created they would find themselves subject to the domination of white settlers. They were afraid too lest they should lose their land; and losing their land meant being proletarianised – like the Kikuyu. But Daudi Chwa's pamphlet – and other sources besides – makes it quite clear that in the view of those Baganda who were primarily concerned the issues at stake ran very much deeper. At bottom there was a profound concern for the integrity and self-generating capabilities of Baganda society, and a deep anxiety lest these should be in any way frustrated. It is only necessary to take a glance at the riots in Buganda in the 1940s (or the agrarian discontents in Luo country in Kenya in the 1950s, quite apart from Mau Mau) to see the acuteness and depth of the frustration which could be built up whenever people in East Africa felt themselves alienated from the régime dominant over them. The delight with which Baganda leaders welcomed (and later recalled) Sir Charles Dundas' speech to the Lukiko in 1944, in which he accorded Buganda the full stature of a native state under British protection – and went further than any other Governor of Uganda towards proclaiming that the kingdom should be left alone to govern itself through its existing system of chiefs – indicates something of the depth of feeling which they could display upon such an issue.[25] For all their anxiety to procure all the advantages which were available to them from contact with outside societies the Baganda have time and again displayed their deep-rooted animosity to any major threat to their indigenous society and culture – from the time of Kabaka Mwanga's order for the murder of Bishop Hannington[26] in 1884 (because he saw him as a threat to his kingdom's autonomy) to the fierce boycott of Asian traders in the rural countryside of Buganda in 1959.

Such an attitude seems to have been part and parcel of Baganda thinking over a very long period. Buganda, it is worth recalling, began as a very small kingdom, which against all the odds (more particularly its originally very much larger neighbour Bunyoro-Kitara) grew by successive stages so that (significantly not until 1965) it scarcely ever seems to have lost territory which it had once secured; and clearly (as so much of its nineteenth century history demonstrated) took great care about incorporating new areas into the body of the kingdom, even when these could be had for the taking.[27] Throughout, it displayed great persistence, great caution, and a great deal of skill.

In the end, as the British discovered on more than one occasion, Buganda became a formidable political achievement. There is not much doubt, moreover, that many Baganda leaders saw it that way. They took immense pride in who they were – a pride which was reinforced by their victories over such proposals as those for East African Federation, and their success in more than one encounter with the British administration. It was they above all that ensured that 'White Man's Africa' had its Achilles heel. Obstinately Buganda remained 'primarily African' and Uganda with it; and in due course successfully blew the first buttress from the settler-dominated order in Bantu Africa.[28]

III

It was with a mind fashioned by all this earlier experience that the Baganda came to face a further set of crises in the 1950s and 1960s. Now finely honed, it contained an element of what the Greeks used to call *hubris*. For a great many of them the new threat constituted no less a challenge to all they had striven for than had been earlier represented by British proposals for an East African federation. Having withstood being submerged in a settler dominated federation, they were now faced by being submerged in a non-Baganda-dominated Uganda. The fear that through the ballot box they would be overwhelmed, in a whole variety of ways, by a combination of their much more numerous neighbours ran deep. For many of them an old-style threat was simply expressing itself in a new-style guise.[29]

It looks as if the nature of the new challenge was first perceived in 1953 at the court of Kabaka Mutesa II, very possibly by Kabaka Mutesa himself. It is moreover, some measure of the penetrating insight which the Baganda have so frequently displayed that it should have been held to at that time in the midst of their last great encounter with the British over the possibility of a British-imposed federation. The federation issue was resolved in 1953, broadly speaking to the satisfaction of the Baganda, by Sir Andrew Cohen's statements late in that year denying that the British had any intention of creating an East African federation. Kabaka Mutesa II still asked, however, for the separation of Buganda from the rest of the Uganda Protectorate, because even as early as 1953 he saw very clearly that, if universal suffrage was being introduced, the numerical preponderance of the non-Baganda parts of the country threatened the position of *primus inter pares* within Uganda which

Buganda had held hitherto; and if he sensed as well that the threat which the non-Baganda could very easily come to represent ran even deeper than this, his prescience was as we shall see truly remarkable. At the time Cohen felt bound to resist any such demand because it would have involved taking the hub away from the wheel – so intimate were the connections between Buganda and Uganda.

There was thus set on foot, however, the political crises of the thirteen years from 1953 to 1966. As a result of the Kabaka's return in 1955 (following his deportation by Cohen in 1953), Cohen managed to restore the equilibrium momentarily. It was a condition of the Kabaka's return that Baganda members elected by a Buganda electoral college should take their seats in Uganda's Legislative Council, as no elected Baganda had ever done before. But in a series of maladroit actions Cohen's successor Crawford threw away in 1957 much of this achievement when he provided several Baganda members of the Uganda Legislative Council with a set of excuses for resigning from it. For thereafter the Buganda Lukiko took its cue from the doctrine first adumbrated by the Kabaka in 1953, that Buganda's future safety lay only in independence – a course of action which eventuated in its unilateral declaration of independence in 1960.

Buganda's UDI was never in itself taken very seriously: but it was now very clear that the concern which both the Kabaka and his associates, and the Lukiko, were expressing had such support in Buganda that had the British (or indeed anyone else at that stage) chosen to have ridden roughshod over it, it would have been a very serious matter indeed. If no-one was prepared to use force (and force on this issue might well have been required) against the Kabaka and the Lukiko – and in the last days of empire no-one was so minded – then some kind of federal status for Buganda within Uganda was a *sine qua non* for the future.

Buganda's campaign had, however, by this time stirred into life the long-standing envy of the Baganda which had become so widespread in the rest of Uganda. It had indeed found expression in the non-Baganda – almost anti-Baganda – party, the Uganda Peoples' Congress led by the rising Lango politician, Milton Obote. But in 1961 Obote too seems to have come to the conclusion that conflict with the Baganda was likely to be much too costly. It would be better to join them instead. He therefore formally accepted Buganda's compromise claim for federal status within an independent Uganda, and created the alliance between his own UPC and Buganda's *Kabaka Yekka* (Kabaka only) party, which swept Uganda into independence before the end of 1962. Obote's *mariage de convenance* was confirmed in 1963 when he was instrumental in procuring Kabaka Mutesa's appointment as President of Uganda. To an outside eye, indeed, this seemed a superbly well-contrived conclusion to the controversies of the previous decade. The Prime Minister of Uganda was a northerner, but the Kabaka of Buganda was President of Uganda. Buganda's autonomy remained intact, and in terms of the status symbols of the day (the ballot box notwithstanding) it remained *primus inter pares*. The resolution of the tense relationship between Buganda and the rest of the country seemed to have been effected.[30]

IV

But in 1966 all of this was swept away. Dr Obote, it seems clear, was concerned to reinforce his own by no means impregnable position – and, to be fair, that of the Prime Minister of Uganda – as soon as possible. He saw that his first task politically was to wean to his own side some of the leaders of the Democratic Party who composed the opposition in the National Assembly. It proved to be not too difficult to persuade a number of them of the grave disadvantages of inveterate opposition in a state where the merits of the two-party system were by no means generally accepted. His major coup came with the crossing of the floor by Basil Bataringaya, the leader of the Democratic Party in the legislature, whom he promptly made a minister in his Cabinet. Previously Obote had been dependent for his majority upon the support of the Kabaka Yekka members. The DP switches, meant however, that by the end of 1964 he had a majority within the National Assembly without having to rely upon Kabaka Yekka support:[31] and he soon demonstrated his new-found mastery by carrying through the previously promised referendum in those western parts of Buganda which the Banyoro had claimed for over half a century were their 'Lost Counties'. A majority there voted for their return to Bunyoro. Buganda thus lost territory which it had held in the past for what would seem to have been the first time for centuries. The whole episode understandably caused a furore in Buganda. It caused the fall of a Buganda government and severely weakened the alliance between Obote and Buganda's leaders.

There is not much doubt that the Kabaka had been moving heaven and earth to frustrate the referendum: and not much doubt either that he was little enamoured of the idea of being simply a constitutional monarch for Uganda; he was now very certainly nothing of the kind in Buganda itself.[32] The fateful clash which subsequently occurred between him and Dr Obote owed a good deal, however, to his increasing fear that the integrity of Buganda could not be assured whilst Obote remained in power. The evidence suggests that early in 1966 the Kabaka sought to seize the opportunity of a potential split in the ranks of Dr Obote's own UPC between Obote's own northerners and the southern – Bantu – members of its leadership group, to bring about Obote's downfall.[33] Had Mutesa been successful he and his immediate associates could have joined with the leaders from the 'kingdom' areas of the country – broadly speaking the Bantu-speaking southern half – in installing a new government. He could thus have headed for the first time a majority grouping in the country and thereby have secured much the most promising guarantee which its political structure permitted for entrenching all which he and they held dear – including very probably the Buganda model itself.

But Dr Obote was too swift footed. He moved against the dissidents in his own party, and then suspended the constitution fashioned at independence. Not for the first time, Buganda seemed to face a major threat to all it had striven for; and its response was true to tradition. The Kabaka protested vigorously, and sought outside help from the United Nations:[34] the Lukiko passed a resolution telling Obote's government to remove itself from Buganda's soil; and out in the countryside some impatient Baganda peasants launched some violent assaults upon some rural police stations – those scattered symbols of the central government's authority, which contained (or so it was thought) policemen who were mostly from Obote's own northern part of the country. Obote immediately riposted by sending his Special Force against the Kabaka's palace. A sharp conflict ensued. Mutesa II fled; and in his second exile called the autobiography which he compiled *The Desecration of my Kingdom.*[35] Given the previous stature which Buganda had enjoyed it seemed indeed an almost sacrilegious *dénouement.*

The irony moreover in the situation could not have been heavier. No part of the country had done more to secure its African character against the slings and arrows of the colonial period than Buganda. In the end, however, it was the African Government that brought it to independence which clove its heart.

V

There was, even so, an anomaly here. For the defiance which the Kabaka and the Buganda Lukiko had hurled at Dr Obote only represented one side of the response of the Baganda people to these events. It has to be remembered that there were Baganda members of Obote's own government who participated in the decision to attack the palace of the Kabaka. Most of them, moreover, remained his associates in the period which immediately followed. (Although at the time of the attack a Muganda who was Attorney General of Buganda was in Britain seeking to win support for the Kabaka's case, he came in the immediate aftermath of another Muganda who was Attorney General of Uganda and had spoken on Dr Obote's side.) It was estimated, moreover, that of Uganda's 200 top civil servants 150 were at this time Baganda.[36] There is no evidence to show that in the aftermath of the attack upon the palace any of them ceased from serving the Uganda government, though it seems very clear that their defection would have faced it with exceedingly serious difficulties.

Furthermore, although many Baganda were clearly greatly disturbed by the attack upon the palace[37], the rural violence which accompanied it very soon ceased, and the overwhelming majority of the Baganda – unlike the Bakonjo of Mount Ruwenzori who throughout these years kept up their violent opposition to the Uganda Government for causes which were in no sense fundamentally different[38] – soon resumed their regular avocations.

Admittedly Dr Obote 'had the maxims and they had not'. But this is far from being the whole of the story. For it has always to be remembered that alongside Buganda's long standing determination to preserve its integrity it has always displayed an equal determination to ensure that its doors should be kept open to the advantages flowing from outside. A century before this policy had been superbly exemplified by Kabaka Mutesa I.[39] Kabaka Daudi Chwa expressed it precisely in the pamphlet whose title has been quoted: he was against the inroads of 'foreignisation'; but he was keenly in favour of securing both 'education' and 'civilisation'. Just three years before the 1966 crisis nineteen Baganda members of the Uganda National Assembly who were members of Kabaka Yekka circulated a pamphlet in which they declared 'that it must be understood by those who don't know it, and particularly by those who have forgotten, that Buganda is a part of Uganda and so it will remain forever'. They went on to state, moreover, that to think 'that Buganda is a separate country from Uganda [would be] to live in the unrealistic isolationistic view that many of us have held up-to-date and *which serves to prejudice Buganda and the Baganda, not only in Uganda but even outside Uganda*'[40]. The signatories included Amos Sempa, for fifteen years the ablest of Buganda's 'loyalists', and Mayanja-Nkangi, the Oxford graduate who was soon to be the last of the Buganda Katikiros, and a fellow exile of the Kabaka. The dual concern that is – that Buganda's integrity should be preserved, but not at the cost of leaving itself isolated in a cul-de-sac – is deeply rooted in Baganda thinking. It has been their great achievement to have ridden it in tandem over so many long stretches. In a period of uncertainty the inherent contradiction between its two sides has, of course, wracked the conscience of many Baganda. The debate in any one of their minds has often been plain to see.[41] But at a crisis neither aspect has been totally abandoned, and only very painfully and tragically have the divisions crystallised out. In 1897 Kabaka Mwanga eventually headed the forces in revolt against the British presence in his country; but his senior chiefs – who were by no means backward in their defence of Buganda's autonomy on other occasions – backed the British against him.[42] So it was in 1966. Whilst the Kabaka and the Lukiko and some of the rural population entered upon a vehement

conflict with Dr Obote's central government, when the roll
was taken the bulk of the educated Baganda elite were found
acquiescing in Dr Obote's regime while the mass of the rural
population protested not at all.

There was, however, one important novelty in 1966, which
perhaps helps fill out the explanation of why the elite at all
events acted as it did.

Ever since the white man established himself here, [the 1963
KY committee had remarked] we in Buganda have been driven
by one fear, that is the fear of losing the Namulondo [the throne] and
so losing our identity. We have persistently resisted anything that
tended to detract from our status and we have objected to every
suggestion of closer union or federation with other territories in
East Africa. [But, they went on] Since October 9 last year [Inde-
pendence Day 1962] events changed fundamentally.[43]

For fifty years, that is, Buganda had brilliantly resisted all
attempts to bring it subject to a European settler society (and
all Uganda, and perhaps East and Central Africa as well,
stood in its debt). But by 1966 this was no longer the issue. It
was not a case of being swamped by a European society. It was
a case of participating in an African one: and there was at
least a fair chance that Baganda could do this without finding
their creative capabilities being suppressed – and to that extent
without losing their cultural identity – if they would agree to
work with the new order. Indeed there might well be more
creative opportunities for up and coming Baganda within a
wider Uganda than within the order which the Kabaka had
wished to maintain. The precedents were not unfavourable, if
one turned oneself back three quarters of a century. The effect
of Captain Lugard's victory in the first battle of Mengo in
1892[44] had, it is true, been to circumscribe Buganda's autonomy:
and the effect of Obote's victory in the second battle of Mengo
in 1966 was probably to destroy the kingdom. But the first did
not radically frustrate the creative energies of the Baganda;
and on one condition – the condition the British accepted: that
the Baganda should be given a full chance to develop their
capabilities – it was by no means inevitable that the second
should either.

This, it seems, is what Dr Obote's Baganda associates discerned like Kagwa and the Christian oligarchs before them.[45] In so doing they were being faithful to one aspect of the long-standing ideology of the Baganda, as Mutesa II was to the other. It entailed in the 1890s accepting the power of the new leviathan, while exploiting its opportunities. But Buganda's deep-rooted ideology – odd as it may seem – provided the justification for this, both at that time, and in 1966.

VI

Yet if the attack upon the palace became in these respects a climactic moment for the Baganda, it was of even greater moment in another respect as well. For it constituted not just an attack upon Kabaka Mutesa and the Buganda kingdom. It was a momentous attack as well upon the Buganda model. 'The problems', one of Dr Obote's Ministers was to soon be saying, 'were tribalism, religionism and what he called "Bugandaism"'.[46]

It is hardly surprising perhaps that immediately after the attack upon the palace the Buganda Government should have been demolished. What is especially significant is that its replicas in the rest of the country were dismantled very soon afterwards as well. If the Kabaka of Buganda was exiled, and the Buganda Government destroyed, the other rulers of Uganda soon found themselves being pensioned off, while all the local governments on the Buganda model were shortly afterwards made legally subject to the authority and direction of the central Uganda Government to a completely new extent. This becomes clear from a comparison between the 1966 constitution (published as it happens just before the attack on the palace) and that which was promulgated in 1967.[47] The latter (and the Local Administrations Act which followed it), the Minister of Regional Administrations was soon to declare, marked

not another stage in the development of Uganda's internal relationships ... but a break with the past, and the start of a new era ... no longer were local authorities encouraged to think of themselves as separate units of Government ... This is the theme behind the new Constitution and the new Local Administrations Act; that all sectional interests must give way before the national will, and that one structure of Government, interlocking from the Presidency down to the miruka, must guide and order all our efforts.[48]

The issues here were by no means new. Back in the 1930s the then Governor, Sir Philip Mitchell, had pointed out that while the prevailing political structures in Buganda and its neighbouring kingdoms in the south met many of the criteria of the then prevalent doctrines of indirect rule, the Buganda-like structures in northern, traditionally acephalous, Uganda were alien institutions, more akin in their operations to direct rather than to anything which might be called indirect rule; and the policies he fashioned were calculated to break the sway which the Buganda model exercised over the whole country. On the one hand he proposed that it should be frankly acknowledged that in the non-kingdom areas the prevailing structures represented direct rule; and in order to mitigate their impact he sought at the same time to hasten the creation of representative district councils. Meanwhile, in Buganda more especially, he set on foot changes designed to bring its government more fully into line with the full indirect rule conception: in particular he sought to expunge the anomaly of the existing dual government in Buganda by which Baganda chiefs and British officials worked along parallel lines, so that (as in Northern Nigeria) the chiefly authority might become responsible for all local government, and British activities could be limited to those under the aegis of a Resident at the centre.[49]

Much of the genesis of the events of 1966 is to be found in the subsequent shifts away from the Mitchell programme. Essentially the distinction Mitchell sought to draw between the kingdoms and the other districts of Uganda was not effected. This was partly because he did not appreciate that even by this time there was as much popular disenchantment with the Buganda model in Buganda itself as in other parts of the country. There were riots in Buganda in 1945 and 1949, very largely against it.[50] And by the 1950s it was obviously just as urgent to introduce fully representative councils in Buganda as in the rest of the country.[51] Soon afterwards, moreover, the Kabaka's apparently dramatic success in his conflict with the British during 1953–5 gave the Buganda model an altogether new lease of life. It was from this moment onwards, for example, that other parts of the country began to top off their version of

243

it, as it was topped off in Buganda, with a ceremonial head – a Laloyo in Acholi, a W'Egwanga in Bukedi, a Kingoo in Sebei etc., etc.:[52] and from this moment onwards as well that those areas which had had fewer ministers than Buganda set about trying to make up the leeway.[53]

At the same time, despite much that Mitchell, and more particularly his successor Dundas, had intended[54], one of the crucial consequences of the Buganda riots in the 1940s had been that the central government of Uganda maintained, or rather restored and elaborated, the Protectorate Government's activities in Buganda, and *a fortiori* in the rest of the country, and thereby reinforced both the centre's sense of responsibility for so many governmental operations at the local level, and its ability to express it. There were sustained attempts in the 1950s to devolve responsibility – for health, education and agriculture for example – upon local governments.[55] Cohen, who was Governor at the time, justified this policy on the ground that 'political advance was bound to bring out the strength of tribal loyalties . . . the view we took was that strengthening the unity of the country would not be furthered by failing to recognize the attachment of the people to its parts'. But such was the strength of the old dual tradition of government in Uganda that every effort to advance devolution was limited by the central government's deep-rooted anxiety to ensure that ultimate control remained in its own hands. When the Munster Commission reported shortly before independence upon relations between Buganda and the central government of Uganda it gave considerable prominence to the problems which this ambivalence entailed.[56]

It was to this situation that Dr Obote and his government succeeded at independence. By East African standards the autonomy of local governments in Uganda based upon the amended Buganda model was very strong indeed. In the decade or so before independence it had been, moreover, reinforced, both because the strength and elaborateness of the Buganda model itself had been enlarged, and because District Councils had been thrown open to locally elected members. At the same time the long term ambiguity in the responsibility of the centre and of the relatively autonomous local governments for government at the local level persisted,[57] and in a variety of ways it seems clear that local governments established upon the modified Buganda model were seen by the ambitious, enterprising and radically minded central government which Dr Obote formed as its chief obstacle. In a series of amendments to the Local Administrations Act it sought to strengthen its hand against them.[58] But both in the economy and in the polity they came increasingly to feel the pressure of limited resources upon which to draw, and it seems patent that when an occasion presented itself the temptation to sweep away the prototype of their troubles so as to make it easier to bring down its replicas became overwhelming.

There were linked considerations as well. For in their assault upon the Buganda model Dr Obote and his colleagues were not only attacking its institutional features. They were attacking its values as well. They attacked the religious divisions which had gone with it. Political parties in Uganda, and the political divisions which had accompanied them, had owed a great deal to the Buganda-based conflicts between Catholics and Protestants which had been replicated in the rest of the country.[59] Divisions along religious lines were now vigorously denounced.[60]

But more than that as well; in his justifications for his actions against the Kabaka, Dr Obote premised his defence upon the interests of the 'common man'. 'The present crisis', he said in February 1966, as it was reaching its climax, '. . . is one of a struggle between the interests of the common man and those persons who are highly placed and occupy positions of influence.'[61] In so saying he was expressing the deep-seated hostility of the traditionally acephalous peoples of his own northern region against the hierarchical values which the Buganda model had displayed.[62] It is vitally important to remember that at the same time he was appealing to the anti-hierarchical tendencies which were present in Buganda and in the other kingdoms themselves – to those for example which were constantly raising their heads amongst those in Buganda who called themselves Bataka (and had been involved in the discontents of the 1920s, the riots of the 1940s, and the populist movements of the 1950s); and to that which was rife amongst the subordinated Bairu in Ankole; or expressed itself in the Rukurato committee in Bunyoro which forced constitutional

changes upon a very reluctant Mukama in 1955.[63] The attack
upon the Kabaka of Buganda's palace represented indeed not
just an attack upon the structural features of the Buganda
model, or upon its religious accompaniments. It was an attack
as well upon the hierarchical, elitist values which were so
closely associated with them. If the Kabaka sensed that (together with everything else which he opposed in Dr Obote) these
things were at stake as well, his prescience was wholly correct.
Obote's actions in 1966 and 1967 represented a major victory
for the populist egalitarian values,[64] more especially, but not
exclusively, of his own northern region, over the elitist and
hierarchical values of the Buganda model with which despite
amendments Uganda had lived for half a century and more. In
the light of preceding history this indeed was its major feature.

The anomaly here is that in taking action against the district
replicas of the model as well as the prototype itself Obote was
reducing the power of the directly elected councils which had
already reformed it substantially – in Lango district indeed
under his own chairmanship. In many areas, that is, to
get rid in the mid-1960s of the Buganda model was to get rid of
the directly elected local councils and the essentially local
governments associated with them. Yet clearly this was
intended. Seen from the centre, powerful local governments
were a curse not a blessing. There is some evidence, moreover,
that despite elections they had by the 1960s fallen once again
into the hands of local elites.[65]

VII

But what remained was the problem of the alternative. For if
there was support for the populist, egalitarian values which
Dr Obote represented, these were hardly adequately expressed
by the autocratic régime which he maintained in the period
after May 1966. There were two central problems here. How
could new political resources be created? How, having de-
throned hierarchical, elitist institutions, could populism be
institutionalised in their place?

The first, and truly delicate, step was to establish a firm link
with the armed services (who in the end had been brought in to
destroy the old order). Back in 1888 resort to violence had

brought a decade of armed conflict. A check to its propensities on this occasion was high on Dr Obote's list of priorities. He was both solicitous of the armed forces, and careful to urge that they should leave politics to the politicians.[66] He was cautious too about his connexions with the Baganda elite; those not against him (he appeared to be saying) could be assumed to be with him.[67] During 1967, moreover, he and his Government eventually promulgated a new constitution. He even allowed the National Assembly to discuss it for three months on end.[68]

This tied in with a more substantial purpose – to secure effective popular acceptance of the legitimacy (in the Weberian sense) of his authority. In 1967 he himself embarked on a speech-making tour in some outlying parts of the country.[69] During 1968 there was a major effort to make progress in this way. A large rally, to which religious leaders and the diplomatic corps were invited, was held at the Lugazi football ground on 27 March.[70] Thereafter steps were taken to nail the support of the country's three most important latent wielders of power. In June a seminar was held for the secretaries-general of Districts – those key local figures whom the régime had decided to retain.[71] Immediately afterwards a UPC Conference was held – the first since 1964; Presidents Kaunda of Zambia and Nyerere of Tanzania were invited, and Dr Obote was elected to its Presidency for the next seven years.[72] Then in September a further conference was held, for senior officers of the army, the police and the prison service.[73]

Simultaneously an ambitious 'meet-the-people' tour was mounted. In April the President went to four western districts, and to Teso in the east. In May he was in West Nile and Acholi, and in June in Lango and Bunyoro.[74] There was now in Uganda, so ran his reiterated refrain, 'one State, one Government, one Parliament, one People'. He denounced the Kabaka and also the educated elite. The emphasis, he insisted, must be upon the 'common man'. 'The Rulers of Uganda', he told an audience in Ankole in the middle of April, 'must be all the citizens of Uganda as a whole';[75] and towards the end of the month he roundly affirmed in Teso that 'he and his Ministers had not gone to Soroti [the District's headquarters] as big chiefs but they had gone there to meet their masters'.[76]

But in August and September it was not the President who went on tour in Buganda but a number of his Ministers.[77] In the newly formed East Mengo District they were accompanied by the new Secretary-General, Blasio Kavuma (who had once been a minister in the Kabaka's Government immediately after the Return in 1955). True to one part of the Baganda tradition Kavuma 'appealed to the Baganda to stop their habit of opposing anything that was new'.[78] But the general response was clearly giving cause for considerable concern. In August the Minister of Education, himself a Muganda, was asking an audience in Bulemezi 'why Dr Obote should be hated?'[79] and at the end of September the Minister of Labour enquired of a meeting at Nagalama 'how long are the Baganda going to be deceived?'[80] There was a great rally in Kampala on Republic Day, 8 September.[81] But the fact that a break-through had not been made into the Buganda countryside did not pass unnoticed. *Reporter*, East Africa's leading fortnightly, declared on 6 September 1968:

Although President Obote has during the past year made several successful 'meet-the-people' tours in various districts he has yet to make an extensive tour of the Kabaka's former kingdom. When he does he will be putting the seal on the Government's efforts to unite the Baganda people with the rest of the nation.[82]

By the end of the year this had not occurred. In December 1968 Obote did hold a meeting at Bombo in Buganda. Scheduled to begin in the afternoon, its start was unexpectedly brought forward to the morning. Troops and police were in evidence: and not more than 1000 people attended. 'Disappointing', a Muganda member of the UPC called it.[83] Clearly, fashioning new political resources and institutionalising populism were proving to be formidable tasks. What was more, the imprisonment at this time of Abu Mayanja, the ablest intellectually of the politicians from Buganda, symbolised the possibility of serious failure in securing effective outlets for the more energetic Baganda. Once again, it seemed, Buganda was haunting Uganda; and if the reports about some of the Secretaries-General of Districts (who even now were often being carefully picked from amongst the available local notables) were true, so was the Buganda model as well.[84]

248

1969 brought at first very little change. In the second half of the year a bold new course was struck, an avowedly ideological 'move to the left'. It was very much in line, however, with much which had proceeded. On 24 October the governing UPC adopted *The Common Man's Charter*, produced by President Obote himself.

We hold it [this affirmed] as the inalienable right of the people that they must be masters of their own destiny and not servants of this or that man; that they must, as citizens of an Independent Republic, express their views as freely as possible within the laws of their country, made, *not in separate Parliaments*, but in one Parliament in which the people as a whole have an equal say through their representatives. [Emphasis added]

And it went on:

With the removal of the feudal factor from our political and economic life, we need to do two things. First we must not allow the previous position of the feudalists to be filled by neo-feudalists. Secondly, we must move away from circumstances, which may give birth to neo-feudalism or generate feudalistic mentality.

Thereafter a 'new political culture' was set forth for Uganda. Its advance was assisted by the death at the end of the year of the exiled Mutesa II, and in 1970 it was elaborated in a series of further pronouncements by President Obote. Of special significance were his *Proposals for New Methods of Election of Representatives of the People to Parliament* published in July 1970 (as this book was in final proof).

The greatest divisive friction which Uganda experienced after Independence [this affirmed] was the struggle between Uganda and the Districts. Due to the nature of administration established during the Protectorate Era, District Administrations saw themselves as alternative centres of power.[85]

New proposals were accordingly sketched out for national elections by which candidates who stood in their own 'basic' constituencies would be required to secure votes in three other constituencies in the remaining three regions of Uganda. The explicit purpose was to break the hold of 'the tribal masters, whether in the form of ideology or individuals', and insist that 'the National Assembly must be national, and Members of it must also be national'.

As the 1970s opened, therefore, not only was President Obote's counter ideology for Uganda being made increasingly explicit, but a strenuous effort was being made as well to give it apposite institutional form. The struggle to be rid of the models which Buganda had provided for half a century past, and establish in their place a quite new order for Uganda, was being pressed with decided vehemence.

NOTES

1. The most vivid, albeit inevitably one-sided account is in the Kabaka of Buganda, *The Desecration of My Kingdom*, London, 1967, Chs. I and II.
2. Uganda Government, *General Notice* of 1 July 1908, clarified the point.
3. H. B. Thomas, 'Capax Imperii – the Story of Semei Kakinguri', *Uganda Journal*, VI 3 (1939), pp. 125–36; A. D. Roberts, 'The Sub-Imperialism of the Baganda', *Journal of African History*, III, 3 (1962), pp. 435–50.
4. Audrey I. Richards, *East African Chiefs*, London 1960, *passim;* D. A. Low, 'Uganda: the establishment of the Protectorate, 1894–1919', in Oxford, *History of East Africa*, Vol. II, Oxford, 1965, p. 91 sqq.
5. Ibid.
6. For a resumé around 1950 see Lord Hailey, *Native Administration in the British African Territories, Part I*, London, 1950, Chapter 1. But see especially F. G. Burke, *Local Government and Politics in Uganda*, Syracuse, 1964, pp. 32, 36–7, 42, 49–50, 53, 55, 230.
7. Low and Pratt, *Buganda and British Overrule*, Ch. 6. See also Burke, *Local Government*, pp. 69–72, 162–3.
8. Provincial Commissioner, Buganda, to District Commissioner, Masaka, 6 July 1917. Masaka District Archives.
9. Louise M. M. Pirouet, 'The Expansion of the Church of Uganda (N.A.C.) from Buganda into Northern and Western Uganda between 1891 and 1914, with Special Reference to the Work of African Teachers and Evangelists', University of East Africa, unpublished Ph.D. thesis, 1968, contains an authoritative account.
10. E.g. Uganda Protectorate, *Report of the Commission of Inquiry into the Disturbances in Certain Areas of the Bukedi and Bugisu Districts of the Eastern Province during the month of January 1960*, Sessional Paper No. 3 of 1960; See also Burke, *Local Government*, p. 198 sqq.
11. See F. Lukyn Williams, 'Nuwa Mbaguta, Nganzi of Ankole', *Uganda Journal*, X, 2 (1946); Burke, *Local Government*, Ch. 5.
12. In October 1914 an Anglican missionary report from Mbale stated: 'At present many of the people are reading that they may "become Baganda" and they say that Baptism is the mark of attaining that

position, the great ideal is to be educated and clothed that "they may pass for Baganda" . . .', *Uganda Notes*, October 1914, p. 216. Writing in reply to a prominent Muganda politician, A. A. Nekyon (who was to become a close ministerial colleague of President Obote) wrote in 1953: 'I think Mr Kiwanuka still mistakes Uganda for Buganda. If Mr Kiwanuka thinks there is a King for Uganda as a whole, he is causing a worse ill feeling than the Protectorate Government does', *Uganda Herald*, 26 Nov. 1953. I am much indebted to Tom Watson and Brian Bowles for these references.

13. A striking example of the doctrine can be found in the opening pages of G. R. Sandford, *An Administrative and Political History of the Masai Reserve*, London 1919.

14. George Shepperson and Thomas Price, *Independent African: John Chilembwe and the Origins, Setting and Significance of the Nyasaland Native Rising of 1915*, Edinburgh 1958; G. S. Mwase, *Strike a Blow and Die*, Ed. R. I. Rotberg, Cambridge, Mass., 1967.

15. Uganda Protectorate, *Native Administration*, Note by the Governor, Entebbe 1939, pp. 10–11.

16. Philip Powesland, 'Economic Policy and Labour, *East African Studies No. 10*. London 1957, and C. C. Wrigley 'Crops and Wealth in Uganda', *East African Studies No. 12*. London 1959, both discuss these matters.

17. See, for example, various memoranda on this subject in the Hobley and Ainsworth papers at Rhodes House, Oxford.

18. 'Memorandum containing rough notes for a despatch to the Secretary of State upon the question of Amalgamation between the Uganda Protectorate and the East African Protectorate', Confidential [unsigned, but by Stanley Tomkins, 1909] London, Public Record Office, C.O. 533/62.

19. See the first and third chapters in this book.

20. D. A. Low, *The Mind of Buganda* (forthcoming), will contain some details.

21. Evidence of Serwano Kulubya, Omuwanika of Buganda, *Report of Joint Committee on Closer Union in East Africa*, Vol. II, Minutes of Evidence, House of Commons Paper 156, 1931, pp. 550–578.

22. H. H. Daudi Chwa, Kabaka of Buganda, *Education, Civilisation and Foreignisation in Buganda*, Kampala 1935.

23. Low and Pratt, pp. 254–8 contains a summary.

24. Ibid, pp. 385–8, 232 ff.

25. The speech was printed as an Appendix to the *Report of the Sub-Committee of the Lukiiko which was set up to examine the recommendations of the Hancock Committee*, Entebbe, 1955.

26. H. B. Thomas, 'The Last Days of Bishop Hannington', *Uganda Journal*, VIII, 1 (1940) pp. 19-27.

27. A. H. Cox, 'The Growth and Expansion of Buganda', *Uganda Journal*, XIV, 2 (1950), pp. 153–9.

28. See Chapter 4.

29. The key document is The Kabaka's Government, *Buganda's Position*, Mengo 1960.

30. For further accounts of these years see David E. Apter, *The Political Kingdom in Uganda*, Princeton 1961, Ch. 14 ff.; R. C. Pratt, 'Nationalism in Uganda', *Political Studies*, IX, 1961, pp. 157–78; 'Epilogue' by A. I. Richards in Lloyd A. Fallers, *The King's Men*, London 1964; Cherry Gertzal 'How Kabaka Yekka Came to Be', *African Report*, October 1964; 'Uganda' by Donald Rothchild and Michael Rogin in Gwendolen M. Carter, ed. *National Unity and Regionalism in Eight African States*, Ithaca, 1966; J. M. Lee, 'Buganda's Position in Federal Uganda', *Journal of Commonwealth Political Studies*, III, 3, (Nov. 1965).

31. See the valuable resumé in Colin Leys, 'Recent Relations between the States of East Africa', *International Journal*, (August 1965), pp. 514–17.

32. Kabaka, *Desecration*, contains some frank passages.

33. Ibid, Ch. 2.

34. *Sir Edward's Appeal to the Secretary-General of the UNO*, Kampala 1966.

35. See Kabaka, *Desecration*, Ch. 1. Also G. F. Engholm and Ali A. Mazrui, 'Violent Constitutionalism in Uganda', *Government and Opposition*, II, 4 (July-Oct. 1967) pp. 585–599; Emory Bundy, 'Uganda's New Constitution', *East Africa Journal*, III, 4 (June 1966), pp. 23–32; M. Crawford Young, 'The Obote Revolution', *Africa Report*, (June 1966), pp. 8–14.

36. Ibid, p. 14; also Crawford Young 'Congo and Uganda: a Comparative assessment', *Cahiers économiques et sociaux*, V, 3, (Oct. 1967), p. 398.

37. See, for example, 'The 66 Study Group pamphlet', *The Uganda Crisis 1966, One Hundred Days after the Battle on Mengo Hill*.

38. Uganda Government, *Report of the Commission of Inquiry into the Recent Disturbances amongst the Baamba and Bakonjo People of Toro*, Entebbe 1962; Tom Stacey, *Mission to Ruwenzori*, London 1964; Burke, *Local Government*, pp. 232 ff.

39. J. M. Gray, 'Mutesa of Buganda', *Uganda Journal*, I, (1934), pp. 22–49.

40. S. J. Luyimbazi-Zake and others, *Fresh Political Approach in Buganda. Basis of MP's Recommendations for KY-UPC Merger*, Kampala, 1963.

41. For example, in that of Kabaka Mutesa II: it may be recalled that he who once asked for the separation of Buganda from Uganda became the first President of Uganda.

42. See Oxford *History of East Africa*, Vol. II, Ch. 2.

43. Zake and others, *Fresh Political Approach*.

44. The most important account is in Margery Perham: *Lugard, The Years of Adventure*, London 1956, Ch. 15.

45. See, for example, Erisa Kironde to *The People*, 17 September 1966.

46. Basil Bataringaya, Minister for Internal Affairs, *Uganda News*, 24 July 1968.

47. Cf. Uganda Government, *The Constitution of Uganda*, Entebbe, 15 April 1966, and Uganda Government, *The Government Proposals for a New Constitution*, Entebbe, 9 June 1967. See also Burke, *Local Government*, p. 43.

48. J. M. S. Ochola, Minister of Regional Administrations, *Uganda News*, 14 June 1968; see also Abu Mayanja, 'The Government's Proposals for a New Constitution for Uganda', *Transition*, XXXII, 7, i, (Aug-Sept. 1967) pp. 22–3.

49. Uganda Protectorate, *Native Administration*, Note by the Governor, Entebbe, 1939; *Relations of the Protectorate Government in Uganda with the Native Government of Buganda*, Note by the Governor, Entebbe, 1939; Sir Philip Mitchell, *African Afterthoughts*, London, 1954, Ch. 9; see also J. C. D. Lawrence, *The Iteso*, London, 1957, p. 36; Burke, *Local Government*, pp. 36–8, 143 ff.; Margery Perham, 'The Model Baganda', *Colonial Sequence 1930–1949*, London, 1967, pp. 169–173.

50. *Report of the Commission of Inquiry into the Disturbances which occurred in Uganda during January 1945*, Entebbe, 1945; *Report of the Commission of Inquiry into the Disturbances in Uganda during April, 1949*, Entebbe 1950.

51. *Memorandum on Constitutional Development and Reform in Buganda*, Entebbe, 1953.

52. E.g. Burke, *Local Government*, p. 166 ff, 217.

53. In the years following the signing of the Buganda Agreement 1955 there was, for example, a sustained campaign to this end by the Kingdom of Toro. See also Burke, *Local Government*, pp. 44, 46, 58.

54. *Native Administration in Uganda*. A Memorandum by His Excellency the Governor, Entebbe, 1941; Sir Charles Dundas, *African Crossroads*, London, 1955, Ch. 13. See also Burke, *Local Government*, pp. 40 sqq.

55. E.g. C. A. G. Wallis, *Report of an Inquiry into African Local Government in the Uganda Protectorate*, Entebbe, 1953.

56. Sir Andrew Cohen, *British Policy in Changing Africa*, London, 1959, p. 58; *Report of the Uganda Relationships Commission 1961 under the Chairmanship of the Right Honourable the Earl of Munster, PC KBE*, Entebbe, 1961. See also Burke, *Local Government*, p. 70.

57. Professor K. Ingham has drawn attention to the Provincial Commissioner in 1955 who remarked: 'I am sure that, so far as my province is concerned, there would be a considerable amount of ill-feeling on the part of my African Local Governments if they felt they were to be subjected to the decision of a body [Executive Council] which is only remotely – so far as they know – connected with them', *Proceedings of the Uganda Legislative Council*, 12 Jan. 1955, p. 63. Professor F. G. Burke in an unpublished paper of 1965 made the essential point at that time: 'Power to mobilize and manipulate the people of Uganda is limited because it is relatively dispersed'. See also Burke, *Local Government*, pp. 41, 47, 58, 156 ff., 228–9; and Aaron Segal, 'The Politics of Land in East Africa; *Economic Development and Cultural Change*, XVI, 2 (1968) pp. 281–295.

58. E.g. Local Administrations (Amendment) Acts 1962, 1963, 1965; also The Western Kingdoms and Busoga Act 1963. See also Burke, *Local Government*, pp. 40 ff., 231.

59. This has been explored by, among others, F. B. Welbourn, *Religion and Politics in Uganda, 1952–62*, Nairobi, 1966; see also Burke, *Local Government*, p. 202; Apter *Political Kingdom*, Ch. 14.

60. E.g. *Uganda News*, 19 Apr, 6, 15 Aug., 17 Sept 1968.

61. Statement by Dr Obote, 24 Feb. 1966, *Reporter*, 11 March 1966. See also among many other examples, his further statements, *Reporter*, 27 June 1966, *Uganda News*, 17 Apr., 7 Sept. 1967, 8 June 1968. It is

perhaps worth noting here an early expression of Obote's thought. On 24 April 1952 the *Uganda Herald* published the following letter from him.

> I shall be highly obliged if you would allow me space in your esteemed paper to express the feelings of young and enlightened Semi-Hamites and Nilotes about some of the aims of the Uganda National Congress. Not long ago, Mr Fenner Brockway, M.P. came to Uganda and concentrated his activities in and around Kampala. He returned to England and gave his version of the "Unification of all Tribes in Uganda". I shall not give here Mr Fenner Brockway's version but it is enough to say that his version of the "Unification of all Tribes in Uganda" is a direct negation of the established traditions of the Semi-Hamites and the Norsemen (Nilotes) and that we are worried about it. It will, therefore, be of great interest to us if the Uganda National Congress will point out exactly what they mean by the "Unification of all Tribes in Uganda". "Self-Government in Uganda" is a target to aim at by Uganda citizens. Co-operation with the Government so as to attain self-government is also recommended but we Semi-Hamites and Norsemen of Uganda who have had no educational opportunity as the rest of Uganda, feel that the Congress is aiming at "Self-Government in Uganda", is hastening and thereby leaving us behind. Because of our present inability to aim so high and in order not to be a burden to the Congress, it must be pointed out to the Congress here and now that with us, the question of questions lies in Education and rapid development of the African Local Governments. It is rather unfortunate that the Congress makes education and the control of Uganda economy subsidiary aims and the height of folly is the apparent omission by the Congress of a definite aim to the slogan, "immediate Local Self-Government in Uganda".

I am much indebted to Brian Bowles for this reference.

62 Dr J. S. La Fontaine remarks in an unpublished paper on 'Tribalism among the Gisu': 'Tribes with an egalitarian tradition ally themselves against the traditional kingdoms. It is worth noting that it was only after Obote achieved leadership in the Uganda National Congress that Gisu joined it in larger numbers. Formerly, under Ganda leadership, it made little headway in the area'. See also Burke, *Local Government*, pp. 177, 199, 209, 219–20.

63. See Chapter 5; and Burke, *Local Government*, p. 95 ff.

64. It is not without significance that the lively newspaper of Obote's Uganda Peoples Congress was called *The People*.

65. On these and related matters see Colin Leys, *Politicians and Policies. An Essay on politics in Acholi, Uganda 1962–65*, Nairobi, 1967; also Burke, *Local Government*, pp. 107 ff. 150 ff., 158 ff.

66. E.g. *Uganda News*, 20 Sept. 1968.

67. He did not react publicly, for example, to the call for elections in an important letter to *The People*, 17 Sept. 1966.

68. *Uganda News*, June-Sept. 1968, *passim*.

69. Ibid, 18 Mar. 17 Apr. 1967.

70. Ibid, 28 Mar. 1968.

71. Ibid, 14 June 1968.

72. Ibid, 7–14 June 1968.

73. Ibid, 20 Sept. 1968.
74. Ibid, 9 April – 25 June 1968, *passim*.
75. Ibid, 17 April 1968.
76. Ibid, 27 April 1968.
77. They included Kalule-Settala (Finance), Luyimbazi-Zake (Education), Lubowa (Labour), Kalema (Commerce and Industry), ibid, Aug.-Sept. 1968, *passim*.
78. Ibid, 12 Sept. 1968.
79. Ibid, 26 Aug. 1968.
80. Ibid, 23 Sept. 1968.
81. *Reporter*, 20 Sept. 1968, pp. 12–13.
82. Ibid, 6 Sept. 1968, p. 11.
83. Personal interview, 30 Dec. 1968.
84. E.g. George Bennett 'Patterns of Government in East Africa', *International Affairs*, XLV, 1, (Jan. 1969), p. 92.
85. A. Milton Obote, *The Common Man's Charter*, Kampala, 1969. *Proposals for New Methods of Election of Representatives of the People to Parliament*, Kampala 1970.

BIBLIOGRAPHICAL NOTE

Substantial bibliographies of printed, and other, material on the history of Buganda, and of Uganda, will be found in:

H. B. Thomas and R. Scott, *Uganda*, London, 1935.

M. C. Fallers, *The Eastern Lacustrine Bantu*, London, 1960; and in the volumes of the Oxford *History of East Africa* (in which there are also a number of relevant chapters); Vol. I edited by Roland Oliver and Gervase Mathew, 1963; Vol. II edited by Vincent Harlow and E. M. Chilver, 1965; Vol. III edited by D. A. Low and Alison Smith, forthcoming.

The following is a selected list of recent publications:

D. E. Apter, *The Political Kingdom in Uganda*, Princeton, 1961.

F. G. Burke, *Local Government and Politics in Uganda*, Syracuse, 1964.

L. A. Fallers (ed.), *The King's Men. Leadership and Status in Buganda on the Eve of Independence*, London, 1964.

J. F. Faupel, *African Holocaust*, London, 1962.

P. C. W. Gutkind, *The Royal Capital of Buganda*, The Hague, 1963.

H. P. Gale, *Uganda and the Mill Hill Fathers*, London, 1959.

K. Ingham, *The Making of Modern Uganda*, London, 1958.

The Kabaka of Buganda, *The Desecration of my Kingdom*, London, 1967.

D. A. Low and R. C. Pratt, *Buganda and British Overrule 1900–1955, Two Studies*, London 1960.

M. F. Perham, *Lugard, The Years of Adventure*, London, 1956.

Philip Powesland, 'Economic Policy and Labour', *East African Studies No. 10*, Kampala, 1957.

A. I. Richards (ed.), *Economic Development and Tribal Change*, Cambridge, 1954.

A. I. Richards (ed.), *East African Chiefs*, London, 1959.

Donald Rothchild and Michael Rogin, 'Uganda', in Gwendolen M. Carter (ed.), *National Unity and Regionalism in Eight African States*, Ithaca, 1966.

M. Southwold, 'Bureaucracy and Chiefship in Buganda', *East African Studies, No. 14*, Kampala, 1961.

J. V. Taylor, *The Growth of the Church in Buganda*, London, 1958.

F. B. Welbourn, *East African Rebels*, London, 1961.

C. C. Wrigley, 'Crops and Wealth in Uganda', *East African Studies No. 12*, Kampala, 1959.

Four important Ph.D. theses soon, one must hope, to appear in print are:

M. S. Kiwanuka, 'The traditional history of the Buganda Kingdom: with special reference to the historical writings of Sir Apolo Kagwa', University of London, 1965.

John A. Rowe, 'Revolution in Buganda, 1856–1900', University of Wisconsin, 1966.

M. J. Twaddle, 'Politics in Bukedi 1900–1939: an historical study of administrative change under the impact of British colonial rule', University of London, 1967.

Louise M. M. Pirouet, 'The expansion of the Church of Uganda (N.A.C.) from Buganda into Northern and Western Uganda between 1891 and 1914, with special reference to the work of African teachers and evangelists', University of East Africa, 1968.

INDEX

Achimota College, 173
Acholi, 189, 241, 247
Africa, kingdoms, 1, 6; European scramble for, 27, 56, 84; British policy in, 56–7; British attitude to, 76–7, 78; independence in, 101–3, 114; nationalism in, 139; development of political parties in, 167–8, 173–4; and the African Personality, 214
African Development Fund, 169
Aga Khan, 173
Agreed Recommendations of the Namirembe Conference, 129, 131
Albert, Lake, 58, 86, 227
All-Buganda Party, 186, 196
All-Uganda Party, see All-Buganda Party
Ajayi, Professor, 7
Anderson, Sir Percy, 58
Anglican Church, Anglicans, 25, 26, 30, 38, 42, 48, 62, 119, 148, 229; see also Protestants
Anglo-German Agreement 1980, 55
Ankole, 1, 7, 45, 126, 187, 191, 195, 217, 228–30, 245, 247
Anti-Slavery Society, 60, 67
Apter, Professor David, 139, 161
Arabs, 20–23, 25, 27, 29, 34, 52, 86
Asians, in Uganda, 102, 104, 168; representation of, 106, 107, 125, 126, 127–8, 130, 187; in commerce, 151, 157–8, 168; UNC attacks on, 155; boycott of, 156, 157–8, 201, 234; political organization of, 173
Awolwo, 180
Azikiwe, Nnamdi, 180

Basigu, 5
Bairu, 245
Baker, Sir Samuel, 85
Bakonjo people, 4, 239
Bakungu, 15–17, 140–41, 144, 148, 151, 152, 158, 160
Balfour, Arthur, 61, 73
Balokole, 148
Bataka, 15–17, 140, 141, 144, 148, 151, 152, 158, 160

Bataka Party, 94, 167, 176, 245; see also Butaka Union
Bataringaya, Basil, 237
Batongole, 141
Bechuanaland, 57, 79
Bell, Sir Hesketh, 88
Berkeley, Bishop, 117
Binaisa, Godfrey, 197
Birch, J. P., 124
Birmingham, 67–8, 71, 72, 78
Britain, British, and Baganda Christians, 1, 35–6, 87; in East Africa, 31, 55, 85; in Buganda, 35–8, 86–7; and Buganda oligarchy, 38–9, 40–41, 42, 51–2, 170; deportation of Kabaka Mwanga by, 39; administration in Buganda, 50, 87–90, 91–2, 94, 97, 114, 149–50, 153, 155, 175; and Kabaka Mutesa II, 94–8, 105, 109–14, 151–2; and proposed East African Federation, 94, 96, 108, 110, 174, 178, 223; and Uganda Legislative Council, 96–7, 110, 187–8, 192–4, 207–8; and African self-government, 101–3, 105, 203; and proposed Central-African Federation, 101–3, 105, 108, 174; proposed constitutional changes, 105–9; and the Buganda crisis, 105–12; support for Mutesa II in, 112–13; setting up independent inquiry, 114–17; and the Uganda Constitutional Committee, 192–3, 206–8, 216–18; and the London Conference, 216–18; in Nigeria, 243; see also IBEA Company; Namirembe Conference; Uganda Agreement
Bristol, 64–5, 66, 72, 75
British East Africa, or IBEA, 81
Brockway, Fenner, 150
Buddu, 37
Buganda, development of, 1, 211; religion in, 1, 8, 14, 17–29, 30–38, 41–2, 45, 47, 85–7, 142–3, 168, 170–71, 229–30; arrival of British in, 1, 7, 35–8, 40–41, 55–9, 86–7; importance of, 1–2, 5–7, 13; popula-

259

tion of, 1, 168, 205; size of, 1, 190, 234; administration in, 2, 45–7, 88–90, 93–5, 97, 103–4, 140–42, 144–9, 232–3; populism in, 8, 10, 112–13, 149–60, 176, 245; authority of chiefs in, 9, 15, 16, 141, 144, 152; agriculture in, 13, 45, 89, 146–7, 168–9; social structure in, 14–17, 47–52, 140, 169; rebellion in, 29–32, 143; civil war in, 32–40; oligarchy in, 40–46, 87–8, 143–4, 153, 159, 170; autonomy of, 40, 149, 206, 211, 212, 215–16, 233, 237, 240; and the Kabakaship, 43–4; land settlement in, 44–5, 89, 93, 145–6; religio-political parties in, 47–52, 90, 170–71; establishment of Lukiko in, 48; Europeans in, 84–5; economy of, 89, 92, 104, 145–6, 149, 156–7, 168–9; discontent in, 90–91, 94–5, 148–53, 159; and Uganda, 91–2, 94–9, 105–10, 114, 133, 158, 187–8, 192–6, 211–12; riots in, 94, 105, 149–51, 198–9, 243, 245; and the Legislative Council, 96–7, 107, 125, 127, 129–30, 133, 187–8, 201, 204–11, 237; Asians in, 104, 106, 126, 156–8, 201; education in, 105, 106, 190; proposals for constitutional reform in, 106–7; and the 1953 declaration, 106–7; and the 1953 crisis, 108–17; opposition to East African Federation, 106, 108–10, 211, 233, 235; demand for independence by, 110, 235; effect of deportation of Mutesa II on, 112–14, 115, 194; and the Hancock Committee, 115–23; and the Namirembe Conference, 123–33; electoral reforms in, 151, 204–5, 212; development of political parties in, 154–5, 157, 160, 167, 176–84, 190–92, 194–205, 218–20; influence in Uganda of, 171, 190, 227–30, 232–3; opposition to chiefs in, 176–7, 199–201; and neo-traditionalists, 184–6, 188, 190–91, 193, 201, 204–5, 210, 213–14, 218; and the 'Lost Counties', 189–90, 237–8; and the Constitutional Committee, 192–3, 201; struggle for independence by, 206–11, 215–16; declaration of independence by, 208; and Uganda Constitutional Conference, 216–18; elections for National Assembly in, 218–20; and the struggle with central government, 237–9, 242–6; Ugandan attempts at reconciliation with, 246–9; see also Uganda Agreement

Buganda Agreement 1955, 132

Buganda Appointments Board, 128, 131, 132

Buganda Land Law, 146

Buganda's Position, 206

Bugisu, 4, 179, 189, 195

Bugisu Coffee Union, 179

Bugisu District Council, 188

Bukedi, 195, 230, 244

Bulemezi, 248

Bunche, Dr Ralph, 115, 116

Bunyoro, 1, 7, 13, 18, 85, 87, 90, 126, 189–90, 211, 217, 228–9, 234, 243, 247

Busoga, 90, 179, 187, 189, 191, 195, 220, 229

Busulu and Nvujo Law, 89, 147

Butaka Union, 151, 160, 176, 184

Buvuma, 6

Cairo, 183, 192

Caledonian Society, 173

Cambridge, 64, 72, 105, 180

Cameron, Sir Donald, 233

Catholic Action movement, 183

Central Africa, 1, 75, 101–2, 107–8, 112–14, 130, 133, 174, 203, 231, 241

Central African Federation, 102, 113

Central Council of Indian Associations, 173

Central Council of Muslim Associations, 173

Chamberlain, Joseph, 67, 73, 78

Chandos, Lord, 174, 203

Chester, 70, 72, 75, 76

chiefs, authority of in Buganda, 9, 15, 16, 141, 144, 152; appointment of, 15–17, 140–41, 152, 159, 179, 199–200; rebellion by, 29–32, 142; during civil war, 32–5; and the Kabaka, 42–3; and county chieftainships, 45–6; and the British, 87–91, 96, 143, 145, 149–50, 199; discontent among, 90–92; and the people, 141–8, 148–51, 152–3, 159,

chiefs–*contd.*
200; in administration, 145, 148, 151, 171, 228
Chilembwe, Rev. John, 23
Christians, Christianity, Baganda converts to, 1, 8, 14, 17–18, 22–7, 41–2; persecution of, 28–9, 85–6; in Kabaka Mwanga's army, 30–31; rebellion by, 32, 142; during civil war, 33–7, 56, 58, 86–7, 143, 153; and the British, 35, 37–8, 40, 86; during the oligarchy, 38–40, 42, 45–52, 58, 87, 170–71; in political parties, 160; in Uganda, 229–31; *see also* missionaries; Protestants; Roman Catholics
Church Missionary Gleaner, 81
Church Missionary Society, 25, 56–8, 60, 62–5, 67, 68, 74, 78–9, 81
clan heads, *see* chiefs; lineage heads
clans, 14–19, 169, 186
Cohen, Sir Andrew, 95, 105–16, 119, 122–31, 133, 182, 192, 233, 235–6, 244
The Common Man's Charter, 10, 11, 249, 254
Congo, 58
Conservative Party, 8, 61, 67, 73–4, 82, 113, 172
Convention Peoples Party, 167, 172, 204
Co-operative Societies Ordinance, 93
Council of Bataka (Landowner's) in Buganda, 46
Council of Clan Elders, 129
Cowan, Sir J., 68, 74
Crawford, Sir Frederick, 133, 187–8, 191, 236

Daudi Chwa, Kabaka, 39, 42, 43, 51–2, 90, 91, 95, 110, 143, 233, 240
Democratic Party, formation of, 182–3, 184; Roman Catholics in, 182–4, 209; Presidents of, 184, 197, 209; in 1958 elections, 189; opposition to, 190, 210, 218–21; success of, in 1961 elections, 209–11; in 1962 elections to National Assembly, 220–21; alliance of, with UPC, 236–7
Dilke, Sir Charles, 81
District Councils, 167, 182, 187, 189, 191, 195, 244
Dundas, Sir Charles, 234, 244

East Africa, independence, 3, 9, 101, 114, 130, 133, 174, 231; district aggregations in, 4–5; conversions in, 18; British in, 31, 55, 57, 85–6, 101–2; Germans in, 55, 85; proposed Federation in, 96, 101–3, 107–9, 122, 130, 174, 211–12, 235; settlers in, 101–2, 241; political movements in, 178
East African High Commission, 108–9, 174, 211, 233
East Mengo district, 248
Edinburgh, 68, 69, 71, 72
Education, Civilization and Foreignization, 233, 251
Edusei, Mr, 204
Egypt, 3, 20, 24, 58, 78, 81, 82, 84–6, 183, 211
Eishengyero, *see* District Councils
Emin Pasha Relief Expedition, 78
Entebbe, 110, 111, 150
Europe, Europeans, in Buganda, 3, 22, 55–6, 112, 118; in Africa, 7, 27, 34, 84–5, 86; and African independence, 102; population of, in Buganda, 104; representation in Uganda Legislative Council, 126, 127, 129, 187; in Uganda, 168, 173; *see also* Christianity; settlers
Evans-Pritchard, Professor E. E., 20–21, 52

Fashoda, 55
Federation of the Bataka, 89, 151
Federation of Rhodesia and Nyasaland, 177, 178
Federation of Uganda African Farmers, 151, 178
Fort Hare, 172
Free Church of Scotland, 63, 68

Gabunga, 141
Germany, 55, 85, 183
Ghana, 105, 167, 169, 172, 186, 203, 204, 214
Gladstone, W. E., 57, 58, 74, 75, 78, 81, 82
Glasgow, 68, 69, 71
Gold Coast, 121; *and see* Ghana
Gordon, Colonel C. G., 78, 85
Grey, Sir Edward, 80
Griffiths, James, 102, 113
Gusii, 4

Hancock, Sir Keith, 95, 114–17, 118–23, 130, 131, 132, 133

Hannington, Bishop James, 70, 85, 234
Harcourt, Sir William, 58, 81
Haya people, 5
Hicks-Beach, Sir Michael, 64, 65, 75

Iliffe, Dr John, 8
Imperial British East African Company,
   55–60, 78, 81, 86; see also Lugard,
   Lord
India, 101, 114, 139, 172, 203, 214
Indian Congress of Kenya, 173
Indian National Congress, 172, 178
Indian Nationalist Association of Zanzi-
   bar, 173
Iseera, 195
Islam, 1, 14, 17, 20–23, 25, 28–9, 35,
   38, 170; see also Muslims
Ismailis, 175
Italy, 115, 150, 183

Jinja, 179
Johnston, Sir Harry, 40–41, 42, 87

Kabaka, authority of, 1, 14–17, 19,
   43–4, 122, 140–43, 151, 159, 169–70;
   position of, under Uganda Agree-
   ment, 95, 103–4, 131; position of,
   discussed during Namirembe Con-
   ference 122, 128, 129, 130
Kabaka Yekka (KY), 158, 160, 218–21,
   237, 240, 241
Kadu, 168
Kagwa, Sir Apolo, 2–3, 46, 51–2, 87–90,
   92, 97, 149, 213, 215, 233
Kagwa, Kawalya, 2, 93, 149
Kajubi, Senteza, 197
Kakunguru, Semei, 6, 228
Kalibala, Dr E. B., 115, 116, 173
Kamba people, 4
Kampala, 92, 104–5, 119, 120, 195, 198,
   248
Kamya, Augustine, 220
KANU, 168
Karamoja, 187
Kasuli, Father, 119
Katikiro, office of, 2, 42, 51, 95, 104
Katwe, 120, 195, 198
Kaunda, Kenneth, 247
Kavuma, Blasio, 248
Kenya, territorial aggregations in, 4;
   political movements in, 168, 169,
   173, 195; poverty in, 169; elections
   in, 188, 198; under colonialism, 228,

232; see also Mau Mau conflict;
   settlers
Kenya Africa Union, 169
Kigezi, 189, 228
Kikuyu people, 5, 233
King's College School, Budo, 92, 183
'King's Friends', 185, 201, 213
Kintu, Kabaka, 35
Kintu, Mikaeri, 185, 187, 204
Kipsigis, 4
Kironde, Apolo, 97, 115–16, 119, 121,
   125, 127, 197
Kironde, Erisa, 197
Kitakule, Rev. Henry Wright Duta, 51,
   52
Kiwanuka, Archbishop, 49, 119, 129
Kiwanuka, Benedicto, 181, 184, 190,
   197, 209, 210–11, 215, 216, 217
Koki people, 6
Kulubya, Serwano, 90, 91, 96, 124,
   128, 149, 213, 215, 233
Kunuka, Dr B. N., 197
Kyambalongo, 119
Kyaze, Mr, 119

Labour Party, 8, 112, 172
Lango, 5, 189, 192, 246, 247
Lavigerie, Cardinal, 23
Laws, Dr Robert, 69
Lennox-Boyd, Alan, 126, 127
Liberal Party, 57, 63, 73–4, 82, 172
lineage heads, 14, 151, 169, 176; see also
   clan heads
Liverpool, 71, 72, 75
Livingstonia Mission Committee, 69
Lonsdale, Dr John, 8
'Lost Counties', 238
Lubogo, David, 197
Luganda language, press, 111, 118,
   131, 182, 196
Lukiko, origin of, 42; during oligarchy,
   42, 48, 170–71; and British adminis-
   tration, 88–9; and the Kabaka, 91;
   chiefs in, 92–4, 121, 177, 201;
   possible repudiation of Hancock
   Committee by, 95; under Uganda
   Agreement, 104, 144; elections to,
   106–7, 112, 158, 180, 181–2, 185–6,
   219–20; and opposition to Uganda
   Legislative Council, 110, 201, 208–
   9, 217, 236; effect of deportation of
   Mutesa II on, 112, 113–14, 115;
   demand for elections to, 149, 151,

Lukiko–*contd.*
199; declaration of independence by, 208, 236; and Buganda's autonomy, 212, 236, 238; and the Constitutional Conference, 217
Lugard, Lord, in Buganda, 35, 36, 55–6, 58, 86, 241; in England, 60–61, 64, 67, 68, 72, 74, 81
Lule, Dr Y. K., 119, 122, 185
Luo people, 4, 234
Lutaya, James, 185
Luyia people, 4, 5
Lyttleton, Oliver, 108, 113–14, 116

Mabega wa Lukiko ne Nnamulondu, 220
Mackinnon, Sir William, 55, 56
Macleod, Iain, 218
Macmillan, Harold, 130
Magezi, 181
Mahdi revolt, 85
Mair, Dr Lucy, 140, 161
mailo tenure, *see* Buganda, land settlement
Makerere University College, 122, 207
Makumbi, Thomas, 115, 116, 119, 127, 197
Malawi, 173
Malawi National Congress, 167
Malayan emergency, 113
Manchester Guardian, 59
Masagazi, Father, 119
Mau Mau conflict, 113, 133, 178, 234
Mawanda, Kabaka, 15
Mayanja, Abu, 213, 248
Mayanja-Nkangi, 240
Mbale, 179
Mbaguta, Nuwa, 230
Mboya, Tom, 180
missionaries, 23–7, 33–4, 50–51, 78, 85–6, 88, 142, 144, 147, 168, 215; *see also* Church Missionary Society
Mitchell, Sir Philip, 91, 98, 231, 243–4
Montagu declaration, 101, 130
Morning Post, 60
Mounteney-Jephson, 78
Muganda, 16–17, 43, 140, 186
Mugwanya, Matayo, 121, 127, 184, 190
Mujasi, 46, 141
Mukasa, 23, 32
Mukasa, B. J., 173
Mukasa, Hamu, 91
Mulira, Eridadi, 115–16, 119, 121–2,

125, 127, 181–2, 183, 190, 193, 197
Munster Commission, 244
Musazi, Ignatius, 173, 178, 180–81, 192–3, 197–8, 208
Muslims, 28, 30–34, 37–9, 41, 45–6, 48–9, 52, 86–7, 184
Musoke, 119
Mutaka, 32; *see also* clan heads
Mutesa I, Kabaka, 19–20, 22–7, 41, 85, 110, 215, 240
Mutesa II, Kabaka, riots against, 94, 105; opposition to Ugandan unitary state by, 94–5, 106–12, 235–6; deportation of, 95, 111–16, 120, 151, 174, 178, 185, 236; restoration of, 97, 98, 132–3, 152, 236; career of, 105; joint proposals for constitutional reform, 106–7, 110, 199; attack on and escape of, 134, 239, 242; and chiefs, 152, 199; popular support for, 152–6; and Kabaka Yekka, 158; as President of Uganda, 237–9; and the 'Lost Counties' referendum, 238; and conflict with central government, 239, 240–41, 242
Muwanda, Paulo, 197
Muwazi, Dr E. M. K., 197
Mwanga, Kabaka, 27–41, 47, 56, 85–7, 143, 216, 234
Mwoyo gwa Gwanga, 218, 220

Nadiope, 189, 191
Nagolama, 248
Nairobi, 90, 174, 214
Namirembe, 119
Namirembe cathedral, 42, 51, 93
Namirembe Conference, 123-34 *passim*
Nandi people, 4
National Council for Nigeria and the Cameroons, 167
National Liberation Movement, 186, 204
National Union of Conservative Associations, 61
native council *see* Lukiko
NCNC, 168
Ndebele kingdom, 86
Nehru, Jawaharlal, 214
Negritude, 214
Ngoratok, 195
Nigeria, 3, 105, 168, 175, 228, 229, 243
Niger River, 101

Nile River, 78, 102, 179
Nkrumah, Kwame, 180
Nsibirwa, Martin Luther, 90, 91, 93
Nuer, the, 20
Nyasaland, 57, 69, 167, 178, 231; *see also* Malawi
Nyerere, Julius, 180, 247
Nyeri, 5

Obote, A. M., 10, 134, 189, 192, 205, 209, 236–42, 244–9
Obwangor, C. J., 189, 190
Omulamuzi, office of, 104
Omuwanika, office of, 104

Pan-Africanism, 3, 214
Pastoral Letter on Church and State, 49
Perham, Dame Margery, 35, 114
Peters, Carl, 55
Portal, Sir Gerald, 58–9, 80, 81
Pratt, Professor R. C., 159, 161
Presbyterians, 62, 68–9, 74
Progressive Party, 155, 182, 183, 189, 190, 193, 200
Protestants, Buganda regiments of, 30; during civil war, 34–6, 86; conversion of Kabaka Mwanga to, 37; oligarchy, 37–9, 47–8, 170–1; and distribution of chieftainships, 45–6, 183–4; in England and 'Uganda question', 65, 69; in Uganda Leg. Council Elections, 189, 210–11; and development of political parties, 189, 210–11, 218; *see also* Progressive Party

Queen Elizabeth National Park, 179

Relationships Committee, 208, 211, 216–17
Rhodes, Cecil, 79
Rhodesia, 173; *see also* Northern Rhodesia
The Rise of Our East African Empire, 81
Roman Catholics, Catholicism, arrival of, in Buganda, 23, 25–6; regiments of, 30, 47; and struggle with Protestants, 34–7, 47, 52, 86, 168; and distribution of offices, 37–8, 39, 42, 45–6, 119, 171, 183–4; under oligarchy, 47–9, 170, 171; pastoral work of, 148, 229; and political parties, 176, 183–4, 209–10; *see also* Democratic Party

Rosebery, Lord, 57–60, 65, 68, 79–80, 81
Royal Colonial Institute, 81
Royal Scottish Geographical Society, 74
Ruwenzori, Mount, 239

Salisbury, Lord, 55, 57, 59, 61, 69, 73, 82
Saul, Dr John, 8, 9
Saza chiefs, 104, 119, 121, 128, 132–3
Sebei people, 4, 244
Sekabanja, S. M., 187
Sempa, Amos, 118
Sesse islands, 18
settlers, 102, 113, 211, 231, 233, 235, 241
slave trade, 76–7, 78
Singo, 185
Smythies, Bishop, 61
Society for the Propogation of the Gospel, 62, 66, 70, 72
Soroti, 247
South Africa, 1, 85, 102, 172, 174, 178
Southern Rhodesian African National Congress, 214
Sowter, Rev. G. A., 64–5
Stanley, 22, 60, 61, 66, 78
Standard, 60
Statement by the Governor, 129, 180
Stonehouse, John, 150
Sudan, Sudanese, 3, 20, 24, 39, 85, 178, 181

Tanganyika, Tanzania, 5, 169, 173, 178, 188, 198, 233, 247
Tanganyika African National Union, 167
Teso, 189, 190, 195, 230, 247
The Times, 59–60, 68, 80, 81, 114
Toro, 1, 4, 7, 126, 179, 188, 217, 229
trade, 21, 56, 76, 78, 85, 86, 158; *see also* Asians
trade unions, 195–6
Tucker, Bishop, 56, 57
Twining, Lord, 178

Uganda, importance of Buganda in, 1–2, 6, 92, 97, 104–5, 227–30; administration in, 1, 96, 104, 175–6, 227–9, 244–5; assault upon Kabaka's palace by, 2, 227, 239; minorities in, 4, 104, 150, 156–8, 168, 173–4, 193, 201; development of political

Uganda–*contd.*
parties in, 9, 103–4, 154–5, 167–8, 171–84, 187–94, 200–2, 207–11, 218–22, 236–9; IBEA Company in, 55–9; British retention of, 52–82 *passim*; economy in, 88, 92, 147, 150, 155–6, 168–9, 174; relations between Buganda and, 97–9, 107–8; size of, 104; and the unitary state, 105, 109, 129–31, 133–4, 206–9, 216–18, 244; independence of, 108, 113, 121–2, 124, 133, 194, 202–3, 216–18, 236; Buganda demands for independence, 110, 206–7, 212–13, 225–6; and result of Namirembe Conference, 129–31; populism in, 139, 150–51, 156–8, 160; lack of anti-imperialist nationalism in, 154, 167, 174, 202, 203, 222; attitude to Buganda in, 190–91, 227–31, 236–7; and Relationships Commission, 206–7, 208; and federalism, 207, 237; Christianity in, 229–30, 245; final struggle with Buganda, 237–9, 242–6; attempt to unify, 246–9; *see also* Buganda; executive Council of, 106, 107, 132; legislative Council of, Buganda opposition to, 8, 96, 110, 121, 201, 211–12; Baganda members in, 97; and representation, 106–7, 109, 125–31, 187–9; reconstitution of 1955 of, 132; Baganda resignations from, 133, 181, 236; direct elections for, 187–9, 195, 207, 208–9; opposition to Buganda in, 191–2, 193–4, 201; national assembly of, 217–21, 237, 240
Uganda Agreement 1900, and position of Kabaka 41, 95–6, 103, 111, 131; and land settlement, 44–5, 89, 91, 103, 143–4, 146; and administration, 45–6, 104; and Baganda cooperation, 41, 88–9, 103; and the wider protectorate, 97; and Saza chiefs, 104
Uganda Constitutional Committee, 167–8, 192–3, 201–2

Uganda Constitutional Conference, 216–18
Uganda Labour Party, 184
Uganda National Congress, 97, 106, 110, 118, 155, 173, 178–80, 189, 197, 209, 213
Uganda National Movement, 157, 160, 167, 193, 201–2, 205, 209–10, 218–20
Uganda National Party, 155, 200, 209
Ugnada Nationalist Party, 184
Uganda Peoples Congress, 193–4, 205, 209–11, 217, 219–21, 236–8, 247, 249
Uganda Peoples National Liberation Movement, 190
Uganda Peoples Union, 189–91, 193, 205, 207
Uganda Reform Party, 184
Uganda Taxpayers Party, 184
United Congress Party, 155, 181–3, 190–93, 197–8, 200, 202–3, 205
United Nations, 3, 115, 238
United Presbyterian Church of Scotland, 68

Victoria, Lake, 13, 18, 31, 88, 227
Volta River, 101

Wamala, 93
Wanga chiefs, 5
Weber, Max, 15, 32
West Africa, 3, 101, 172, 203
Western Province, 191
West Nile district, 247
White, Eirene, 113
Wild Committee, 130
Wilson, George, 228

Young Baganda Association, 89

Zake, Luyimbazi, 197
Zake, Sengendo, 119, 127
Zambezi River, 102, 133
Zambia, 173, 247
Zanzibar, 51, 58, 173, 211, 215, 227
Zimbabwe African Peoples Union, 214